LOCAL HEROES CHANGING AMERICA

for **Joe Wood**

INDIVISIBLE

LOCAL HEROES
CHANGING AMERICA

EDITED BY TOM RANKIN

WITH THE INDIVISIBLE PROJECT STAFF

FOREWORD BY RAY SUAREZ

A LYNDHURST BOOK

PUBLISHED BY THE CENTER FOR DOCUMENTARY STUDIES

IN ASSOCIATION WITH W. W. NORTON & COMPANY   NEW YORK • LONDON

Indivisible is a project of the Center for Documentary Studies at Duke University in partnership with the Center for Creative Photography, The University of Arizona. Funded by The Pew Charitable Trusts.

A museum exhibition of the original photographs and recorded voices of Indivisible, as well as two postcard exhibitions, will tour nationally. Exhibitions were organized by the Center for Creative Photography, The University of Arizona. Museum venues include:

The Terra Museum of American Art, Chicago, Illinois
October–November 2000

Akron Art Museum, Akron, Ohio
December 2000–February 2001

**Center for Creative Photography,
The University of Arizona, Tucson**
July–September 2001

North Carolina Museum of Art, Raleigh
October 2001–January 2002

**Museum of Contemporary Art, San Diego
La Jolla, California**
January–April 2002

John and Mable Ringling Museum of Art, Sarasota, Florida
May–July 2002

Philadelphia Museum of Art, Philadelphia, Pennsylvania
August–October 2002

Anchorage Museum of History and Art, Anchorage, Alaska
October–December 2002

San Antonio Museum of Art, San Antonio, Texas
Dates in 2003 to be announced

Additional support for educational programs accompanying the exhibitions was provided by the National Endowment for the Arts.

The text of this book is composed in Bulmer and Univers with the display set in Trajan.
Book design by Catherine Mills Design, Seattle
Manufacturing by Mondadori Printing, Verona, Italy

Library of Congress Cataloging-in-Publication Data

Rankin, Tom.
Local heroes changing America: indivisible / Tom Rankin; foreword by Ray Suarez.
    p.   cm.
"A Lyndhurst Book published by the Center for Documentary Studies in association with W. W. Norton & Company."
1. United States—Social conditions—1980- 2. Community life—United States. 3. Community development—United States. 4. Voluntarism—United States. I. Suarez, Ray, 1957- III. Title.
HN59.2 R36 2000
306'.0973—dc21   00-24128

ISBN 0-393-05028-9

W. W. Norton & Company, Inc.
500 Fifth Avenue, New York, New York 10110
web.wwnorton.com
W. W. Norton & Company, Ltd.
10 Coptic Street, London WC1A 1PU

1 2 3 4 5 6 7 8 9 0

Lyndhurst Books publish works of creative exploration by writers and photographers who convey new ways of seeing and understanding human experience in all its diversity—books that tell stories, challenge our assumptions, awaken our social conscience, and connect life, learning, and art.

Center for Documentary Studies at Duke University
1317 West Pettigrew Street
Durham, North Carolina 27705
http://cds.aas.duke.edu

To order books, call W. W. Norton at 1.800.233.4830.

For more information about Indivisible, call 1.877.INDIV99 toll free or log on to the the project Web site at www.indivisible.org

The images and interviews in *Local Heroes* were edited by Tom Rankin and Trudy Wilner Stack. The principal editor is noted in each chapter.

FOREWORD

BY RAY SUAREZ

Journalists don't like to admit it, but they often head out into the world with a pretty good idea of what they intend to find. The story is already writing itself when they should still be wondering, searching, curious. We go to bad places to live to report the news. We write little morality plays. We talk to local people armed with our pads and pencils and our own expectations that they are as anxious to get out of there as we would be. We emissaries from the middle class dropping by to pass our judgment on them. It's not that we're insensitive creeps, exploiters, or worse. It is more often the rushed nature of our business. We parachute into people's lives, cast them in our dramas, and move on. We are also prisoners of the conventions of journalistic narratives: local heroes, self-sacrificing neighbor, tragic victims, bright promise ending in sorrow. We get few opportunities to know, or to show, the struggles of our neighbors. Their problems are presented formulaically, not as dispatches from the other side of town, but from what might as well be the other side of the world. Every night, in cities large and small, we commit the verbal equivalents of drive-by shootings.

Once in St. Louis, I talked to a young single mother in a rundown part of that once thriving city. We met by the school where she was a volunteer. She introduced me to other members of her neighborhood crime watch. I asked her where she would go if she could get away from this corner of north St. Louis, and she immediately set me straight. She loved her neighborhood. She had struggled for years to make it a better place. Why would she leave now that she could see some of her efforts finally bearing fruit?

She shut me up. (Well, for a minute, anyway.)

And she gave me plenty to think about. As a reporter and interviewer, I've heard thousands of stories from people struggling to control their own fates and the destinies of their neighborhoods. In places as different as the people themselves, they've worked to take back their streets, improve schools, build houses, fight drugs, reclaim shattered lives, and exert local control over their economic destinies. Whether you live in one of these places, or live the kind of life in which you may never see one of them firsthand, you should thank your lucky stars that so many, in so many ways, come forward to work.

There is a common thread running like a vein of ore through these stories. It's the surge of confidence, in themselves and in their neighbors, that comes to people when they take those first, tentative steps toward acting instead of being acted upon. For millions of Americans, this kind of control is expected, a normal part of everyday life. As you move down the wage ladder, from high-income neighborhoods to the homes of the struggling classes, this potency and power gradually morphs to a kind of resignation. What sets these places apart, physically and socially, is often the widespread feeling that the people with the say-so will write the story of the places they live, not the people who live there.

We may not always recognize it, but one thing I've learned in decades of reporting from urban ground zero, the one thing the Indivisible project (of which this book is one result) illustrates so clearly, is the tremendous gulf between being poor, and being poor and powerless. The shame so many Americans immediately attach to poverty may come not from the state of poverty itself, but from the passivity and powerlessness that so often accompany it. That powerlessness can even creep into middle-class life. The "muscles" of civic engagement grow slack. People with a stake in the system grow disconnected from it. Community organizing has been a powerful antidote to the despair that comes from the inability to comprehend your own circumstances and rise above them.

In many of the most successful organizing projects I've seen close up, the people or the places they affect so powerfully don't end up looking very different. The houses are still old. The city services may still fall short. But the places and the people who call them home are altered in ways that register with even a casual observer: people who need to deal with officialdom lift up their heads instead of staring at their feet; young women who need prenatal care don't hide in the shadows without getting what they must have; voting doesn't seem like a counterintuitive act. The people who are organized deal with the rest of their world with a sense of entitlement—not entitlement in the sense of someone who confidently demands something for nothing, but the entitlement that comes from a wakening sense of citizenship, a connection to the whole of society. The potential had been there all along. It was finally unlocked by the demand that an individual step forward and join the wider enterprise of living in society. The tremendous isolation of so many American lives can make their manifest difficulties so much worse. The inability to see your own role in shaping your own future is an epidemic. The work profiled in *Local Heroes Changing America* is an antidote.

We've come through several decades of depopulation, deindustrialization, disinvestment, and decline in much of urban America. There was a time when the big, powerful voices in the culture were aggressively throwing their weight around in the toughest neighborhoods: closing plants, creating programs, clearing "slums." The fate of the community was not in the hands of the people who went to work there, the people who swept the walks, and paid the bills. The people who had been good enough to make steel, and shoes, and cardboard boxes were not going to be able to make decisions about their own future. This condescension, this steady lecture from city hall, the state house, and the federal government finally brought a backlash. Lowell, and east L.A., and north Milwaukee, and east Cleveland, finally started to say no.

From the figurative sons and daughters of legendary community organizer Saul Alinsky, to parish priests ready to incite their flocks to march, and from people who had left the old neighborhood and come back with the training and skills their people needed, came a thousand new organizations. After banks and factories and the federal government had left these places to their fate, the people left behind had to find a way to make it on their own. This book is a collection of those stories, gathered with the conviction that people are experts about their own lives.

This isn't about revolution.

This isn't about getting rich.

It is about nothing more revolutionary than harnessing the energy and common sense of common people. You'll find, as I have found, listening to their stories, and watching their hard work, that people are rarely more heroic, rarely more beautiful, rarely more fully alive, than when they find fulfillment in each other and in community.

The causes and the methods aren't always "right." Successes like the ones you find within these pages often come after failures. Maybe the last time the community didn't fully understand what it was up against. Maybe the time before a strong idea was there, but the foot soldiers needed to make it work couldn't commit to the end. No matter. Each attempt teaches lessons. Each is another step in the making of a citizen.

Perhaps you'll admire their self-realization. Maybe you'll find comfort in their strength. But will you wonder about yourself? In the stories and powerful first-person narratives of people engaged in the difficult work of wrestling hope out of despair will you wonder, "If I had grown up here, would I have been crushed by it?" "If my neighbors called out in their suffering, would I step in to help, even at personal and material cost?" "What makes someone who could go elsewhere and make a pretty decent buck, throw in her lot with these people?" Even if you were ready to put yourself in a harness in a time of crisis, could you keep it up long enough to see it through?

I'm not sure how to adequately express what it is that sets apart those who come forward when so many others can't be bothered. I am reluctant to celebrate them in a way that gushes too much, that sentimentalizes the serious obstacles these neighbors face every day. To make them into selfless Mother Teresas would only make them unreachable, comforting in their remoteness from everyday experience. But to make them too ordinary would understate the real risk and sacrifice often faced in making a challenge your own. Long

before the pats on the back and the thanks of the grateful comes suspicion of motives and resentment of prying. "It's always been this way. Who do you think you are?"

All right. This particular road to redemption is not for everybody. But if you look at the deeply distressed communities across the country, from the south Bronx to Brownsville, Texas, to Chicago's West Side to East Palo Alto, what will you find about the people and places that are going to make it, and the ones that aren't? The places with the most active citizens' sector are the ones with a chance. They may be even poorer than other neighborhoods nearby in all the conventional measures: years of education, household income, single heads of households. But people looking out for each other have a tool for forging a better life more potent than a few extra bucks.

They are more able to extend their control—what sociologists call the "social control of normative behavior"—from their front doors to the corners and alleyways where drug dealers and gang-bangers lurk. Citizen power informs the political process and sends impulses up the political ladder from the streets to the councils of government and grant-making institutions. In what writer Malcolm Gladwell calls the "tipping point," a new ambience created by citizen action can make other problems appear more soluble. The free-floating anxiety many Americans, rich and poor, feel about the places they live disappears once they are engaged. You can see the real threat and real potential for what they are.

The attention you couldn't get as one person on the phone is suddenly paid to organized neighbors, by schools and police, by banks and hospitals. With each individual battle a little more is learned about what doors need to be knocked on and what powerful people need to be consulted. Each battle, won or lost, leaves its residue. That residue eventually becomes part of the memory banks of neighborhood groups that one day makes them powerful—even one day, God help us, makes them the Establishment.

The authentic and necessary leaders who rise up from the grass roots have become mayors and city council members and state representatives. They have perfected community models that have been exported and met needs around the country. Perhaps most important, they have served as a constant reminder to the rest of the society that the "problem people" are not passively sitting packed away in declining neighborhoods, in ghettos and public housing, waiting for the rest of us to help.

Local heroes also do something subtle and necessary: they remove the oppression of low expectations from the arsenals of the arrogant. People rising to help themselves cannot as easily be dismissed, forgotten, or marginalized. Each successful project is a claim on the goods of the wider society that would have been snubbed or ignored before. These stories act as a wake-up call to those who hold the power and the resources and before could very easily turn away.

The needs are innumerable: in housing, public health, employment, crime, education, safety, environmental protection, and sustainable hunting and fishing. A domestic Marshall Plan is not just around the corner. But the potent and infectious example of the street workers, organizers, volunteers, trainers, and the trained light the way all over the country.

It would be ludicrous to imagine that all the unmet needs across America are just waiting for a plucky band of organized neighbors to come to the rescue. Some problems are too old, too deep, too serious to be overcome simply through community organization. However, when help does arrive from some far-off somewhere, the well-organized neighborhood will be able to absorb that help far better than the one in which alienation from neighbor and local government leaves people scattered and suspicious, bitter and pessimistic. Connection to these local institutions turns a floating free agent into a citizen. Suddenly, a neighbor can see his or her self-interest tied to who is mayor in a way never possible before. A government that had only shown itself as hostile, or at best neglectful, seems reformable. This should come as no surprise, since these same citizen volunteers have already made a journey in which unlikely events became possible. Gang-bangers, welfare mothers, dropouts, and street people suddenly melt away; in their place are citizens.

Citizens see themselves as actors. They are no longer waiting for someone to save them. They are now ready to transact: to have expectations and to meet the demands of others. This is not a small thing. It is everything.

In *Local Heroes*, testimony is strong. People talk into being the complex relationships they have with their causes. The people you'll meet have been transformed themselves by the transformative work they do for others. They are keenly aware of their own selves, the assumptions and suspicions they brought to the work of change. Now they are stronger, affirmed, clear, and coherent. They can see what they've done and take satisfaction from it. I know these people too, from the forgotten places in the American landscape that only make the late news when there's bad news.

By definition, half of all Americans earn a below-average income. Half of all families are not excitedly logging on to the NASDAQ Web site to see how their high-tech shares are performing. They aren't getting in on the ground floor of a hot new IPO or feeling burdened by the "wealth effect" that Alan Greenspan believes is fueling an overheated marketplace.

To watch and read our news in this country it is hard to remember how many tens of millions of Americans are not powering up their Palm Pilots or chatting into a cell phone while strolling down an airport concourse to their next flight. That world of pleasurable consumption is too much with us, and the real lives of the other half are not shown enough. In *Who Wants to Be a Millionaire?* America, the heroes of this book are investing lives with dignity, telling their own histories, coming to America with clean hands and Martin Luther King's check, marked "insufficient funds."

If you take the subway in New York City to Grand Central Station and reach the sidewalk from underground at 42nd Street, walk toward the Daily News Building. Above the impressive front doors is a bas-relief, in fabulous art deco style. Spanning the urban street scene in the panel, the to and fro of men and women, is the legend "He Made So Many of Them." Some 140 years ago, a man who grew up in crushing poverty, Abraham Lincoln, is popularly reported to have said that "God must have loved the common people. He made so many of them."

This sculpture is one of my favorite sights in my hometown. Down at sidewalk level, far below the stylized skyscrapers, sun rays, and clouds, are the jumbled masses of the American street. Men and women of various shapes and sizes and stations of life are the representatives of the plain folk, the demos of our democracy. I like to think that Lincoln was right about the Almighty. But I'm convinced those common folk are ready to become uncommon gifts to the world around them.

INTRODUCTION

BY TOM RANKIN

Local Heroes Changing America is about the work and vision of committed individuals and communities across America. Through the images of our country's finest photographers and the voices of extraordinary citizens as collected by renowned documentary fieldworkers, this book takes us to twelve distinct places, to witness what it means to live responsibly and actively in one's own community. We often hear and read the tired cliché, "think globally, act locally." Rather than ringing hollow like so many clichés or much of the rhetoric about contemporary political and social life, the stories that follow evoke most meaningfully the real potential, even the necessity, for all of us to be engaged in local life and change. In an age when cynics remark glibly that we no longer practice the principles of democratic activism for the betterment of our home places, what is said and pictured here tells another story, a story of the vitality and passion of individual people who work for change with the humble tools of their own wisdom, experience, and commitment.

This book is one part of a large national documentary initiative, Indivisible. Initiated and funded by The Pew Charitable Trusts, Indivisible is a firsthand examination of grassroots American democracy. Indivisible matches documentary expression—photographs and narrative voices—with the story of these twelve locales and the efforts of the people there to effect change. By giving form to the stories of these people and places, Indivisible affirms the value of collective action, the necessity of our mutual interests, and the recognition of our deep interdependence. In addition to this book, Indivisible includes a major exhibition that is traveling to museums throughout the country; postcard exhibitions that will tour nationally to public spaces and disseminate the images and text of Indivisible on free postcards; and a Web site featuring photographs, audio pieces from interviews, and information on the twelve communities and their institutions. In addition, Indivisible creates a permanent record through local archives in the twelve communities and project archives accessible at Duke University and the Center for Creative Photography, The University of Arizona.

Like the communities it portrays, Indivisible is the result of the work of many people. The Center for Documentary Studies at Duke University and the Center for Creative Photography, The University of Arizona, partnered on many components of this project. From the outset, project codirector Trudy Wilner Stack and I envisioned a project that would cross many of the conventional boundaries of exhibition and publication; a project that would be embraced by the art museum and be comfortable in public spaces, such as an airport, a city hall, or a community center; a project that would commission some of this country's most compelling and insightful photographers and fieldworkers to spend time documenting communities; a project that would connect two major universities in an endeavor intended for a wide public audience; and, finally, a project that in addition to bearing witness to community life through powerful words and original images would aim to create conversation and reflection about participatory democracy by citizens throughout the country. To move anywhere near those ambitious goals meant forming collaborations with a vast number of people, many of whom are represented in the pages of this book. Trudy Wilner Stack contributed to nearly every piece of *Local Heroes Changing America*, including writing introductions to five chapters; lending her sharp photographic eye to the editing of the images; listening to, selecting, and editing oral history interviews; and providing endless editorial counsel. Her extensive and thoughtful contributions help make this book what it is. Likewise, the entire staff of Indivisible contributed to the creation of this book, which could not have been moved from idea to form without their collective contributions.

How does one go about looking at community-based democratic action in this country? Where does one go? What constitutes community? How does one choose communities, and on what grounds? The questions go on and on. Beginning this project under the aegis of and with funding from The Pew Charitable Trusts, the two of us—with much help—set out not to locate the "best" examples of local democracy in action, but rather to assemble a group of geographically diverse places where people are joining together to shape the future at the local level. We consciously looked for communities in different parts of the country, hoping to reflect regional differences. We looked for communities where activism is rooted in citizen initiatives, rather than cases where the impetus is institutionally driven or comes from the "top down." We looked for racial, ethnic, and gender diversity; for class differences; for youth communities; and for communities dealing with a range of issues such as housing, health, labor, and the environment. We talked to hundreds of people, visiting them to talk in person about our project, its goals, and the potential collaboration, to assess just how well a community's story could be told through our primary mediums of photographs and oral history. Our selection process was not based on any quantitative data or scientific indicators, but was the result of careful canvassing of the country. Our hope is that Indivisible—with its local initiatives and thousands of people—presents a cumulative portrait of this country, of people working to have a positive impact on contemporary society, to shape their own destinies, and succeeding.

The photographers and fieldworkers spent up to thirty days in their respective locales, informed by our interest in and knowledge of each place, but also with the freedom to follow their own cultural and artistic interests, developing independent points of view on the story. This method—directing documentarians toward the goals and principles of Indivisible and also encouraging artistic and documentary freedom—was intentional, blending the approaches of a structured ethnographic project with that of a more flexible art commission. During the fieldwork phase of the project, we relied heavily on local contacts, cultivating relationships between documentarians and people in the communities. While not all photographers and fieldworkers worked together "in the field" at the same time, we encouraged close communication between the two, knowing that the interview material and the images would ultimately need to form a coherent whole. There was great variety in how the various photographer/fieldworker "teams" chose to meet this need for their own collaboration. For us, the codirectors, how images and texts were to relate to each other in the book was a crucial decision. We decided to vary that relationship from chapter to chapter, and we invite the reader to approach these pages as though entering a conversation between images and words, a conversation that we hope the reader will fully join.

"Local" and "community" are two words that have resonated throughout this project and appear often in this book. While each term has its own distinct meaning, people often used them here interchangeably to evoke a common spirit or shared concept. We, too, have used them similarly at times. "If the word community is to mean or amount to anything," argues Wendell Berry in his essay "Sex, Economy, Freedom, and Community," "it must refer to a place (in its natural integrity) and its people. It must refer to a placed people. Since there obviously can be no cultural relationship that is uniform between a nation and continent, community must mean a people locally placed and a people, moreover, not too numerous to have a common knowledge of themselves and their place." For Berry, as for Indivisible, our nation is made up of a constellation of many local communities, different in their place and all that place defines, but with a commonality made possible by a shared interest, a simultaneous respect for differences, and a recognition of our ultimate interdependence. Local communities here stretch geographically from the town of Delray Beach on Florida's Atlantic coast to an assemblage of coastal residents throughout Alaska, from birth supporters and expectant mothers in Stony Brook, New York, to housing activists in the Rio Grande Valley of Texas. Diverse as the geography they represent, these communities are made and live through the heroic, often gritty, work—efforts small and large—of local people who have in common the vision that the present and the future require our personal commitment and participation; and that to reach toward that envisioned better future demands that we locate what we share even while we acknowledge our differences.

How can these people be called heroes, you might ask? Just what is a "local hero"? Hero is used here not to put certain folks on a pedestal above others or to shine some kind of divine recognition down on particular individuals, by definition excluding others. Rather, I have in mind the countless parables in almost all cultures of the lone, ordinary soul whose modest act reverberates throughout a group as heroic, as an act that brings about a positive change. Such an act can work to unite others in a common goal, igniting the fuse of grassroots action. Way down the list of definitions for a hero in the *Webster's Collegiate Dictionary* is this: "the central figure in an event, period, or movement." The heroes here are not larger than life, nor are they lone actors in a predictable drama. They may not even be "central" figures, but they somehow figure prominently in the day-to-day work of changing and improving their places. They are common folks of uncommon decency with a concern for justice and the common good. Part of any heroic act is a large dose of strength and persistence, and we see throughout the twelve communities portrayed here the collective courage, confidence, and commitment necessary to inspire and cause change.

The narratives that appear in this book were all recorded by our documentary fieldworkers and carefully transcribed and then edited from those recordings. They represent only a small fraction of the material recorded in each community, and in the selection and editing of narratives we had to leave out far more than we included. Such is the nature of a project of this magnitude. We transcribed these interviews for presentation in print, often deleting interviewers' questions and editing with the reader in mind. We also recognize that while many stories that are told in interviews make for good stories in print, nothing replaces hearing the original speaker. For that reason, this book includes an audio compact disc, highlighting sounds and sentiments, and giving voice to each community. This audio component is not meant to literally follow the book text or necessarily to provide audio versions of all narratives found in the book. Instead, the five-minute audio "portrait" of each community compiled by project coordinator Elana Hadler evokes the spirit and local context, introducing listeners to particular individuals and events, and providing an additional dimension to the photographs and transcribed texts.

We begin at the beginning with "Birth Stories," the story of a group of wise and engaged women and their medical community who are changing and personalizing the birth experience of Long Island, New York, mothers. What more powerful metaphor for heroic change within community than to begin this book—and any life—with efforts to enhance the birth experience of mothers and their families. From New York we trek to the Navajo Nation— home of some of our oldest American citizens, representing another kind of beginning—where the agricultural and traditional weaving ways of the past are helping to forge a meaningful and vital future. Seeing sheep as a key ingredient in everyday Navajo life, a group of Navajo activists are working to ensure the future of the traditional Churro sheep breed, the source of wool that Navajo weaving depends on, and to rediscover the rich history of the Navajo way of life.

"Faith, Race, and Renewal" lands us in Columbia, South Carolina. Most recently, Columbia has been in the spotlight as the center of the important debate to remove the Confederate battle flag from official display on state property (what historian Charles Reagan Wilson has called "the effort to desegregate Southern symbols"). Alongside these efforts stand the less known attempts of a biracial, ecumenical group of residents in the community of Eau Claire–North Columbia, who are working to improve their part of Columbia through cooperation. Anchored in the United Methodist Church, but extending into a variety of interested groups, the Eau Claire example provides a vivid window on how communities can foster change on their own terms, improving race relations, education, real estate development, and housing. Housing is the center of a different vision in "Building on the Border," where we witness the work of Proyecto Azteca, a farmworker-founded organization that helps move Mexican American workers from marginal housing to quality homes in San Juan, Texas. In the heart of the Rio Grande Valley, Proyecto Azteca is focused on the principles of self-help and hard work, where families receive low-interest loans in exchange for helping to build their own houses.

With "Growing Up, Coming Together" we move from the agricultural landscape of Texas to the city streets of southwest Chicago where an ethnically diverse community is coming together around the needs of youth. The Southwest Youth Collaborative also is run partly by young people. A persistent theme running through this chapter, however, is the need to bring all kinds of people together, to foster a language and tradition for communicating across societal and generational differences, and to begin this work with local residents in their early, formative years. The search for ways to communicate across conflicting opinions toward a common goal extends to the next chapter, "A Forest Home." In the Yaak Valley of Montana we witness local efforts to maintain a livelihood in a rural, land-based economy while managing forest resources. Though the opinions of just what constitutes "proper" forest management are varied, residents of the Yaak Valley rely on their love of place to build democratic consensus for the preservation of both environment and ways of life.

"Citizens on Watch" takes us to Palm Beach County, Florida, to the city of Delray Beach, a place completely transformed by Haitian immigration during the 1980s and 1990s. As is often the case, the great numbers of immigrants that arrived unexpectedly shook loose the hinges of community stability. A collateral effort, largely led by law-enforcement officers, social-service workers, and citizen volunteers, has brought confidence, understanding, and safety to neighborhood streets. We move from this Florida coastal city of complex racial and class divisions to the coastal communities of Alaska, rich in marine resources, where a coalition of fishermen, environmentalists, and coastal residents has formed the Alaska Marine Conservation Council to restore and protect marine life. Working on many fronts—public education, legislative advocacy, and marine ecosystem research—this group seeks solutions that consider both the needs of the ecosystem and the cultural and economic needs of fishing families and their communities.

In San Francisco, depicted in "Youthline," young people are helping other young people through a powerful community of support and connection. A project of CHALK (Communities in Harmony Advocating for Learning and Kids), Youthline uses the telephone to offer noon-to-midnight access to "listeners," young people who help their peers by directing them to information and resources in their times of need. A youth-employment opportunity formed around shared concerns and the ease of communication through technology, Youthline provides a glimpse of the care and commitment of American youth in this West Coast city. Nothing is more needed in many American places than access to capital, and in "Local Money" we get acquainted with the work of the Alternatives Federal Credit Union—locally referred to by some as the "hippie bank"—in Ithaca, New York. While banking can seem a mundane or even invisible necessity, the impact of Alternatives, whose policies are based on a not-for-profit community development principle, is significant and is clearly seen and heard.

American cities small and large grapple with how best to ensure a viable, healthy future. The final two chapters look at two distinct examples of civic renewal: the attempts to revive and enrich small towns in western North Carolina and the Village of Arts and Humanities' catalytic work to reimagine and reinvent a section of North Philadelphia. While the small town of Marshall, North Carolina, and the city of Philadelphia have little in common at first glance, their portrayal in both of these chapters attests to the universal need to protect and improve local places in ways appropriate to the needs, dreams, and hopes of residents. We close our journey to these American places and the people and forces that are reshaping them with a reimagined inner city, created through collaborations between artists and local people, educators and youth, volunteers and staff, interns and residents. We can see in the Village of Arts and Humanities the glow that emanates from individual and community hands, brought together through leadership, the shared desire for a better future, and the spirit and vision of possibility. This impulse—to move from notion to action, from hope to committed struggle, from alienation and indifference to connection and common trust, from abstract idea to visible change—is the essence of Indivisible.

INDIVISIBLE

This book is part of the national documentary project Indivisible—
an exploration of community life and action in America by some of
this country's most accomplished photographers, radio producers,
and folklorists. This book and its compact disc audio collection of
American voices are companions to a major traveling museum exhibition, *Indivisible: Stories of American Community*; postcard exhibits;
events; an interactive Web site; and major research archives.

Indivisible is a project of the Center for Documentary Studies at Duke
University in partnership with the Center for Creative Photography,
The University of Arizona. This book and the Indivisible project are
funded by The Pew Charitable Trusts.

PHOTOGRAPHS BY **SYLVIA PLACHY** · INTERVIEWS BY **KAREN MICHEL**

BIRTH STORIES

MIDWIFERY PRACTICE AND DOULA SERVICE
UNIVERSITY HOSPITAL AND MEDICAL CENTER

STONY BROOK, NEW YORK

The impersonality of hospital-based birth, together with increasing medical intervention and the growing isolation of new mothers, has led to the development of doula service, a new community role with deep roots in traditional practice. "Doula" is a Greek word denoting a woman's servant, or someone who acts in service of another person. Today the term describes a person who is trained to offer prenatal and labor support, as well as emotional and practical assistance through the early postpartum weeks at home.

Historically, and in cultures where medical attention is less valued or unavailable, new and expectant mothers have relied on the care and guidance of elder women who carry the knowledge of experience and oral tradition. When the role of extended family members falters in a society where relatives are widely dispersed; when a woman's mother and grandmother have no experience with natural childbirth, breastfeeding, or balancing a professional and domestic life; when many pregnant teenagers and single women approach their new parental status alone and unsupported—doulas provide a tried and simple solution to a contemporary problem.

When technology, drugs, and surgical procedures contribute to the clinical and intimidating atmosphere of hospital births, a return to natural approaches to childbirth and newborn care combined with sound medicine makes increasing sense. An educated network of individuals who offer gentler, less invasive approaches to normal birth and greater agency for parents has emerged both from health professionals who recognize the pitfalls of excessive medical intervention and from a lay community of women who have felt regret, frustration, and powerlessness with their own experience.

The Doula Service of University Hospital and Medical Center in Stony Brook, New York, trains Long Island women to be doulas, and provides the option of doula support to expectant mothers regardless of their ability to pay. In tandem with Suffolk County's first hospital midwifery practice, a small group of women, led by in inspired trio of obstetrician, nurse-midwife, and doula instructor, serve as doulas for mothers of all ages and backgrounds.

While the work of doulas during childbirth largely consists of encouraging words, wiped brows, massages, hand-holding, and help with walking and position changes, the presence of a doula in the delivery room results in remarkably lowered rates of cesarean sections and use of anesthesia, particularly epidurals. Their postpartum service includes breastfeeding advice, companionship and conversation, and such necessary tasks as babysitting older siblings, cooking, cleaning, shopping, and newborn care. A doula intends never to supersede the relationship between mother and child, nor the role of the father, family, and friends, but rather to help create a supportive environment for those relationships to flourish in the presence of new life.

The doulas help build fellowship among women, increase trust and balance between patients and healthcare providers, and underline the rich, essential value of the first bonds between parents and children. At Stony Brook, a committed, impassioned corps of local doulas and healthcare professionals advocate and advance this ancient, humanizing approach to supporting birth.   *T.W.S.*

Jane Arnold, director of Midwifery Practice and founding coordinator of the volunteer doula program

Sometimes you don't actually make things happen; sometimes you just stand in the place of what you believe in, and then other things begin to happen from that. I feel that's what I've done here, and I feel that's what midwives and doulas need to do nationwide in America. If we don't stand for normal birth, then normal birth will disappear. Someone has to stand in the place of that and say, "Birth can happen, birth is a natural process." You need to be vigilant. You need to be watchful. You need to have position collaboration, but birth is a natural process and you don't necessarily have to intervene. There is a great integrity of the body, and there is a great integrity that families bring to birth that needs to be honored and protected.

Marshall Klaus was on the *Today* show talking about doulas. He said, "If a doula was a machine, we would have one in every labor and delivery room all across the nation, no matter where you were." One of the labor and delivery nurses here, who is very supportive of this project and who had worked with doulas in New Mexico, said, "Let's bring in the VCR and let's just put the tape in and run it. And let's just put up all these studies that Dr. Klaus has done around labor and delivery." And so we did. We didn't say anything; we just left them. And, pretty soon, people started to come up to me to say, "Hey, you know, what about doulas? What about this? It sounds like a good idea."

The important thing in a place like this is to not take credit for anything—just let it happen. It doesn't matter whose idea it is as long as it happens. So if other people think it's their idea, that's fine. The important thing is, it happens.

Now, a lot of our births have doulas at them. And a lot of women are asking for doulas, and a lot of doulas are going to other hospitals, and other hospitals are calling and saying, "How did you set up your doula program? We want to do that." So, in order to do it right and to win people's confidence and to build community again, we had to go very slowly and I had to be able to stand behind every person I've placed at a birth. I had to be sure that I could stand behind the women I was asking other people to trust.

Jane Arnold shares her impressions with the doulas she works with as a midwife in labor and delivery.

When we're doing labors together, it's like you're totally egoless. I think that that's really what it means to be in service of another person. You're not doing it for a reward, you're not doing it to get something, but you're really just working in tandem with this family.

When this nurse said in exasperation, "I didn't know what to do with midwives here, and now I don't know what to do with doulas," I think what she was saying was that we really bring a new perspective to a medicalized institution—that birth is normal and that you can follow your body and you can follow your natural instincts. People do feel secure in a medicalized unit where they can intervene. They gain control like that. If you're having someone just follow her body and push with her body, then really what you're saying is: "I'm a facilitator. I'm just here to guide you. You're really in control and you're really doing it." And I think that was very frightening to nurses and even some of the physicians.

Opening image: Midwife Jane Arnold attends Sunshin and Robert Gordon hours before the birth of their first child.

Opposite: Laboring Sunshin Gordon with her husband, Robert, and first-time doula Jacqueline Shepard

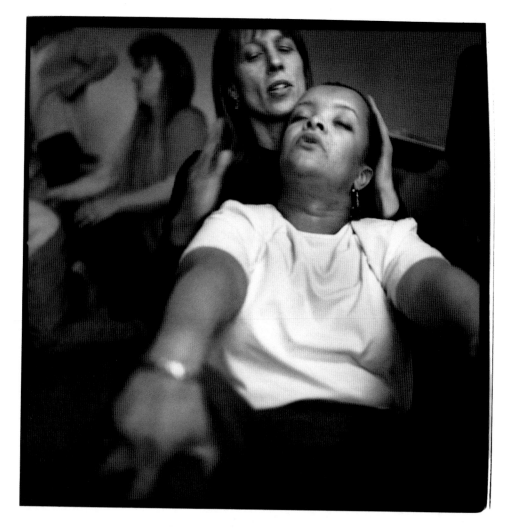

Jacqueline Shepard, doula-in-training

How amazing that it's this thing called delivery and everybody's experience is totally different. What's important to one is different from another: wives' tales; family values and beliefs, and disbeliefs; priorities, concerns, issues; status, finances, occupations, and professions. From bus drivers to nurses, it is amazing that we all came to the same calling, and our backgrounds are totally different. And yet we all feel the need to do what we've been doing naturally, because I think that all of us, in some way or another, actually had been doing it anyway, not knowing that it was a profession, and we're able to do it and give back.

As a child, I wanted to know how we got here. My mom explained to us that men and women should be in love and marriage and all those nice dynamics that we hope for. She explained to us about intercourse, you know, how to prepare yourself, and what our cycle is about, the twenty-eight-day cycle, and egg meets sperm, etc., etc., and how life begins. My mom was always very open, so I think I had the answers before I was nine. My mom never held anything back. She didn't make up names for private parts, she didn't call your private parts "cookies," or anything like that. She just said, "You're a lady. You're a woman. These are your body parts, and they will change, and they are yours, and you honor them, you respect them, you keep them, you cherish yourself." So, that's where my interest, actually my foundation, my basis in this, all began.

Dr. Bruce Meyer, director of Maternal Fetal Medicine and father of four, paved the way for the establishment of the Midwifery Practice and Doula Service.

The truth is, none of us is giving birth the way our moms did. In the fifties we gave everybody twilight sleep and did a forceps delivery on everybody as soon as they got completely dilated. You woke up four or five hours later, and they brought you this baby and said it's yours, and you didn't remember what happened. So we've come a long way from there. To suggest that there isn't another long way we can go says that we can't grow as people, and I don't believe that.

What I hope and what I would like to come out of doulas is that you must have a childbirth experience that is positive. There doesn't have to be a specific experience for you that's the same as the experience for the lady next door or for the lady last week. But it has to be a positive experience; it has to be something that you come out of saying, "There is value. I feel good about the birth of my child."

Jacqueline Shepard and a fellow student in a doula class train for labor support through role-playing.

Opposite: Jacqueline Shepard holds up portraits of her role models, her mother and sister, in her brother's backyard.

Laboring mother Ana Fox Savillo and her husband, Alain Savillo, with doula Darlinda Donlan in the delivery room

DD: That's it, great. Terrific. Really slow, deep breaths. That way you won't be fighting the muscles. You'll relax and you'll dilate quicker.

AFS: Is it almost time yet? [Laughter.]

AS: Yeah. About thirty minutes.

AFS: No, tell me the truth. How long?

DD: With each contraction you have, you're just a step closer.

AS: [Moans.]

DD: The baby moved.

AFS: How far away are the contractions supposed to be if it's, like, time?

DD: It varies with each person.

AS: I think this is what? Two minutes apart?

AFS: Yeah.

DD: So the job of contractions is just to dilate the cervix.

AFS: It's got to—

DD: Thin out, yeah, so the baby's head can go through. Stretch it out.

AFS: Oh, no!

AS: One question. How can the baby breathe right now, through the umbilical cord? Right now, since there's no more, like, water?

DD: Not until he comes out. There's still water.

AS: There's still water.

AFS: I'm going to keep leaking until after I have the baby, right? Yeah. And then I'll start bleeding. [Laughs.] I'm so hungry! One part of my stomach is growling, and the other part is contracting. Ow!

DD: OK, nice deep, slow breaths. Slow. Slow. Slow. That's it. Great. Terrific. Great.

As wonderful as birth is, it's very scary, and women really need that support, that continual support that they are not able to get in hospitals. Because of staffing situations, nurses really can't provide one-on-one care. Their partners, although they've prepared themselves for labor and birth, find it very different when they get into a labor unit. The partner tends to get totally stressed out watching this person he cares about in pain and doing things that may not be working for her, and feels helpless. And she, on the other hand, although she needs her partner there, is feeling scared to death because this person doesn't know what the hell to do. Having a doula there puts her at ease.

I just feel that birth is such a wonderful thing, and a lot of women are alone, even though they do have their partner, they're basically alone. We really provide a necessary—I can't even say a service, because I don't like that word, but support. We, as women, have strength that we can share with other women in an event in their life that is just so meaningful to them as individuals, to their families, and to their communities. There are a lot of women out there who don't have support of a significant other person, and the thought of them going through such an event by themselves is just not acceptable.

So I am going all over Long Island just talking about doulas and what we do and how we affect the families that we're working with and how we can be part of the team that is helping women have their babies. The team, meaning the physician or midwife, the nurse, and the family and the mother—we're all working together to give you the best birth experience that you can have because you will bond with your baby much better. You will sense that this is an important event in your life, whether you wanted it now or not. It's an important event, and you are completely surrounded by people who really, genuinely care for you. You are not alone. You are not. Sometimes we think that nobody cares, but you know what? We care. And I would treat you just the way I would treat my own daughter if it was my daughter having a baby. So you're in luck, honey.

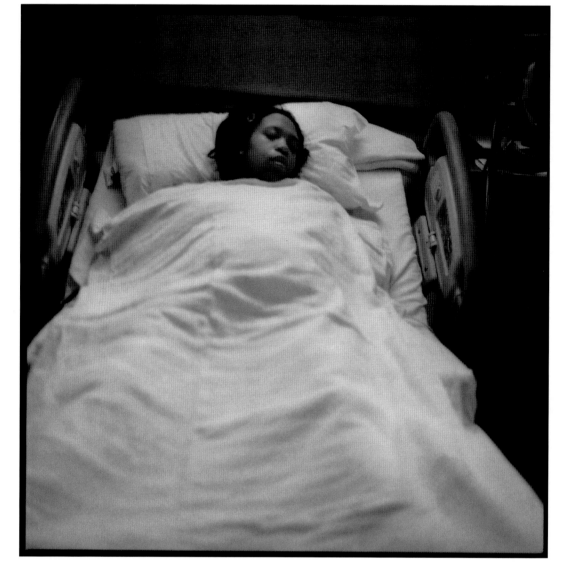

I knew that I enjoyed being there. I didn't know what part I would play. I knew I didn't want to be a nurse. I knew I didn't want to be a doctor. But I did know that I wanted to be holding her hand—that's all I wanted—to be right there by her side. I felt that was missing in the delivery. My first impression was it was mechanical. Everyone knew their place; everyone knew what was about to happen, and it just happened. I sat in the corner, and I was very observant to the whole thing. I just remember not liking the fact that she was alone; she didn't have any support. I mean she got support from the nurses, but there was no one that she bonded with, like a family friend. I remember feeling that a long time ago, but I didn't know what a doula was at that time.

Sunshin Gordon rests in the delivery room.

Opposite: Sunshin Gordon in labor, being attended by doula Jacqueline Shepard and midwife Jane Arnold

Lise Golub, a doula who is also a nurse and the wife of an obstetrician

Even though she says, "I can't do this, I can't do this," you tell her, "You can do it and you are doing it, and everything's going to be fine, you're safe, and we care about you." She needs that sense. "You're not just a number. You're not just another person. And we don't care if you have money. You are a person, and you mean something. You have tremendous value, and your value isn't just for this moment. It's doing everything that we can do to make you have the best experience, that you'll walk out of here feeling valuable, that, hopefully, it will carry on, and that your baby's valuable, and that whatever's gone on in your life before, good or bad, that that value can continue."

To be part of an event that is so important to this woman and her partner and her family, and to be really invited to that birth—because basically you're being invited there—is an honor for me. To be part of something in their life that is going to change them and to know that I was able to help them in either a small way or a major part to birth their baby. My husband laughs at me when at every birth I get tears in my eyes. He says, "You've seen so many births, you'd think you'd sort of get over this." I say, "Well, that's your Y chromosome talking." This is really a wonderful event, and when you see a woman birth her baby and where that baby started and where it's come to, it's just unbelievable. When a woman or her husband looks into your eyes and says, "We don't know how we would have done this without you being here, and we'll never ever have another baby unless you show up again," it is a validation that you really did make a change, or make an impression on their life. And you just can't get enough of it.

Dr. Bruce Meyer, medical school professor, obstetrician, and proponent of the doula movement

There is a lot of the sentiment that doula equals acupressure, equals echinacea, equals other kinds of herbal remedies, equals somebody in a smoking jacket in a dark back room grinding something in a mortar and pestle that they then put in a spoon and hand to you. It has that kind of a hocus-pocus element to it. The data says it really does decrease the cesarean section rate, but why? We don't really have good explanations for that. It deals with that mind-body duality issue, and if you're not comfortable with the idea that the mind plays a significant role in health, then you're not going to be comfortable with the idea that a doula may have value to your health.

There's a lot of resistance, but you know, nothing worth doing is incredibly easy, or I should say, anything worth doing that is incredibly easy has already been done. So we're left with the stuff that isn't so easy to do. Our philosophy is that this is a process and not a product and that it is going to take time, and it is going to take potentially a generation of people working in our labor and delivery and in other labor and deliveries. If we let ourselves get intimidated by the "We've been doing it this way for twenty years and there's nothing wrong with the way we are doing it" philosophy, then you know, when you stop growing, you die. You just have to persuade people that this kind of growth is a positive thing.

Sarah Matematico and her new baby, Physeria, wait with midwife Jane Arnold for their ride home from the hospital.

Opposite, left: Doula Debra Pascali-Bonaro helps Paula Restivo-Wilkens create a plaster cast of her body to commemorate her pregnancy.

Opposite, right: Lise Golub makes a postpartum visit and delights in Olivia Gordon, a baby whose birth she recently attended as a doula.

Carol McLarey, doula

This woman was transported to a degree I had never seen anyone in labor. She had us telling her and describing to her a scene of snow, and she just kept wanting us to talk her through, and that's how she was getting through her contractions. By the time the baby was born, she was so far away, it actually took her a while to come back. It was a confusing transition for her, and she was upset, feeling like something was wrong with the baby. We were telling her, "The baby's beautiful, the baby's wonderful and fine." And she was crying and saying, "Oh, I'm sorry. I'm sorry." And I said to her, "You know, you've been so far away, it's just going to take you a little while to come back to where we are right now. But you're all right. You're getting there, and everything's fine." And she looked way into my eyes, and it just felt like that connection was what helped to bring her back then, and she was OK.

Doula Darlinda Donlan works with Ana Fox Savillo to relieve her back pain and progress her labor.

DD: OK. Is the contraction gone now? OK. See if you can kind of slow your breathing down a little bit. Take some nice, deep breaths. Just kind of sway back and forth till the next one comes. Is it coming?
AFS: Yeah, yeah.
DD: OK. So I need you to start breathing in through your nose and out through your mouth.
AFS: I can't breathe through my nose.
DD: OK, breathe through your mouth. Good. Come on, Alexander. Come on down. Your mommy is waiting for you. She's been working hard here. Try to slow your breathing down. Slow. Good. Is it over? I want you to take a nice, deep breath now. Let's just see if you can relax. Let your body go limp. Let it just melt into the floor.

New mother Sunshin Gordon recounts how her labor was assisted by doulas Lise Golub and Jacqueline Shepard.

SG: I can just imagine, if you guys weren't there, how empty the room would have felt. It helped that he was there, that Rob was there, but it wouldn't have been the same without all of you. I think what helped the most is the fact that the doulas were there, Lise and Jackie were holding my hand. I knew they weren't leaving. I knew that the nurse had to leave, and the midwife had to leave, but I knew that Jackie and Lise were going to be there. For me, I want someone there to tell me that it's going to be OK. I'm a baby in a way.

LG: That you're not going to die.

SG: Yes, that I'm not going to die. It was just really painful, and I wanted someone to say it was OK. They did different techniques that helped a lot. The dancing part, I don't know what to call it, but that helped.

LG: You can call that labor dancing, that double-hip squeeze, squeezing the hips to take the pressure off your back.

SG: That helped a lot. I wouldn't have initiated things like that during my labor without the doula there. The best thing about it was how Lise kept saying this is the extent of the contractions. And it was. She was telling the truth, and it really helped a lot.

Sunshin Gordon in labor

Jacqueline Shepard witnesses
her first birth as a doula.

Debbie Rotunno, doula and mother of two young children, attended one mother who gave birth at home.

The caregiver didn't arrive in time, so I was on the phone with the midwife, who was en route, and she was coaching me as I was coaching the dad, and I was able to help them deliver their own baby, which was quite a beautiful thing. And right after the baby was born, the sun came up through their bedroom windows, and the little girl runs across the room, and you hear her footsteps up there, and she came down, and I got to videotape her expression as she saw her new sister. It was beautiful. It really was an unbelievable experience. And I'm new to all of this doula work, but as I come up on my one-year anniversary next month, one birth is better than the next.

Lise Golub, doula

Last night I was on the phone, oddly enough, with this woman whose baby died last year. I had sent her a card on the anniversary of the baby's death, and I just wrote her a note, and she said, "Lise, that was the most beautiful note that I have ever read." One of the things that doulas do—it's sort of a tradition—they have bead necklaces, and for every birth that they have, they add another bead to this necklace. I had been collecting beads, and when this baby died, it really touched my heart. I was in a bead store, and I found a bead that was in the shape of a heart, but was an iridescent heart. I put it in the center of all the beads on this necklace, and I wrote to the mother and told her I had done this, that I could never forget Francesca, because she really changed my life, and she changed my view of birth.

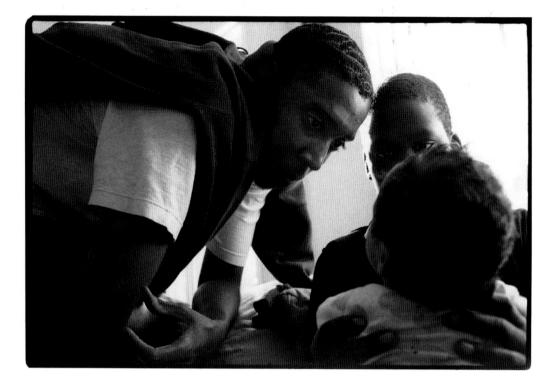

Jane Arnold tells her story of becoming a postpartum doula.

I felt so isolated when I had my four children. Soon afterwards, we moved from New York City to New Mexico, and I was carrying this incredible question with me, "Do other women when they give birth—and I had wonderful births, they were easy—do women feel so isolated, do they feel so cut off, do they feel so unsupported? What do they do? What do women do in America?" I decided that I must find this out; it became almost a hunger in me. I started this service called the M.O.M. Service, Inc. I named it M.O.M. for Maintenance of Maternity. I advertised that I would do anything for a postpartum woman. I would clean, I would cook, I would teach breastfeeding, I would teach newborn care, I would listen to their birth story. I used to go way out into the hills and park my car and walk way up to people's homes that were very isolated. I watched them and I thought, "What do they need, what do they want?" And I realized that they needed the same thing that I had needed— they needed support and they needed validation of their innate mothering abilities. They needed encouragement. They needed community. My question was answered.

Phayseria Karla Mitchell with her father (left) and her uncle

Opposite: Sarah Matematico and Phayseria wait for the baby's father at his mother's home.

Philip Mitchell, 20, talking to his new daughter, then only a few hours old

You a little heartbreaker. You know daddy gonna spoil you, right? You gonna think you better than everybody else 'cause your daddy taught you that way; there won't nobody be able to compare to you, Boo, nobody. See, my baby a mix of everything, my baby got black, my baby Chinese, my baby Philippine and Indian. She a mix of four different things. She a true mutt. But she beautiful.

Carol McLarey, doula

My third birth actually was twins, and that's when I probably could have used more support. It was a little scary. The time I had after they were born was one of the most difficult in my entire life. That's probably the part of my experience that makes me feel the most committed to making a difference for other women—because I desperately, desperately needed some kind of help afterwards at home. I had a son who was not yet five years old, and he was starting kindergarten three weeks after the babies were born. And I had a two-and-a-half-year-old daughter, and my twins were born three and a half weeks early. I was in the hospital for four days, and my mother had come to help out. The babies were in the hospital almost two weeks, and when the second one came home, she had to leave. I can still remember my husband pulling out of the driveway to take my mother to the airport. I'm sitting on the couch with a baby beside me and a baby on my lap and the two little kids running around and thinking, "What am I going to do?"

I did what I had to do, but it was really difficult. I wasn't depressed, but I was just under a tremendous amount of stress, and alone. I can remember standing in the middle of the kitchen crying. I can remember standing at the living-room window looking out just to see if anybody was going by because, if they had been, I would have said, "Come on in!" All my friends were having babies. They were of no help. They were in their own houses looking out the window.

I feel really committed to helping women get through that postpartum period without the same kind of difficulties that I had. A lot of people are just happy if you're there with them, and I know I would have been. I wouldn't have cared if anybody did anything, except just to be there in my house with me, talking to me and supporting me emotionally. It's a very fragile time. It's a very precious time. Babies deserve that kind of start, and certainly parents do. The better start they get, the better off they're going to be for the rest of their lives.

What is important is that the woman and her family have a sense of community, a community of caring and a community that acutely is trying to improve her and her baby's outcome. A C-section is not necessarily bad, and vaginal delivery is not necessarily good, but what is important is that there be a process that everybody goes through that results in a healthy mom and a healthy baby, and that a bond is created in that family.

Do I think that philosophically people need to think about these kinds of issues and to address them in the way they provide care? Yes. Would I like our program to be a model? Do you have to create a program like our program in order to do it? I don't think you do. Every community is different, and the barriers you face and the resistance you face is going to be different in different places. I would not presume to tell people in Minnesota how to create a doula program in Minnesota because I don't know enough about the culture in their labor and delivery or the culture in their community to know whether this is the right way for them. But should we be talking about and addressing these issues of midwifery care and childbirth companions and doulas? I think we should. If having a program sparks interest in other people and makes them think about it, then yes, in that sense, I think the program should be a role model.

Ana Fox Savillo with her just-delivered son, Alejandro Antonio Domingo Savillo

Keith Swarthout holds his new child, just born by cesarean section, as mother Tammy Price lays her hand on the baby's head.

Opposite: Soubia Asim and her baby receive a home visit from Lise Golub, their doula.

Jacqueline Shepard, doula

My grandfather taught me that the most important value in life is what you have within yourself. He taught me that when I was a baby. I was a very, very sick child, very sick. And my grandfather used to babysit me and, when I was with him, I didn't need my medication, and I was able to eat my lunch, and my headaches went away, and I think it was because he gave me such comfort. He taught me that early on.

Being a doula is going to allow me to give back, allow me to enhance a delivery for the mom—and the dad, offering them memories that are going to be positive, offering them a chance to reflect on the most enjoyable moments of their delivery for the rest of their lives. I'll probably be a part of their story when they're telling their child about how many pounds they weighed, what time they were born, that "Jacqueline was there."

Marie Faulkner, doula

I have seven children, and they're my life. Everything comes after them that I do, and they know it. They know they're first place, and seeing my friends now developing that same relationship with their kids, not something like, "Well, I need to go to the gym." Not that we can't have other things, but just that bond. I think it all comes from your birth experience, and having a good experience, and going into the nursing and having someone you can call on the phone who can answer questions because there are times the baby's crying and crying, and you don't know why. Having someone who you can call on to help you through it and hold your hand changes your whole outlook. I see women who didn't have that. They have a baby that's crying and crying and crying, and they're passing it off on anybody that they can get to take the baby, and you can see that a negativeness comes into the relationship. Yet when they don't go through that and they have loving support, the bond is a lifetime thing, and so I feel that what I do makes a lifetime situation between that mother and father and that child.

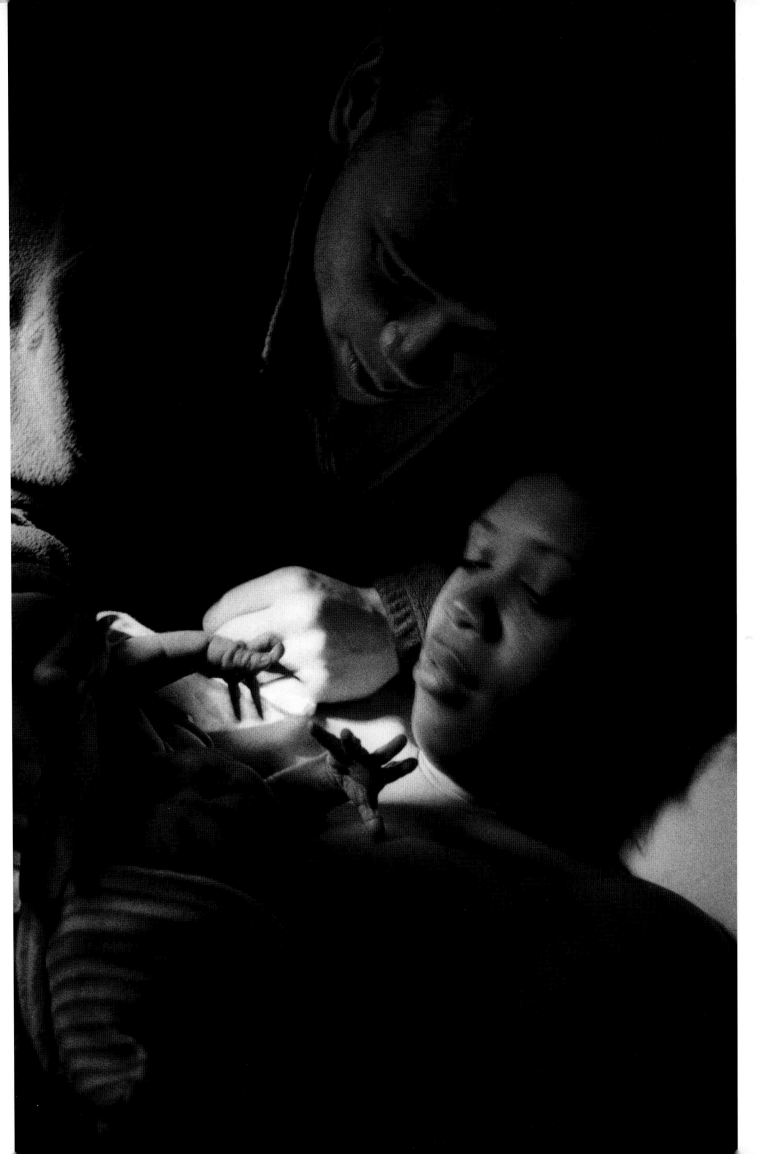

Robert and Sunshin Gordon's
first look at their new daughter

Opposite: Ana Fox Savillo at
home with her son, Alejandro

Olivia Sunshin Gordon is my baby's name. Nobody in our family's name is Olivia. We just couldn't think of a name for her for the longest time until the eighth month. Finally, we looked on the Internet and we said, "Oh, Olivia! Olivia's nice!" We didn't find out until later that it means peace. A long time ago, one of the baby's godfathers told us, before she was born, that she would be the peace between our families. They don't argue—it's just, my family never really supported me that much in this whole situation, and his family didn't agree with my family's not supporting me. So, now my family's easing up, and she *is* our peace! She *is* our little Olivia! Meaning peace.

Doula service founder Jane Arnold on why giving support is central to a doula's role

When I say support, I mean it in a really profound sense, in a way that we don't give service to people that much anymore. It means really putting another person's needs above your own for a period of time and for a specific reason.

It's very important that we have the opportunity to offer this kind of support to birthing women, either in labor or in postpartum. It is very much a part of caring for women and babies, and I'm not sure that in America we do such a good job of that. We talk a lot about it, but I don't know that we do a lot about it. And this is a very simple, loving, grassroots way to care for the heirs of our civilization.

Olivia Gordon looks at her father, Robert, moments after delivery.

Robert Gordon kisses his newborn baby daughter.

Opposite: Sunshin, Robert, and Olivia Gordon pose for their first formal family portrait.

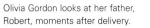

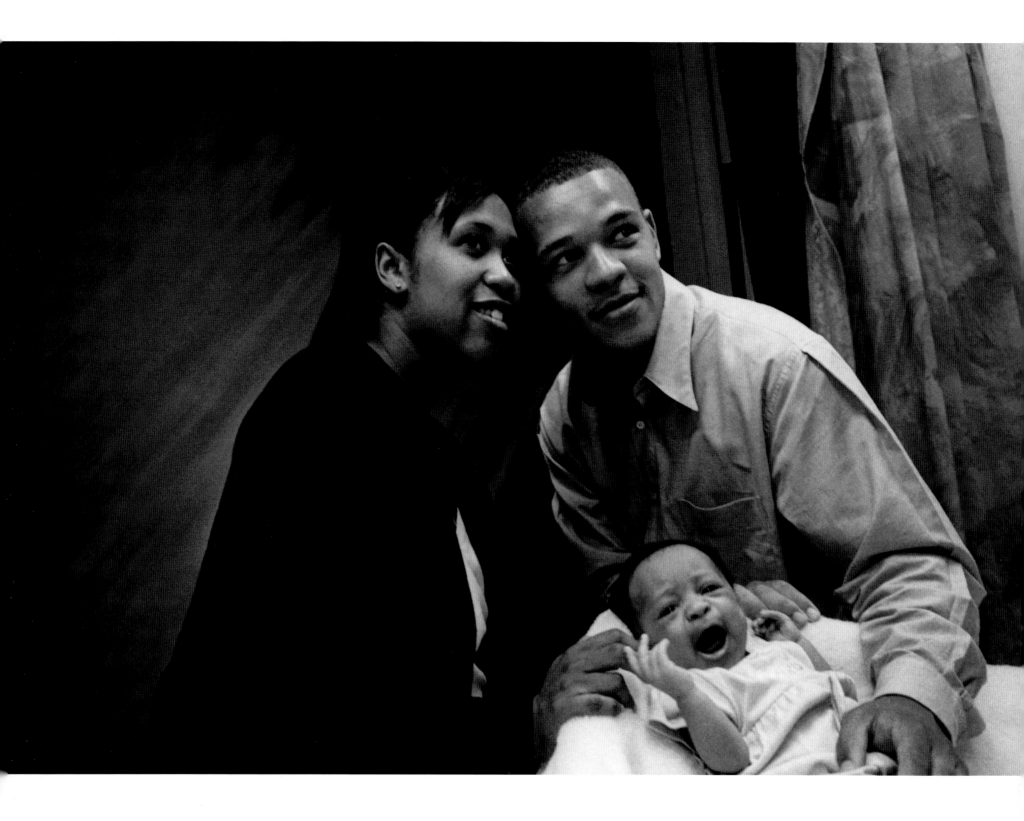

PHOTOGRAPHS BY **LUCY CAPEHART** • INTERVIEWS BY **JACK LOEFFLER**

A TRADITIONAL FUTURE

DINÉ BÍ' ÍÍNA', INC. (NAVAJO LIFEWAYS)

NAVAJO NATION

Building a future on the shoulders of the past is the goal of a group of Navajo herders, weavers, and cultural activists working under the name Diné bí' íína', meaning "Navajo lifeways." Sheep, say Navajo elders, will unlock a prosperous future for the Navajo Nation. Self-consciously identifying with deep cultural traditions, Diné bí' íína' organizers, who represent the Navajo Nation Sheep and Goat Producers, see long-term economic and cultural benefits in increasing sheep and wool production and in nurturing awareness of the history of sheep to the Navajo way of life. Founded in Arizona in 1991, the group is committed to supporting traditional ways of life and economic opportunity. While a Navajo organization primarily led by Navajo women, Diné bí' íína' works with anyone interested in raising sheep or working with wool.

Here in the Southwest desert, tribal leaders have helped revive sheep farming among the Navajo with the reintroduction of the Churro sheep, which were once widely raised by the tribe. Churro sheep are believed to have entered Navajo country with Spanish explorers, who came to New Mexico in the 1600s. The Navajo, ever adaptive, embraced the practice of raising sheep and using the wool to weave exquisite rugs. The Churro can withstand intense drought. The Churro produces lambs at a higher rate, grows more wool, of better quality, for traditional rug making and other uses, and produces lean, healthy meat. The Churro was central to Navajo life for a very long time and was deeply connected to Navajo agriculture and day-to-day life until the late nineteenth and early twentieth century when the sheep were nearly exterminated by a combination of agricultural policies, herd reduction incentives, and the introduction of other breeds by the U.S. government. In recent years the Navajo, recognizing the importance of this breed to tribal lifeways, spirituality, traditional arts, and economic independence, have been raising the Churro in increasing numbers. This old breed of sheep is in effect a symbol of the tribe's past through which one can see a promising future.

Diné bí' íína' works closely with the Navajo Sheep Project, founded in 1977 by Dr. Lyle McNeal, an animal geneticist who became familiar with the Churro breed while working with Navajo farming families. At that time the Churro was on the brink of extinction, and McNeal worked with Navajos to reintroduce the breed, placing Churro breeding stock throughout the Navajo Nation. The work of Diné bí' íína' and the annual Sheep Is Life festival builds on the foundation laid by McNeal and traditional Navajo herders. Sharon Begay, Diné bí' íína''s president and daughter of the effort's spiritual leader Goldtooth Begay, contends that the sheep give the Navajo people all they need to connect them with the past and sustain them in the future: wool to weave Navajo rugs, lean mutton to eat, and the understanding of the spiritual history of Navajo life—all are elements essential to forging a strong future for the Navajo Nation. *T.R.*

Alta Begay, Sharon Begay's sister and a Diné bí' íína' volunteer

Historically, from the non-native perspective, the sheep came with the Spaniards in the 1600s. When you go back to the traditional history, and the mythology of the Navajo, the sheep has always been here. The spirit of that sheep has always been here, and with the coming of the Spaniards, the physical sheep came. That's my understanding of sheep—it's always been here; it's always been part of the culture and who we are as people. So I think that's the fiber that continues to help us as a people to grow and expand because with sheep you're mobile, too. You can go different places with them, they're part of your family, so people move with them.

Sharon Begay is a school teacher and the founder of Diné bí' íína'.

Through history, the way that we got the sheep was through the Spanish and the conquistadors. The Navajos used to go out and steal them, and found out that they were good to eat, and they could do things with the wool. They learned how to weave the wool from the Spanish people and then from the Pueblo people. Then we learned and did our own style. We're very adaptive that way.

The way that the medicine people talk about the sheep is that there was a young warrior that went out to go hunting, and he was out near one of the sacred mountains—it was this legend—the Eastern Mountain. He was out there hunting, and all of a sudden he heard something in the bush, rustling around in one of the bushes. Then he went over there, and he thought, "Did I hear something?" So, he went over there four times. Then he listened to the bush. On the fourth time he opened the bush, and he opened it really wide. Pretty soon, at the bottom, he saw a little white fetish, and he picked it up and put it in his hand. And he looked at it, and it was like a little animal figure. Then he took it back. He folded it into one of the cloths and put it in his pouch.

When he got back to the medicine man that evening, he showed him. He said, "This is what I found in a bush up by Tsis na jin." And the medicine man said, "Yes, you will see that animal come to us soon." And that was the sheep. He had found a fetish of the sheep, and said, "Keep it here in this basket." So he put it with the bundle and pretty soon, sure enough, during his lifetime, the sheep came with the conquistadors. And that's how we got the sheep.

Leo Natani is a shepherd and a former tribal councilman.

The way I understood it from my parents was that the Churro sheep can withstand the cold weather. They can go through snow, heat, rain, and they would still be around the following year. Whereas when the Western people brought in these other types of sheep, they started dying on us. They wouldn't last. They wouldn't last the winter, and they'd have to be penned up inside in a warm place to be kept warm. But the Churro sheep can withstand staying out in the corral in a blizzard, in the rain, or any type of weather.

They're tough—that's why our parents always urged us to hang on to the Churro. We tried some other types of sheep. They'd last for a while, but not as long as the Churros, so we just had to go back with what we started.

Opening image: Sarah Natani and sheep corral,
Table Mesa near Shiprock, New Mexico

Opposite: Mountain-sheep rock art, near Bluff, Utah

For me, that's what it's about. It's a healing process. Whether it's sheep or something else that becomes the focal point of people's lives, that's where it is, that's what it means to me to be part of it. That's why I continue to invest my time, volunteer, and continue to be one of the leaders, and promote Diné bí' íína' and the sheep culture, because I think it's very important. The sheep is what helped the Navajo to survive to this point. When you look at what might happen in the future, it's going to be the sheep that saves us. Whatever's going to happen, the catastrophes people talk about, that's what I envision we go back to—even when people leave the reservation and go to work or go to school, it's like it ties you, we have to come back. Many of the families out here have lost their sheep, but the sense of having them and the sense of that culture is still there—because of the sheep. So that's my understanding of it, and my involvement in this project. I try to promote that as a philosophy.

To me, as to the Navajo people that lived through it, the elders, the annihilation was a corollary to the Jewish Holocaust, because this was part of their families' net worth. Their values were tied to the sheep, and it was a very sad time in history, and we mismanaged it as a government, obviously. There are still a few down there who carry those feelings.

Lyle McNeal

The Churro is the first sheep in North America, the first domesticated sheep, and the first sheep and first animal that led to what we might call the agrarian development of society in America, before Jamestown. But Jamestown did not make a significant impact on agriculture, particularly sheep, cattle, and livestock, so the Churro truly, even more so than the longhorn cattle or the *corriente* cattle, symbolizes civilization as we know it, in terms of providing a reliable food and fiber supply.

I always believe things happen for a reason. The creator puts things in our path and people in our path so that we can take up whatever it is that we need to. I always feel that the Creator put Lyle McNeal in our life that way at that time. My dad, not knowing English, just seeing the picture of the sheep meant a lot to him, especially the picture of a Churro sheep. He said, "That's called a Churro sheep, the leader of the sheep. It's got the long hair, and our ancestors used to have it a long time ago, and this is the first time I've ever seen one. Even a picture of one makes me feel in awe of that sheep." He said, "I wonder where we could get some." So, through him—he's the one that really started the organization, Diné bí' íína'—he was the one that said, "Go ask him if he's got any sheep for sale." So that's how we got hold of our sheep—through the Navajo Sheep Project.

The Begays' house, Jeddito, Arizona

Sheep near Polacca, Arizona

Leo Natani, who was born in 1939, grew up herding Churro sheep near Toadlena, New Mexico.

The weaving is part of our culture. If the sheep would disappear, then our culture would disappear. Everything is tied together. I have a circle over at my office which I call the balance of life. It has all four sacred mountains on it, and you are in the middle of that circle, and you have to learn all of your surroundings. You have your disagreement and you have your agreement, but you've got to learn to live with what is around you in order to survive, in order to be where we are today. Why do you think I have a hogan here? Because we put our heads together and started thinking about what our parents taught us. This is part of Sarah's teaching when she teaches weaving, because it starts from here. It starts from that round circle, which is the hogan.

Why do you think our front door is facing east? That's where our Mount Blanco is over here. That is part of our teaching. And everything goes clockwise. If you go outside when it's windy, you can watch the whirlwinds. Some are going clockwise, and some might be going counterclockwise. And that was taught to me by my father—that those that are going counterclockwise are the evil ones. You go out on a windy day and look at some whirlwind and think about it. It'll make you think. Just like what Sarah says, once you start doing your weaving, then it makes you think. You forget about your worries, and it puts your spirit, yourself into high spirit, high esteem. You don't think about all your problems. You don't think about somebody that cussed you out this morning or yesterday. You've got your mind wide open. Open space, like where we are here. You're not in a congested area.

If you can picture yourself, in that circle that I'm talking about, the balance of life, if one person can learn to live with what is around them, then they've got the problem solved. They can endure, and that's what our people did when they went to Fort Sumner in 1864 because they stuck together. They had that unity. Even though it was not written, they had their language. They had their ceremonial, and they endured that four years and they came back over here. And that's what they were trying to teach us by telling us, "Don't ever forget your values. Don't ever forget your language." But most of us did.

Sarah Natani weaving, Table Mesa, near Shiprock, New Mexico

Four-horned Churro sheep, Navajo Sheep Project's herd, Bloomfield, New Mexico

Sharon Begay

My mom told me one time—she said, "We're very vulnerable when there's only one person." And she said, "Think about the sheep that way. When I take that wool and when I spin it into many strands and when I twist it, we become intertwined and we become strong like many, many people together helping each other. That's how I think about my rug. There's a lot of history, there's a lot of things woven into that rug."

The Churro sheep are like the Navajos. That's how I see them, almost like warrior sheep. At one time, they were the first ones killed, and the Navajo people were the first ones killed of the Indian people. Then they came back. They flourished. Now they're coming back in great numbers, because more people are becoming aware, and they are coming out of extinction.

Even through the reduction, they lived in canyons where they survived, and through the help of Dr. McNeal they've come back. More people are learning about them. That's the way the Navajo people are. They went down through the genocide, even through that relocation. It seems like the government is always trying to eradicate us in that way.

That's one of the reasons why I feel an anger, but it's a quiet anger. Through this project we're saying, "We've got to fight back in some way, and why not do it through the Navajo lifeway, and that's the sheep." We're bringing the sheep back and reintroducing it to my people, who acquired a lot of wealth through it in the old days, and now they can do it again.

Goldtooth Begay, at 103 years old, is the visionary leader of all the contemporary sheep initiatives. Originally in Navajo, the interview was translated into English by interpreter Al Largo.

I want the people to know that the sheep is my life. I have followed the path of the sheep since I was little, but through time, they have put a reduction on me, and my herd has gotten smaller and smaller. So I wonder now if more reduction will only reduce my chance of ever seeing another way of life. What can they replace it with, if they make a full reduction?

Sharon Begay grew up in Jeddito, Arizona, on the Navajo Nation.

My dad's leg is straight on one side, from polio that happened when he was fifteen. He always told us, "I might be handicapped, but that has never disabled me. Go to school. Get your degree, and learn the white man's ways, because if you don't, some day they're going to take advantage of you." He said, "Learn the language; learn their ways; and then you can come back and use it with your own people and teach your people."

That's probably one of the reasons why I became a teacher. It was really through my dad's inspiration. He always told us, "Go to school" and then he always says, "I will always be of one mind," which means that he's going to only learn one language, and that's Navajo. He said, "But you have the capabilities of having two minds—you have English and Navajo—and that makes you more powerful in one person." If you learn your two languages, it'll make you strong like two people—is what he was saying.

He was the one that always encouraged us about getting educated. My mom was just the opposite. She always told us, "You need to stay home and you need to be a traditional Navajo woman. Do what you have to do at home, and let the men be out there and do their work outside the

Churro rams, Navajo Sheep Project's herd, Bloomfield, New Mexico

Opposite: Sharon and Goldtooth Begay, Jeddito, Arizona

Mary Oskie in front of her log
cabin near Ganado, Arizona

Terrell Piechowski, school counselor and Diné bí' iína' volunteer

The Long Walk was a defining point in Navajo culture. It affected people in many, many different ways. What has been true of all native cultures in the United States and other places like Canada, Mexico, is a huge sense of loss after the conquest. Something was lost. It's a defining moment to say, "Here's where we lost something." It has also for the Navajo people been a defining moment of rebuilding. When they came back from the Long Walk, they had to rebuild a nation, a society, and the rules of the game had changed. I see the Navajo people suffering from the loss yet. This sense of loss is intergenerational—it gets passed on down from father to son to mother to daughter—a sense of despair.

What is needed and what is happening on the Navajo Nation is a discussion right now, and the question that Diné bí' iína' poses—that Sheep Is Life poses—is a very important question: "What is the value of what we had in the past? What is the value of the sheep culture itself, and how is that culture going to be translated into the future to our children?"

This morning I was asking Al if it should be "Diné bí' iína'," with an *i*, or "Diné be iína'," with an *e*. He thought about it, and we started talking about it, and he said, "You know what, Sharon? It really doesn't make no difference whether it's with an *i* or an *e*—it's still the lifeway of the people. Think about how the Navajo people feel about sheep. We are sheep. We eat it, and that's the reason why people take care of it. We have to take care of what we eat. We have to take care of our food." If everything else was gone, and there were sheep, we can still make a living and we can still live our life. With just sheep. We can weave the cloth, and we can use it for food, and it's part of our spiritual life.

Al Largo and Marlene Benally at
the Begays' ranch, Jeddito, Arizona

Sarah Natani holding a newborn lamb,
Table Mesa, near Shiprock, New Mexico

Opposite: Mutton case, Native American
Traditional Meat Store, on Highway 64
between Shiprock and Farmington,
New Mexico

Leo Natani

I'm a shepherd. I started herding sheep when I was big enough to walk. I was taught that I had to count our sheep before we brought them back. That's the first thing that we were taught. Make sure that you bring all of them back, even though we were playing half of the time. But we made sure we counted every one of them before we brought them home, or our parents are angry with us, because we had to go back and hunt up the ones that were missing.

Being a sheepherder is the same as raising your own family. They're your kids. If you look into the eyes of those sheep to butcher one of them, it's really hard for you to pick up one that you're going to eat, and use as food, if they look at you just the same way that your kids look at you, and you treat them the same way, whether it's your sheep or your horses. I guess our Creator put them there for a reason because we use them for our food. We use them for our bedding. We use them if we're in need of financial assistance. They're there for a reason because she uses them for her weaving. Sarah uses them for her teaching and to tell other people about our culture, because weaving is part of our culture. It's a very important part of our culture. A shepherd is really important. A shepherd is the one that overlooks and takes care of sheep so they don't get chased down by a coyote. They don't get chased down by a human coyote, especially.

When you talk about traditional Navajo grassroots, you're talking about a system of life that was based on a small, extended family group of people, who took care of each other. They might have a spokesman, but they basically took care of each other. They got done what needed to be done in a harmonious fashion, which was part of their spirituality. Then after the conquest, the Navajo people were told to departmentalize, that you needed leaders, you needed divisions, and you needed all of this. All of a sudden, it's no longer grassroots—it's no longer family members taking care of their own and operating as a family, as an extended family.

Now it's leaders of departments and leaders of systems, and they don't consult anymore in a real way. They consult for votes or they consult for popularity to stay in office or power to stay in office. So it became a real power game and not a game of love and belonging. It became a game of power, and everybody wanting to survive through walking up the hierarchy, the chain of command. All of a sudden the grassroots people, the ones who still believe that we need to sit down and talk like a family and work this out together in a harmonious way, have all been lost in the decision-making process.

So Diné bí' íína' is saying, "Let's sit down and let's talk again, and let's not have these divisions." We're not talking about going back and seeing what grandma has to say, and then building a society based on what grandma has to say. We're saying grandma should sit down with the kids, and the kids should sit down with the politicians and the superintendent of the schools and the medicine men, and let's have a dialogue. Let's get back to how decisions used to be made. If somebody emerges as a leader who really cares about the people and not the dollar or the power it brings in, then we will acknowledge them as leader, and they can become our spokesman. I think that's what's happening through Diné bí' íína'. We're beginning to see some spokesmen coming up, a new generation of spokespeople who are not tied in any way to any political, economic, or educational system. They are just spokesmen for dialogue.

Leo Natani shares the belief of many Navajo elders about the importance of passing on traditions to younger generations.

Our parents told us that the sheep is the one that keeps nature in balance. If it wasn't for the livestock, then we'll be overgrown with wild forage. In other words, they're the lawn mowers. In the spring or in the fall, they're the ones that plant the seed, when they push the seeds down into the ground because there's no one else to do it. Because the seeds come from the skies, and the sheep are the ones that push the seed down into the ground to make the grasses grow over and over again, year after year, generation after generation.

This is the teaching that was brought down to the kids when they were small. As soon as they start talking, or as soon as they start learning to comprehend, this was taught to them orally. Nothing was written. So it just passed from one generation to the other until we started forgetting, until the Western people came in, and they started telling us that our teaching was wrong, our teaching was evil. Forget about your teaching. Just go with the written language. That's when we started forgetting our language, our values.

Leo Natani, husband of Sarah Natani, on one of the primary principles of Navajo teaching

Peace and harmony is knowing who you are. Peace and harmony is greeting other people. Peace and harmony is saying hello to somebody that you meet. Peace and harmony is respecting an elderly person. Peace and harmony means you're helping a small child. Peace and harmony means that you're assisting whoever is in need. If we can get the meaning of peace and harmony to everybody in this world, we wouldn't have any problem. That's how we teach our peacemakers. That's how I teach my peacemakers. Regardless of the color of their skin, or their clans, peace and harmony is being able to help somebody.

Lena Benally, a member of Diné bi' iiná's
board of directors, and her grandson, Donnie,
at the Begays' ranch, Jeddito, Arizona

Sarah Natani, a weaver and spinner for many years, lives in Table Mesa, New Mexico.

Weaving, it's part of the culture. If you're a troubled person, if you sit down to your weaving, your bad feeling all goes away and the good one comes in. Then you start thinking about your pattern, and when you have a real fine and very good wool to work with, it really builds up your design. The pattern comes to you naturally. You don't put a sketch in it because it'll never come out the same way you drew it. Your whole rug would show how your pattern would be. Some people say that the pattern tells you different stories, but that's not the way I was told. Other people are that way. Your pattern just comes to you, I think.

Interior of Sarah and Leo Natani's hogan, with rugs woven by Sarah

Alta Begay has worked with Diné bí' íína' since 1990.

One of the things that people always ask, "What's the Navajo philosophy?"
What's important about that is that there's not one philosophy. The Navajos
have never really had one to say, "This is the philosophy, this is it." It's an
evolving kind of thing. And in each individual person you see a philosophy
that might be a little bit different from the next person. To me that's what
Navajo has been about. It's the evolving of things; we're adapting to new
things and bringing it in and making it a strong part of the culture. There's
some underlying balances that are there that equalize these things, the new
things that come. That's how I see it. That's my philosophy.

Antonio Manzanares is a Hispano shepherd and founder of Tierra Wools, a community-based weaving store and workshop.

See, what I find is people romanticize a lot of this stuff. We're trying to make a living with this stuff, and it is damn hard, let
me tell you. They see the land; they see the sheep. They don't know the work. You don't know how hard we've worked to
lamb these sheep. Every year I think, "Why am I in this business? Why am I in this business when I'm seeing dead lambs
mounting up." It's great to want to save Navajo sheep culture, but I'm wondering what the hell are we saving it for—so it
will be a museum, so it's a green space for all these developments around us?

I'm thinking to myself, "Why are we working so damn hard? What are we trying to save here, anyway?" I've gotten a
little burned on this whole grassroots movement. I mean I'm still in it, and I still believe in it, but Jiminy Crispers, what are
we working for? In the end I can't see; I can't see the end. What are we saving? Culturally, are we just going to be saving it
so it's a museum piece? Is that it?

Veterinarian Adrienne Ruby treats sheep
for pinkeye near Polacca, Arizona.

Terrell Piechowski credits Lyle McNeal with an important role in the long-range effort to reintroduce sheep.

It's one man who has a vision to do something, and then it becomes a crusade and a struggle to do it. His goal was to save the Navajo Churro sheep from extinction. He has succeeded in that against all of the forces. These were major forces in academia, in agriculture, that said, "Why? Why do you want to have this particular animal survive extinction? It's a domesticated animal, it's an animal that has no value, and we've tried to breed this animal out of the genetics of sheep for a long time, and you're just as stubborn and as unreasonable about this as some of these Navajo people that refuse to give up this animal." So he was bucking a movement that did not see value in this particular animal, and he did it for years and years and years. I think he upset a lot of people.

His salvation right now, as a man, as a human being, is that he has made contact morally, spiritually, with the heart, with some Navajo people, and they're the ones that are supporting him. They're the ones who understand what he does and the importance of it. This is what keeps Lyle going—his Navajo family.

My sensitivity to Mother Earth was not taught to me in college. My grandparents were farmers, ranchers, but the Navajo people have taught me to look at land and animals in a whole different perspective. I think it's been a two-way learning street. We've shared with them some things that we've learned, but I've learned a whole new respect for Mother Earth and Father Sky and what we need to do to maintain some holistic balance. We're definitely out of balance right now. We forced the Navajos to live, and to manage those animals, in a system they weren't accustomed to. Before the formation of the reservation, they were migratory, and the livestock moved seasonally to those ranges and rested on the other ranges while they moved, and then they came back. A lot of our ranchers here in the inter-mountain area still practice that, but we didn't allow the Navajo people to do that when we incarcerated them on a fixed amount of land in that reservation location. We removed them from Dibensa, the northern sacred peak, and Mount Taylor, and all those areas that they grazed their livestock on. So we threw the ecosystem off balance. We should not blame the Navajo people. We are at fault, our government. We took the natural grazing system for those animals, those herbivores, and forced them, like putting them into confinement. I challenge any Anglo rancher to make a success on the reservation raising livestock like they have. It would be a miracle, because we couldn't.

I am impressed by an organization like Diné bí' íína', that is surviving on volunteers. It survives on people who are committed to the mission, who believe in the mission, who see the vision, and want to put their time and effort into it. They're not concerned about who's going to pay me, who isn't going to pay me, they just believe that this needs to be done. On the Navajo Nation we're going to have a groundswell of people who are going to say, not "What can you give me?" or "What's the next federal program coming down the pipe that I can get onto?" They're going to say, "What can we do for ourselves, where do we start working together as a community again?" I think tremendous things are going to happen when that idea and that concept starts to hit.

Navajo Sheep Project sign, Bloomfield, New Mexico

Opposite: Tony Venderver, Al Largo's stepfather, in the Venderver home near Haystack Mountain, New Mexico

PHOTOGRAPHS BY **ELI REED** · INTERVIEWS BY **GEORGE KING**

FAITH, RACE, AND RENEWAL

EAU CLAIRE COMMUNITY COUNCIL · EAU CLAIRE COMMUNITY OF SHALOM

EAU CLAIRE–NORTH COLUMBIA, SOUTH CAROLINA

Eau Claire, South Carolina, with a population of approximately thirty thousand, sits just north of Columbia, the state capital. At one time Eau Claire, the city's first suburb, was solidly white and middle class. During the 1960s, Eau Claire saw changes like those in many American neighborhoods close to downtown areas. As urban renewal and redevelopment changed the landscape of greater Columbia, African Americans were uprooted from their inner-city homes and began to settle in Eau Claire. Many white residents moved out into newer suburbs, selling their former homes to absentee landlords, who created a community of renters. As the civil rights movement progressed, African American families bought or built homes in the Eau Claire area, and they eventually became the majority population, determined to play an active role in local politics.

This slow but profound transformation left Eau Claire with an abundance of local assets and a desire for neighborhood stability. Current residents use different terms to describe the changes and perceived decline of the area, citing absentee property owners, inadequate funding for public schools, discriminatory practices by realtors, banks, and insurance companies, which collectively contributed to a lowering of property values and apparent community indifference. In the last ten to fifteen years, a group of residents began working to revive Eau Claire. Beginning with biracial, faith-based efforts, blacks and whites came together to build grassroots support to improve the community for all. With over seventy churches and at least thirty neighborhood associations, Eau Claire leaders formed two primary community initiatives: the Eau Claire Community Council and the Community of Shalom.

The mission of the council, founded in 1984, is to work collaboratively with a diversity of neighborhoods and community interests to improve Eau Claire–North Columbia. From its inception, it was a biracial group confronting problems affecting both blacks and whites. Recognizing the need for shared leadership, the council rotates the presidency annually between black and white leadership, fostering a profound sense of biracial ownership.

The Community of Shalom, a national initiative of the United Methodist Church, encouraged a historically black church, Frances Burns Methodist Church, and the historically white College Place United Methodist Church to join together in a faith-based, ecumenical effort. Led by local ministers and lay church members, Shalom builds partnerships with other churches, community organizations, and institutions to inspire racial understanding and improve health care, education, housing, and safety.

The renewal of Eau Claire results from the commitment of many residents. Born of a desire to restore property values, promote self-esteem, and advance political influence, the Eau Claire leadership sustains local activism and advances the common good. Through regular meetings and dialogue marked by both patience and frankness, a cadre of residents converted talk to tolerance and communication to collaboration. With purposeful effort they forged initiatives across lines of race and class, positioning Eau Claire to confront and solve problems with vision, decency, and the promise of sustained success. *T.R.*

Opening image:
An Eau Claire street at dusk

Above: Church members at
Wesley United Methodist Church
prior to a baptism service

Bottom: Scott Trent Jr., former
president of the Eau Claire
Community Council, looking at
graffiti on the Norfolk-Southern
railroad trestle on North Main Street

Henry Bracey, former president-elect of the Eau Claire Community Council, at the thirteenth annual Eau Claire Community Thanksgiving Celebration at College Place United Methodist Church, November 1998

A long time ago, years ago, some visionaries came upon some acreage in the northern sector of Columbia, South Carolina, and they contemplated what it represented, and they decided that it had a lot of features, a lot of very powerful qualities. It would be a nice place to come and raise your family. It would be a nice place for young children to grow up and play. It would be a nice place to build institutions of education. It would be a nice place to build places of worship. And they coined the name "Eau Claire," which means "clear water."

They raised families. They attended the educational institutions. They went to the religious institutions. And through this the community thrived. Then some of the visionaries lost the vision. They moved out of Eau Claire. They moved to the suburbs. They moved out of the state. But there were some who stayed.

Some of those who stayed lost the vision also. They stayed because they couldn't go anywhere. They didn't have the funds or the resources to buy or build in some other location. But those who left rented property, and it became a community of renters. And because of this Eau Claire became a community not unlike many other communities. And because it was a particular segment of time and it had a particular segment of problems, the news media and other segments of our community began to label it. And the vision continued to fade away. Like the phoenix that rose from the ashes, new visionaries were born, and they looked at this community, and they saw the possi-

bility that it represented. Bill Manley was one of those visionaries, and I would be remiss if I didn't mention Dorcas Elledge, who welcomed me when I came to this community and said, "Henry, don't come and just watch. Henry, get involved. We need to save this community. Henry, let me tell you what this community represents." And although I arrived with little or no vision—I just saw a piece of property that I liked—she instilled the vision.

And then there was Leroy Moss, who fought to make this place a better place to live. And there was Henry Hopkins, and there was Fran Potter, Scott Trent, Rhett Anders, and many, many others who got involved in developing the vision of the community called Eau Claire.

And so I welcome you to the Land of Clear Water. The water is not so clear anymore, and the stream that once ran through the heart of the city has been covered and paved. But there's a lot of things going on that represent a clear vision. We have a new survey building that's been revived. We have a strip mall that's been revived. And there are many, many programs for our youth in the community to make them better citizens—because the visionaries that live in Eau Claire today decided that we could create the reality, that we would not let this reality be destroyed by anyone or anything. And so I thank each and every one of you who came to share in this celebration and this Thanksgiving. When you give thanks tomorrow for all the many blessings that you've received, give thanks that God created a community called Eau Claire.

Playing baseball at a trailer park on Fairfield Road

Reverend Wiley Cooper, pastor of College Place United Methodist Church and cochair of the Eau Claire Community of Shalom

Every Shalom is different because every community is different, and every group decides what it needs to do. We're bound by that wonderful passage from Jeremiah where the children of Israel are in captivity in Babylonia, and old Jeremiah is writing to them and, of course, they don't want to do anything except come home. He says, "Build houses, plant gardens, get married, give your children in marriage." In other words, you're going to be there for a while. "Seek the Shalom of the city where you are in exile, for in its Shalom you shall find your Shalom."

Shalom is a very small group. A lot more people are involved in doing than are involved in meeting. There are only a very few people these days who find it rewarding to sit in meetings and plan what's going to happen. But they come out to work on a house. They come out to go to the Zoning Board meeting. They come out to lobby city council. And so we have this tremendous network of people with the different neighborhood associations. There are twenty-eight active neighborhood associations in Eau Claire. All of those are brought together with the Eau Claire Community Council.

It's amazing what a small group of people can do and how people think it's big. There are a few folks who are going to be there, and are going to be working, and are going to be responding. For two years we had no money. We even refused to take the United Methodist Church's first grant of two thousand dollars for about a year and a half because we were convinced that if we got diverted into money, we would lose the mission that we were about. I think we had a thousand dollars from the church I'm pastor of, to help with stamps and stuff like that for about a year and a half. That was it. And we worked houses. We did this other park. We had a lot of wonderful things going. Don't let anybody tell you that money is the problem. Money is not the problem.

I got interested in Shalom because it was a vehicle through which we could make a difference in Eau Claire. I had sold real estate, so I knew what the fair housing laws were. When I started calling about houses in Eau Claire, it became evident that there was some problem there, and Wiley and I were discussing it, and I said, "I wonder what would happen if I called some realtors and said, 'I'm looking for a house. It has to be in the city limits, and I want something $100,000 or under. A fixer-upper.' I wonder where they would send me?" Well, they sent me everywhere but to Eau Claire. In fact, they refused to show me houses in Eau Claire. And I, being a reporter, documented it.

We went to Jesse Washington at the Community Relations Council and said, "Help us set up this meeting." And he did, with the Association of Realtors, and we said, "We don't want your licenses, but we do want change." We told them some positive things about the community, and we handed them that documentation and said, "Change it. You're red-lining and you're steering." I knew if they were protecting this little, southern, white lady from coming into Eau Claire, they were only bringing black people into Eau Claire. They were being as unfair to them as to me.

Scott Trent looking into the old Monteith School, the oldest black school structure in South Carolina

Opposite: Lee Bolton and a Shalom member do yard work as part of their housing rehabilitation effort with the Eau Claire Community of Shalom.

Becky Bailey, who attended Eau Claire High School, is currently editor of the *New Survey*, the newsletter of the Eau Claire Community Council.

It has to do with racial issues and community issues and generational issues—all the things that make a community a community. By coining the notion of Shalom ("We'll have peace among all of us"), they help people who are down on their luck with cleaning up their houses. They've actually helped restore some houses, and they've done a lot of things like that.

One of the biggest things that they did was they went before the Board of Realtors. What was happening was that the Board of Realtors was telling people, "You don't want to live in Eau Claire. Let me show you this nice house over here in Rosewood. Let me show you this pretty little place out in Saint Andrews." Once we realized and Shalom realized that, they said, "Cease and desist. You know, that's illegal. You can't do that. There are nice houses out here, and there are nice people out here, and it's not fair to stereotype the entire community because of incidences that happened in the past or that happened in isolated areas."

Since then the community has just opened up. It has just blossomed. The realtors are bringing people out here. They're realizing the error of their ways.

Women's church group at Reverend Wiley and Emily Cooper's house

Opposite: Wiley Cooper teaching children about the many portrayals of Jesus

James Soloman Jr., the son of a Georgia sharecropper, moved to Columbia in 1975.

I like people. I like working with people. I get satisfaction from seeing people with a sense of accomplishment. Basically I believe that the average person that you bump into on the street is just like me—they like people, they are friendly, and most of the time will go out of their way to help somebody. A lot of them are afraid now because they think the other person isn't friendly. But once they get to know that other person, they find that they are probably just as friendly as they are. There is a lot of fear in our communities. People are afraid of one another. The young people are afraid of the older people, or dislike them. The older people are definitely afraid of the younger people. They think they're on drugs. They see them with their pants down on their hips, and they think that they are going to hurt them. They talk loud; they see the way they walk. When I see somebody like that, what I see is myself fifty years ago because I was wearing drape pants and zoot suits and listening to Louis Jordan. My folks thought that was the worst thing in the world. It was natural for me. Well, these kids have their own culture; they aren't bad kids. They're just like we were, it's just a different time. I think they want the same things. They want people to be interested in them. They want people to work with them. They want advice from older people.

The white policy makers were rough. They seemed to want to be harmonious in their relationship but they didn't want to relinquish any power. They wanted to hold on to the power. You could be there, as they say, as the chaplain or the vice president, but as far as getting in the policy making and being the head of something, that took some time. People just have that kind of mentality. It's all right to be richer, but you can't supervise nothing, you can't make the decisions, you can't be in charge.

When Interstate 77 plowed through here, everyone said that this is not the place for me to be no more. We couldn't go nowhere. Where are we going? "We," meaning blacks. So we stayed, and the whites left, and then that was the opportunity. If you want to leave, and we want to stay, then we should run it. They had a lot of problems with that. Lots of problems. Believe me. Even the ones that were left did not want to cooperate with us. I guess that's human behavior. I don't sit down and drill on that. You know, if you don't accept me—who I am, where I am, regardless of my cultural background—then that's your problem. It's not mine—because I'm not going to be put in bondage by you. So that's just part of our philosophy. There's nothing humanly possible to make people accept you, even if they work with you.

They used to say, "Don't move to Eau Claire. There ain't nothin' out there." Now they've found that the land is cheap, and it's right in the inner city, and the city has taken so much interest in it. They drive by and see all this. Columbia College has just completed a building and is still building. New schools are all over the place; we're tearing down all the old schools—putting in new schools. The schools that are left are being turned into community places. So I would say, definitely, you can have bricks and mortar all you want, but you have to change the minds of people, you know, because bricks and mortar are abstract. They ain't going to do nothing but be bricks and mortar. Now, all of a sudden, with the Empowerment Zone money and all the rest of it, everybody wants to lead. The preachers want theirs. The educators want theirs. The community people want theirs.

Henry Hopkins, local organizer and executive
director of the Eau Claire Community Council,
at a meeting on the prevention of violence

Opposite: Eau Claire High School Color Guard
practicing a routine

Arnold Williams moved to Columbia from Florence, South Carolina, in 1992.

I'm forty-five, be forty-six this December. Growing up in the country, growing up around a mixed group of people, we had blacks, we had whites, and we all was poor and we didn't know we was poor. One of my childhood best buddies was a guy named Billy Taylor, a good friend. We played together. I spent many nights at his home. He spent many nights at mine. I went to his church. He went to our church—for years, until we started school in 1961. That's when Billy and I realized that the world saw us different. He was white. I was black.

That great-great-grandmother who was born a slave was so instrumental for me—and I hope it helped Billy too. She said, "The world sees you different, but God always saw you're the same because you're a part of his creation." I guess from her always being there for me, if anyone could have been angry with the circumstance or condition of prejudice and racism, it should have been her, but she never exhibited any anger or any hostility about it. She'd always say, "Son, that's just how it was."

Josephine Spry, a beneficiary of
home rehabilitation efforts by Shalom

Opposite: Fran Potter, longtime
community activist and artist

Fran Potter, a member of the zoning board and former president of the Eau Claire Community Council

I was a tomboy and my first activism that I can recall was in the first grade, when it became apparent that the boys ran the school ground and the girls were not going to be able to play on anything and I organized a girls' vigilante committee—took control of the school ground. I guess that was my first community activism. I also recall that I had a tremendous aversion to the boys with their BB guns, because they used to shoot all the birds. I took care of that by taking their birds, if they shot them in my yard, and making the boys come in the yard, dig their grave, and do a funeral service for the birds. So at least they didn't shoot birds in my yard.

James Soloman Jr. was formerly state commissioner of the Department of Social Services for South Carolina.

I've been around a long time. The times are different now. People are very occupied with stuff and with things and with doing things. People are not as community-minded as they were even when I first moved here. People are, by and large, more concerned with addressing their own needs. When you start trying to promote a sense of community, it's very difficult work, because it is difficult to get people involved at the level at which it makes a difference—people who ought to be involved. Sometimes it is because of a sense of powerlessness. A lot of times people feel that they just don't have the power to make a difference or to bring about positive change, and they try two or three times and it doesn't work, so they just cease to try. Communities age. People who were interested at one time because they had kids in elementary school now have kids that are grown, and those kids have families and they no longer live in the neighborhood. Things just change. It's really not easy. It is easier when there is a problem, when people perceive that there is a problem which affects everybody. It is easier to get people to rally around a problem, to demonstrate, to complain, to try to fix the problem. But to get people to come together and work together, to develop a vision for the neighborhood and strategies and plans of action for achieving that vision, that's a good deal more difficult. So it just isn't easy, but it is rewarding.

Toliver's Mane Event barber shop

Rhett Anders, a local real estate agent, is the president-elect of the Eau Claire Community Council.

My parents ran liquor stores. And while I lived in the white middle-class and upper-middle-class suburb and went to private school, the poor, predominantly black communities supported that lifestyle for me. So I think a lot of the things I do is because of that. I owe them, to give back to the community that gave me that. It's a good feeling, and I'm very blessed that I recognized it. A lot of people wouldn't.

Rhett Anders, current Eau Claire
Community Council president and real
estate agent, in front of a historic property

Opposite left: Shadow of Rhett Anders at
the old Olympic-size swimming pool, built
in 1910 for the Ridgewood Country Club

Opposite right: Lee Bolton, former director
of Hold Out the Lifeline and a member of
Shalom Community of Eau Claire, in the
parking lot of Zesto's, a popular restaurant

Judy Williams and her husband, Arnold, are both ministers in the Eau Claire community.

My husband is known in this community by the kids and their parents, as Mr. Reverend. Never heard that term until we came to Columbia. Mr. Reverend. If a kid would walk up right now, and my husband was there, you would hear them say Mr. Reverend. That's his name. If you would talk to almost anybody walking along the street and you asked them, "What's your church?" they would probably tell you, "New Hope, and Mr. Reverend is our pastor." We have never seen them darken these doors, but they will tell you that because they feel we are part of this community. We had to earn that. Not until last year, did we really make an inroad to build that trust with this community.

I'll never forget one of the moms in the housing unit that sits right back here from the church. She made this statement probably a year after we were here, and it went something like this—she really didn't care whether we were here or not because we were like everybody else who came to Eau Claire. We were knights in shining armor on our little white horses, coming in with all the answers for this community. She said—these were her exact words—"As soon as you get the next star in your crown, you'll be gone too." That has stuck with me ever since. That made us begin to look, because we were following a tradition of what we had learned in church and what they taught us in school. But we had to literally go in the community and find out what they needed, so that they could take ownership of what was happening to them and for them by us.

Baseball game at Hyatt Park

Arnold Williams is a pastor with New Hope Ministries, part of the Church of the Nazarene.

It's got to start from the grassroots level and work its way up. People need to buy into the concept that we can make a difference in our community. People need to buy into the concept that this is what we need to do. For somebody dictating from the top down, it's what the top wants and not what the people want, and if the people can't see, they won't do it. People do what people see.

Chris Geise, a student at Eau Claire High School

The one thing that everybody looks at is TV. If you wanted to change a lot of things in the world, you would get somebody on TV, not nobody famous, because most people who are famous don't know about poverty. You would get somebody straight out of the projects who really cares about themselves and what goes on in the projects and put them on TV, or put a bunch of them on TV, and let them just talk it out with somebody in politics. If it was up to me, I would go on TV and interrupt all the shows, interrupt all of them, and just have it out.

Mary Hunter is president of her neighborhood association in Eau Claire.

You feel guilty when you start complaining and ask other people to do things for you. Well, I feel I need to do some of it myself. So I started going to the meetings, and I did want to help, but I wasn't ready to take on the responsibility of being the president. I was thinking, "I wonder why they didn't have a woman." It was time for elections, and I was really thinking about one of the strong women wanting to nominate somebody. I didn't hear a word about who they had nominated. The nominating committee came that day and called my name, and I know I got hot. There was no way I could say no, because I was thinking all these things to myself, so I just took it on. Somebody needs to do it. We have a lot of people working. It's just a few that are not involved, and it might not be that they don't want to be. I don't know what the reasons are. People have all kinds of reasons.

Playing basketball at Lorick Park

Scott Trent Jr. has lived in the same house in Eau Claire for nineteen years.

Luther Battiste, a former councilman who came of age during the 1960s, is a native of Orangeburg, South Carolina, and a longtime resident of Eau Claire.

They would have sessions at church at night, and you would go and you'd have choirs singing and you would have fiery speeches, and you felt a part of something that was making a positive change in South Carolina and the country. I felt very lucky to be a part of that. When I think about my service on city council and my public service now, that is a foundation for me to be vigilant, to be forceful on issues, because I have that civil rights experience of wanting to produce change. So I see that what I do now is an extension of that, and I always feel the need, no matter what public forum I'm in, to try to produce positive change. That's the basis for everything I do.

Sam Davis, Columbia City Council member and former president of Eau Claire Community Council

Opposite: Leroy Moss, a community worker and activist who is blind, at the recreational center that is named in his honor

To me the thing to be proud of is the head of steam, the fact that we have more people involved now than we did ten years ago. It takes a while to build up a momentum, to get people activated, where they can do things. You help them find a niche in which they can work. You get neighborhoods organized. You get them meeting regularly. You get them participating in the council on a monthly basis, quarterly basis. You have little success stories, and those stories in themselves generate an interest, a need for something bigger. Then you get that bigger thing and end up where we are now. With the big head of steam, we can get the city of Columbia to invest two million dollars to save one old building. That is something that you don't get done overnight.

A lot of folks want things to change, and they complain, and think because they fuss, the government will respond, and it will be changed next week. Well, in very few cases that may happen, but that's rare. It takes more than one time of complaining, of raising an issue. It takes more than one funding cycle, more than one grant, from more than one foundation, to get that momentum. After ten years Eau Claire is almost like a steam engine. We've got that momentum going where everybody knows that Eau Claire is on the move.

Every neighborhood that gets activated probably does that. If not, then I would wonder, how do urban neighborhoods, how do people really make change in their environment that they want done? It's not the process that corporate America operates on, where you got a boss and he says, "This is our project, and George, Bill, Sam, Sue, and Mary, it's your job, you go do it and come back in thirty days," and it's done. "Here's the resources, the money, to go do it." Neighborhood activism, neighborhood change, doesn't work that way. To me, it's all this fussing, almost like a ball of fussiness, and everybody is in that ball of fussiness, moving and fussing and carrying on and demanding and activating and doing. All of a sudden that ball starts rolling—it's gotten the attention of the folks who needed to be told—city government, county government, federal folks, foundations, local corporations. All of a sudden they say, "Well, gee, something is happening in Eau Claire–North Columbia. Gee, something's going on out there. These folks are saying we need to be a part, so let's go be a part." Without us really knowing it, they get pulled in, and then all of a sudden the momentum, the critical mass is reached, and so we're off and rolling.

Scott Trent Jr., a founding member of the Eau Claire Community Council

So many of us had been out there working and talking among ourselves. We bounced ideas off of each other; we raised issues. We were concerned enough to always meet. It seemed like there was something negative that needed to be undone, that we had to be concerned about, and we worked ourselves into a frenzy, really, in a sense. We were constantly talking and constantly meeting and constantly demanding that something be done.

Then after about eight years, Mr. Moss was one of those who got to the point of saying, "Well, all we do is meet and talk, and I'm tired of meeting and talking. I want to do something. I want some action." The critical point, the critical mass had been reached. There had been enough of everything going on and enough movement that, without us being aware of it, like an ocean, the wave broke. Like a water pipe, it busted. All of a sudden, in the last couple of years, everything has just happened, like, "Boom!" There's all kinds of activity taking place all over Eau Claire–North Columbia.

Columbia chief of police
Charles Austin Sr. baptizes
Brandon Hawkins at Central
Baptist Church.

Charles Austin Sr., pastor and Columbia chief of police, preaches to the
Village of Hope Fellowship on Pentecost Day.

I need to remind you that not only did he say the Gates of Hell,
but he said the hell-raisers shall not prevail against it either.
And when Jesus made this proclamation,
he didn't mention anything about architects.
Because we've gotten real hung up these days on buildings,
and what our buildings look like,
who's got the biggest building,
and who's gonna have the biggest building.
But Jesus never mentioned anything
about architects with sketches of a new building.
Jesus never mentions buildings; he never mentions denominations.
Instead, he defined the Church as the body of believers.
Believers who came from places such as Galatia, Ephesus,
Corinth, Thessalonica, and Colossae.
But he never mentioned Methodist.
He never mentioned Baptist.
He never mentioned Catholic, Presbyterians, Episcopalians,
Pentecostals.
He never mentioned any denomination.
Jesus only saw them as being a fellowship.
And no matter what name we apply to a particular fellowship,
there is only one Church.
And that belongs to no particular denomination.
It is the Church that is made up of those who have placed their belief,
their faith, in the person of Jesus.
And having established who the Church is,
Jesus commissioned those who believe in him to go out
and to make disciples.
And thus I say to you this morning,
that once we come to terms with what we are to do as a body of believers
who make up the Church,
we have a life responsibility to go out and to lead people
into a growing relationship with Jesus Christ.
Amen. Amen.

PHOTOGRAPHS BY **DANNY LYON** · INTERVIEWS BY **DANIEL ROTHENBERG**

BUILDING ON THE BORDER

PROYECTO AZTECA

SAN JUAN, TEXAS

The land along the Texas-Mexico border in the Rio Grande Valley is home to a vital culture and community of families who immigrated to the United States from Mexico in pursuit of better economic opportunity. "The Valley," as residents call it, embraces many who view themselves as simultaneously Mexican and American, seeing the official border between the two countries as merely a passage from one familiar place to another. Proyecto Azteca, an organization founded in 1991 by a group from the United Farm Workers union who saw the need for better housing in the region, works with low-income Mexican American families to build quality affordable homes.

Over the years, many Mexican immigrants settled into makeshift houses in *colonias*. Colonias are unincorporated rural developments, no more than a constellation of small land tracts with disheveled housing scattered along a dirt road. While offering a first-rung opportunity for land ownership, colonias typically have no running water, sewer service, or electricity. Without these most basic utilities, life in the colonia can be harsh and even desperate, and moving to better, more comfortable housing is the dream of many Rio Grande Valley Mexicans. Proyecto Azteca offers just such an opportunity. Founded on the principles of self-help and grassroots activism, Proyecto Azteca works to lift families out of marginal colonias and into fine owner-built homes purchased through a combination of sweat equity and no-interest loans.

Proyecto Azteca means "Project Aztec," Aztec being both the name of the ancient people and the Spanish acronym for "Assembly of Zones of Workers Working in Friendship for Equality Housing." The organization has built 127 houses in the past nine years, constructed mostly by and for farmworker families. Families are trained and assisted in construction techniques and benefit from bulk purchase of building materials. The standard Proyecto Azteca house is a three-bedroom, one-bath home with a kitchen, dining room, and living room, totaling 816 square feet, creating a haven for hardworking families. The houses are generally built three at a time, with groups of people working together, and later each house is moved to the family's lot in the nearby colonia. New houses cost approximately sixteen thousand dollars and are financed without interest—a very small sum indeed to improve people's standard of living and help them build a better life.

An enormous part of the story of Proyecto Azteca's housing efforts on the border is the story of the culture of the Rio Grande Valley. This valley land, taken from Mexico 150 years ago by the Treaty of Hildago, pulsates with the intertwined, and at times conflicting, expressions and histories of Texas and Mexico, creating a world of English and Spanish, cowboy and *norteño* music, long-neck beers, and fajitas. The Tex-Mex culture of the Rio Grande, birthed perhaps by the harsh realities of farmworker exploitation, keeps many rooted in the area. Mexican and American join here, and their profound affinity for the area commits many to the task of building new lives in this valley and the improved housing so crucial to family identity and educational and economic progress on the border.   *T.R.*

Arturo Ramírez directs the Center for Economic Opportunities in Alamo, Texas, a nonprofit organization that works in the colonias.

Colonias are rural unincorporated communities that are impoverished where land developers have taken flood-prone, nonproductive agricultural land and converted them to subdivisions, and planted them under the authority of the county government in south Texas. Lots are sold to people that can't afford to buy and build or own their own home in the city. Cities use the southern building codes, and any home that you're going to build, you need to have licensed plumbers, licensed electricians. In the rural communities where county government doesn't regulate building, they can gradually develop their homes by going up north as migrant farm workers, bringing a little bit of money back, and adding to their one-room shack. They do not have to go through the code enforcement officer of a city because it's a rural community that has no code enforcement laws. You have these rural unincorporated communities that were developed by unscrupulous land developers that got a piece of raw land that was not productive because it had a lot of salinity or because it was flood prone. And they made subdivisions out of these acres and sold them to these poor farm-worker families that mostly are new immigrants from Mexico into south Texas, or young couples that can't afford to live inside the city. They go out into the colonias and buy a lot to build their homes on. So these communities are described as impoverished, rural, isolated communities, with little or no infrastructure.

Opening image: Noe Galindo, Colonia Jessups,
near Monte Alto

Above: Roberto Rodríguez's family near Edinburg

David Arizmendi became executive director of Proyecto Azteca in October 1999.
He was born in Chiapas, Mexico, and spent ten years as a labor organizer in California.

The word "colonia" in Mexico means neighborhood, but in Texas, it is a rural, unincorporated community. It is pockets of poverty where people who didn't fit in the traditional real estate market in the city have ventured out into the rural communities to build their own home. They purchased a lot very cheap that has no infrastructure, that has no roads, that has no electricity, no water, no sewer—none of the basic things that we take for granted when we move into a community. People then begin to build on their own, and little by little they'll get a road, and then they'll try to fight to get electricity, and they'll try to get hooked up to water. But it's a struggle.

María Lopez, Alamo, Texas

A historic marker for the spot "where
American blood was shed on American soil,"
along with murals from Mission, Texas, and
the Farm Workers Union Hall in Pharr

Veronica Cruz, the program director for Proyecto Azteca, was born and raised in the valley.

If I were asked, "Are you a U.S. citizen?" well, of course, the answer's "Yes, I am." You ask me who I am, what I am inside, where do I come from, who am I as a person, and without a doubt there's no other way to point than towards Mexico. I'm Mexican, that's it, because my roots are from there. That's what my history entails. That's what basically made me. A lot of these families understand that, and they know it and they feel it too.

You come from a different country and you come here, land of the free and prosperity and opportunity. You come here, and you work hard, and you're willing to do it. Still you come here, and all of a sudden it's like you're meant to lose that identity, because you are bombarded with the "Hispanic" and with the "Latino" and with "American." Once you've crossed that border, and you've taken that one step over that line, this is what you have to become, and for a lot of people that's so difficult.

You have to become the "Hispanic" or the "Latino" or the "American" or whatever and not declare yourself as Mexican because you're not that anymore. For me, "Latino" and "Hispanic" are basically labels. That's it. I don't see them as any form of identity. "Hispanic" basically was created when they wanted to find something to call Mexicans and Puerto Ricans and Cubans when they were here. They were the three most dominant races that were here in the United States, so they came up with "Hispanic." Later on "Latino" was created, but for me, it's a label that is used because people want to feel because you speak Spanish, you're all the same.

Noe Hinojosa Jr. is an artist and entrepreneur in McAllen, Texas. He and his wife own the Millennium Bookstore Cafe.

There is a great deal of animosity left in many homes among people who felt cheated, who felt that their titles direct from the king of Spain were taken from them, stolen. There are many people involved in litigation to this very day. There's animosity from Mexicans still in Mexico who lost relatives, who lost land in this area. Obviously, as the southern tip of Texas, this is the most hotly contested land. It's soaked in blood, soaked. The Rio Grande Valley was the last wild part of the United States. When people were operating in civilized cities, there was still cattle rustling out here, and there were still bandidos and gunfights. This was really the last wild frontier in the United States.

Veronica Cruz

There has been no atonement for what's happened to our people and for what's been done. And I don't think it will. My heart sinks at the thought, but I don't think it's going to happen because there are things people don't realize.

For instance, here in the Southwest, there were lynchings of Mexicans. More Mexicans were hanged than blacks were during the years of slavery in the entire South. Nobody knows that. There's no atonement. People see the blacks, or the African American race, and say, "You know what? Yes." There's a realization that it was slavery. They call it by what it was. Mexicans haven't had that yet. For me then to call myself Mexican American is saying that I've accepted the American part of the history of my people. I don't feel any atonement has been made.

Mexicans are still coming here. They find Mexicans drowned in the Rio, or they find Mexicans in boxcars or trains dying from dehydration. That has to say something. If they're willing to risk their lives to come here—and not to take anything from anybody, but to earn their own—it has to tell you something. It's not that they're coming here to bombard us. It's not that they're coming here to take our glory and our benefits. No. It's a question of survival.

Leslie Newman, the former executive director of
Proyecto Azteca, is an attorney with many years
of experience in community development and
affordable housing issues.

People who live in colonias are building by themselves. They're doing self-help, but they're missing
some key ingredients. Because of their low incomes,
they're missing quality tools and materials. They're
missing construction knowledge and know-how, and
they don't have the long-term financing. They can't
access traditional mortgages and banks. So that's
what we were created to provide—quality tools and
materials, construction knowledge and know-how
through trainers, and then a long-term mortgage so
that people can pay back for their homes.

Through our program, families come who qualify and build their own home. We'll have a crew
of three families working together to build each other's homes. They work under the guidance and
supervision of our construction trainer. We'll access the interim construction funds to buy materials
and quality tools, which individual families can't usually afford. Families will come to our construction site and use our tools. With the materials that we purchase for them, they'll build their own
homes, and then we'll actually put the house on a truck and move it out to the families' individual
lots around the county.

Our families don't even walk into the bank. They're scared of traditional financing institutions.
They're scared that with one mispayment they'll just lose the whole home. There are a lot of myths
and misperceptions about the financial world. Most of our families, for example, don't have bank
accounts at all. They don't have a checking account, savings account. They operate purely on a cash
economy.

Epifanio Morales

Opposite: Aristeo Orta

Before becoming the program assistant with Proyecto Azteca, Glynis Laing spent two years as a Proyecto Azteca volunteer.

All of us at the office and at the organization believe that a home, a decent home, is really the basic building block of the community. There are all kinds of issues that are out there in the colonias. There are drugs. There are gangs. They don't have sewers, some of them. They don't have basic services the rest of us rely on, like garbage pickup or police patrols. We owe it to them—the government owes it to them to provide them funds to build a home. These are families that are on the very bottom of the economic ladder, and everyone deserves some decent place to live that they can take pride in. That's something that we believe.

Veronica Cruz started out as a VISTA volunteer before becoming a staff member at Proyecto Azteca.

We've never checked credit histories for any of the families. We've built over one hundred homes, and a good 80 percent of them would not have passed our credit checks if we had done them. Yet we have not defaulted on one loan yet. That's a sign. It's belief in the power of a person, in the power of a community.

Everybody deserves the right to prove themselves in this world, and that's what we done. We're just the medium, a way for people to be able to express themselves, to find the happiness that they need, the protection, the necessities that they must have for their families, a safe home, decent, affordable.

We present somebody with an opportunity, then they do the rest. We don't hold anybody by the hand. Whatever they have for themselves now—all hundred homes that we've built—the families did it. We didn't do it for them. All we did was find some money for them and provided them with the opportunity. It was the people.

Arturo Ramírez works with families in rural colonias to address the socioeconomic problems that affect their communities.

The magnet is economic prosperity and development of the family. They come here in hopes that they're going to move into these impoverished communities but eventually grow out of them. Then you have these big alligator gars that are just waiting for the little fish from Mexico to come in, and they'll grab them and take advantage of them by selling them flood-prone areas with underdeveloped infrastructure real estate, and they make a killing out of the desperation of these individuals.

It's a characteristic of the Mexicans from Mexico that immigrate into the United States that they feel that they need to own rather than rent. They want to build equity; they have that embedded in them. They say, "We don't want to be first-, second-, third-generation renters—we want to own a piece of land." With a lot of sacrifice, hard work, and sweat equity, they go out there and buy a piece of land and build on it. It's that desire of ownership, with no landlord knocking on your door wanting to collect the rent every month. These people want to have their independent little plot of land that they can say is theirs—I am the king on my land, and this is my piece of land in the United States. I own it, I've paid for it, I worked for it, and I built my home on it.

Homes and interiors at Colonia Jessups; Lauro Pérez prepares lunch at the Proyecto Azteca site; Jesus tire cover.

Patricia Mejía lives in a colonia near Edinburg, Texas.
Translated into English from Spanish.

I belong to one of the rural colonia that are situated to the east of Edinburg called Subdivision Muñiz. We only had light; we lacked everything. Now that colonia lacks pavement and drainage. I believe that this colonia was founded in 1986, and until now, we have advanced a little—all the services that we need for that huge colonia with more than two hundred families, more than five hundred kids.

I entered the colonia. It is the story of most of the Mexicans that immigrate. Our wish is to work and move forward, have a future with our family. When we arrived here, my family and I used to go to the North to work— that is the same story of the residents of this colonia or other poor colonias that exist in the Valley. We used to go to work to the North; we would get some pennies together there because we earned the minimum. We would get some extra money since the whole family was working. Now, the commissioners tell us, "You ask for the pavement, but why did you buy a colonia that wasn't like that, why did you go here?" And I tell them, "If we had money, we wouldn't be here. Of course, we would choose a place where our children lived with dignity." I tell you, it is impossible when you have a very low income, and it is precisely for that reason that we live in these colonias. We don't have enough money to pay for the piece of land that we wish to have. We dream of having our own house.

Martha Rángel harvesting onions near Mercedes
Farmworkers near Edinburg
Opposite: Family at the market, Pharr, Texas

Olga Valle-Herr is a poet who lives in McAllen, Texas.
Translated into English from Spanish.

First of all I am an American because I was born in the United States. But my heritage and my ancestors were from Mexico, and some were from France, from Spain, from Indians. I'm like a Heinz 57, or a potpourri, like the flowers that you mix. All those differences make a person interesting. I like the word "Latina." It seems casual and light, not necessarily from Mexico and not necessarily from Latin America. It covers a lot. "Latina"—it's a beautiful word. I've never liked "Chicana." For some reason I thought that sounded harsh, but I've grown to accept it. I'm a Chicana writer now. I call myself a Chicana writer and I'm kind of proud of that too. So, as I've grown and read more, I find that these words they call us—labels—nothing to be ashamed about. We are all equal.

David Arizmendi is the founder and executive director of Iniciativa Frontera, a colonia resident empowerment organization.

Most people in the valley consider themselves Mexican. When you say the word "Mexican," you're talking more culture than where you were born. There is a difference between a Mexican from Mexico and a Mexican from here, but they coexist. Because it's a Mexican environment, your identity is considered Mexican, which is very different than when you say, "Where were you born?" Our proximity and our relationship to Mexico—the fact that there's a border here—mentally, the border doesn't really exist. The culture and the tradition and the manners, everything is still Mexican.

Farmworker Rolando García sings
into an onion; the bus schedule
out of McAllen.

Noe Hinojosa Jr. returned to the Rio Grande Valley after attending Harvard University on scholarship.

These four counties are among the poorest in the United States. That doesn't mean that everybody here is poor, but there's a larger percentage of poor people than there are other places in the country. It's easy to sweep the poor under the rug and forget about them. There's a debate going on right now about people who are affluent beginning to live in gated communities, communities with big walls around them and gates at the front where you have to punch a code or go through a security guard. People trying to forget that there is hardship. It's easier to relax in your BMW when you don't have to see that guy sitting in the street wishing he had a bicycle.

People won't admit it, but the Valley has always had a self-esteem problem. Low self-esteem. Because we never did have the amenities that they have in San Antonio or Austin in terms of store choices, schools, infrastructure, in terms of a million different things. The Valley has always felt behind, has always felt like the neglected stepchild, has always felt impoverished. There was a sense of inferiority, then there was a sense of superiority in that inferiority. A sense of "we're different and we're downcast," but the underdog always finds strength in its position. It's almost been a springboard for a renewed sense of pride that is starting to take place now, as we are empowered with the tools that we need.

Farmworkers clear an onion field
near Monte Alto.

Opposite: In the cabbage field

Arturo Ramírez lives in Alamo, Texas.

It's an enclosed security blanket, to live in this area. Culturally, we're very comfortable—we love the fajitas; we love our long-neck beers and the Coronas from Mexico. We love our *corridos* and our music. Every time you change the knob on the radio, you hear a variety of music of our culture. So we love this atmosphere. We always want to come home. It's not the water that we drink—it's the cultural atmosphere that we live in. We love it, and it's in the Deep South, Texas. As migrants, we'd go up to Montana, where the militia's developing real strong, the white supremacists, and we'd go up there and harvest sugar beets. We try to assimilate there with the guys that have black hair and black eyes like us, and they'd end up being Cherokee or Blackfeet, and they didn't want us. They spoke a different language. We'd go to Illinois, and we'd find the same situation. We saw and experienced that. We could not assimilate into their communities. They wanted us to harvest their crops, but they didn't want us up there to stay year-round. So we ended up coming back, and we would love that because we'd come back to our security blanket, a community that we helped develop over the years, that had our music, our culture.

Noe Hinojosa Jr. was born and raised in Weslaco, Texas.

The music along the border is different from Mexican music. It's *norteño*. It's *tejano*. It's an amalgam. The food here is called Tex-Mex. If you eat an enchilada here in the Valley and you go to Mexico City and try to get one of those, you're not going to find it. Neither are you going to find the sauces that we enjoy around here. You'll not find the same kinds of soups. What happened here is that all this runs together into a melting pot—not to overuse the phrase—it has become something rather distinct. It is that way on both sides of the border.

It's not just an American flavor. You can go to a lot of these border towns right across the border, and you'll find the same kind of *norteño* music and the same kind of enchiladas and the same kind of salsa. But, if you

go twenty-five, thirty, miles deeper into Mexico, you won't. Both sides of the border are united in so many ways—for the food we share, for the music, for the coast, the climate, for the wildlife, for the fauna. We all enjoy the same mesquites, the same cactus, and the same shrub, brush, and such. We are also united in the sense that we are the ugly stepchild of our respective countries. I have a sense that the United States at large looks down its nose at the border areas. No doubt in my mind that the cultural elite of New York or the West Coast look down their noses at this relatively impoverished and uneducated part of the world, part of their country. I hear the same thing in Mexico. People have this concept that the trash collects along the fence, collects along the border. I've heard that said so many times—the people in Mexico think that all the riffraff from Mexico migrates north to the border and the same is true for the United States. We are brothers, underdog brothers. Neither one of us fully love each other, and we're not loved in our respected countries. So we are united in that sense.

The dance hall, All Valley Flea Market, Hidalgo County, South Texas

Opposite: The Valley. Elissa Villareal, Benito Castillo, and Heidy Rios Aleman at the All Valley Flea Market dance.

Eric D'Avila, a young Valley resident, is a freshman at Tufts University in Massachusetts on a United Farm Workers scholarship.

It's hard to tell someone from outside of the Valley how great it is. There's something about it. You could do so much with so little here just as long as you try. Whereas somewhere else, you have to have a master's degree before you could earn that kind of money. Here in the Valley, you can do whatever you want. I mean, there's just so much you can do as long as you do it right. As long as you put your mind to it, you can do whatever you want here.

It's just a personal view, because I'm from here. As far as what I feel from culture and camaraderie, to people, to their situation, class things, race things, I just feel that the Valley is somewhere great.

María Felix Nerio is a colonia resident in Donna, Texas.

Life between Mexico and United States is so different. There is a Mexican saying, "Mexico is so far from God and so near to the United States." Well, we are far away from God. Like a people forgotten by God, but near to the United States; like being in heaven. But in Mexico, you suffer because of the corruption, the scarcity. Although they say there is no discrimination, there are a lot of killings, a lot of violence. I imagine it's the same here as everywhere, and now there is violence, drugs, assaults.

Thank God we are at the border, and we can just cross. One sister says, "You only know the little puddle and that's all." Well, yes, thank God. If we lived further north, we couldn't go to our country; it would be too difficult. But, thank God, we are near the border, and, yes, one misses it, but at the same time not that much.

Roxanna Acevedo, a student at the University of Texas Pan American, is a teacher's assistant for McAllen's citywide high school program GUAVA, Girls United Around Video Arts.

A lot of people underestimate us. They think, "Ah, they're from the Valley. They don't know anything." Or, "They're kind of slow," or "They're dumb." Or they make fun of the way we speak English. But we're getting people talking to us in Spanish. We're getting people talking to us in English, so of course we make our own language. We mix it up. Like my mom talks to me in English, and I'll talk to her in Spanish. Or we mix up words. People say, "They can't even speak English right. Listen to the way they say that." And it's not that we don't know how to speak English right. It's just that we have a big mixture, and we just mix everything up. That's the way we talk.

At the Sunday evening
dance, Alamo, Texas

Opposite: Pay phone,
San Juan, Texas

Miguel Angel García moved from Colonia Jessups in Monte Alto to a Proyecto Azteca model subdivision named Monte Alto Acres. Translated into English from Spanish.

My wife was the one who came and helped the carpenters, but I also came, with my brother, my mother. My brother and my mother lived here, and we have three different houses, and then the three of us get together. We paid a young man so he would come to help the carpenter, and my wife and sister-in-law were helping them.

My wife knows a little about building a house now because here they taught everyone. We did not know. They taught us how to put nails, to measure, a lot of things. We came some Saturdays and Sundays. We had materials here, and we came to try to speed up the process, to move forward with the houses.

In that way you get more attached to what is yours, because you are watching it. Also you have more faith, because you can see what materials you are using and what you are doing. When you buy a house, you do not know how they built it, and here you can see step by step, plank by plank. You can see how they are placed and nailed.

A bean field along Route 281, the Military Highway; on the horizon is the Rio Grande River, established as the border with Mexico after the War of 1848.

A poem by Amado Balderas Tijernina, a writer and teacher who was born and raised in the Valley

MexicaNo

(Meshica *no*)

Call yourself anything you want *pero Mexica* **no**. Hide behind the labels. Hide behind the lies. Adjectives become you. Descriptive words of something to do with something tropical and misty.

Act like anything else *pero como Mexica***No**. Hide behind languages, hide behind fake accents. Assimilation becomes you. Playing all kinds of role and gavachoisms are overdone and mask your identity.

Learn somebody else's history *pero lo del Mexica***No**. Hide behind the Conquest. Hide behind Colonialism. Peon becomes you. Searching through the pages of the past but you do not recognize yourself because you hide . . . hide from *el Mexica***No**.

Alicia Nabejas lives in Las Milpas Colonia in Pharr, Texas. Translated into English from Spanish.

When you have something, you want someone else to have something good. When you have learned, you want someone else to learn. When you give something, you want to give something to someone else. That is to give and to receive.

When they gave me the opportunity, they told me, "You can be part of the board of directors. Why don't you write down your name?"

I said, "But, I don't know anything about houses."

They told me, "But you are going to learn."

I said, "Well, I would like that. But who would vote for me? Nobody knows me. But I want to know how to help those people, to guide them when they come here. I want to be a member of the project because I want to do the best for the community. If you elect me, I will try to help those people to qualify if they need it."

When they told me, "You have just been elected," I said, "Oh! So, what I'm going to do now? I don't speak—I just read a little English."

I said, "If I have to go to a conference, I will learn."

I have gone to many conferences, and the little I understand, I say, "Very good, I learned something new!" All the experiences you take as a person, as a human being, and being part of an organization, are experiences for your life.

Yolanda Hernandez owns a Proyecto Azteca house.

I don't think I would feel this happy if I had the money and paid somebody to do my house. It's a different feeling because I got to see and make choices. How did I want this ceiling? Did I want it this way or this way? If you pay somebody, you've got to look at a picture and say, "OK, do it like this." So you have no idea of the work that it takes for it to be done.

I was able to get on top of a ladder and hold the sheetrock up there and somebody nailed, and you're so tired. But once that day was over, I came home ready for another day. It didn't matter how hard the work was, or heavy—for us, it was wonderful.

I'm very proud of myself. For one, I would never have thought of going through a program or helping somebody build a home. Now I know that I can do it. I can help other people. If I have the time and can go, I will help a neighbor.

Everybody deserves to have a home, and a comfortable home, where you can have your own space, your own privacy. My children come home in the afternoons, and how comfortable they feel. I had never seen them so calm in my lifetime until now. My husband comes home to our home, which is going to be our home when we're done paying for it. This is something that we did with our hard work. When our friends come over, they say, "Yolanda, this is what you did? This is what you built?"

PHOTOGRAPHS BY **DAWOUD BEY** · INTERVIEWS BY **DAN COLLISON**

GROWING UP, COMING TOGETHER

SOUTHWEST YOUTH COLLABORATIVE

CHICAGO, ILLINOIS

Once the home of Irish, German, Italian, Slovak, and other European families who made lives along the brick bungalow–lined streets of the area, the southwest side of Chicago experienced dramatic changes after the 1960s civil rights movement. Today, it is home predominantly to African American and Latino working-class families and to many more recent immigrants of widely diverse origins. From a primarily white area, known for its resistance and at times animosity toward people of color, southwest Chicago today is a truly multiracial, ethnically varied group of neighborhoods.

Like parts of many American cities, southwest Chicago has seen a rising incidence of crime, gang-related problems, poverty, and unemployment problems that profoundly challenge the lives of the community's young people. While some might see the neighborhood's diversity as an impediment to improving local conditions, the Southwest Youth Collaborative, founded in the early 1980s, embraces pluralism fully and sees the potential for a rich and vibrant life.

Beginning in 1991 with the Children, Youth, and Family Initiative, Chicago's Southwest Youth Collaborative now provides services to youth and families from a range of racial, ethnic, and economic backgrounds. The Collaborative grew out of very local needs and concerns, and is guided by community residents who believe that youth-driven, neighborhood-based efforts offer the greatest chance to effect positive change for the area and its families. Born of a collaboration between faith-based institutions, social service centers, recreational centers, and neighborhood organizations, the Collaborative seeks to build youth leadership, cross-cultural understanding, and intergenerational dialogue through a myriad of remarkable programs.

Five neighborhoods make up the key service area of the Collaborative: West Englewood, Chicago Lawn, Gage Park, West Lawn, and Elsdon. The Collaborative's organization and governance speak to its commitment to pluralism and youth. The board of directors must, according to the bylaws, represent the five geographic areas and various ethnic groups. In addition, half of the twenty-six-member board must be young people.

Five affiliated programs are central to the work of the Collaborative. Girl Talk, a program for female juvenile offenders, meets weekly to discuss issues of self-esteem, sexuality, abuse, and avoiding repeat incarceration. The Prison Action Committee assists released offenders and works to improve conditions inside the Illinois prison system. The Community Justice Initiative works with young people to probe a range of justice and legal issues through role playing and group discussion. The group educates other young people through events and training sessions on issues of juvenile justice. West Englewood Youth and Teen Center and the Greater Lawn Community Youth Network are neighborhood centers that provide a variety of programs for area youth.

The Southwest Youth Collaborative is evolving to meet the challenges facing youth and families in its particular place and time. To Camille Odeh, the charismatic founding and current director, the collection of programs represents a responsible and active local leadership. As the Collaborative improves and enriches its own local area, its members hope to provide an example for the entire city of Chicago.   *T.R.*

Sherry Brown, age nineteen, had a summer job at the West Englewood Youth and Teen Center four years ago. She is now a mentor with the Southwest Youth Collaborative and serves on the board of directors.

I like talking. I like doing trainings. I like to teach people what I know, especially youth my own age that have a hard time growing up and dealing with society. I don't feel that I have the perfect life, but I have so much help and support that I can be the same support for someone else. That's why I got into it. To just support people. To teach what I know. "Each one teach one." I like giving back to my community because I see how it was when I was growing up, and it's so different now.

I never thought I'd be doing anything like this, especially helping my community—because our community was never going to be nothing because of what was going on. I first came and I learned that it's like this because people don't want to help themselves. We have to get out there in our own communities and help our community. There's a lot of people that don't want to do anything, but if there's one out there that wants to do something, the next person can tell the next person, and we can do something. But I never thought I'd be doing anything like this when I was twelve years old.

The biggest problem is the lack of communication between youth and adults. A lot of people will say it's the gangs and the violence and the police. But if adults and youth can sit down and not be afraid of each other, not be afraid to talk to each other, to help each other, those things wouldn't go on.

We only know and only can learn what our elders teach us. So we have to learn from them. Just like they have a lot to tell us, we have a lot to tell them. The community is changing. The generations are changing. There's more younger people in communities now. Once the older people move on, we're going to be left. Right now a lot of the stuff that they figure out and do, it affects us. We should be able to let them know how it feels to us, how it does affect us. If they gave us a chance, we do know what we're talking about because we grow up in this society every day. We walk around in our neighborhoods every day.

They're scared to come outside, but we come outside, and it's like we know what's going on. No one wants to listen to us because they feel we don't know what we're talking about because we're youth. They really do need to listen because we do have a lot to say, and we really do know what we're talking about because we experience it. Just like they experienced a lot of things and we should respect that, they should respect the things that we experience.

I learned if I stand up and speak up, my voice will be heard. When I first came, I used to be shy and never said anything. But when I learned how to talk—going to media classes—and learned how to present myself and learned that if I just sit and think these things, they're not going to happen. I have to get up and get my voice heard.

I have to be able to speak bold and clear about what I have to say. I can't be shy, especially when it comes to my community. You can say that I don't like what's going on. If you had the power to do something about it, you should do it instead of always complaining. I learned how not to complain about things in my community, but do something about them.

Camille Odeh, executive director of the Southwest Youth Collaborative since the doors opened in 1992

Our plan really reflected the genuine needs and concerns of the community. We didn't evolve out of a group of people sitting in an office saying, "This is what needs to happen on the southwest side of Chicago." It was community residents who came together, and it represented the diverse population of the southwest side—this group who decided, "We really need to look at the parks. Are the parks addressing the needs of the kids in our community? Are they reaching out to the new Latino families in the neighborhood? Can they speak the language of the people in the neighborhood? What are the barriers that prevent the kids and the families from using these great facilities that we have in the parks?"

This organization is not a static organization. It's very fluid. It's very broad. Its goals are developing community justice for our children, youth, and families. It needs to be that type of organization if we're going to be able to work with a diverse population. It's our role to create that space and opportunity for communities to develop.

Creating an intergenerational organization is not a simple task. Many youth organizations are adult-driven. Our youth organization is youth-driven to a large extent. We take a backseat role in many cases, and we are a support for the youth. And that's an appropriate role for us to play. We should create the space for the youth to learn, and through their experiences, they will learn, they will make mistakes, they will grow, they will become critical thinkers, and that's what's important. If we can create that time in their life where this work is impacted on them, critically—to impact their thinking and to create an opportunity for them to think about their future and the direction that they want to go— then we've done a tremendous job creating the opportunity for youth to develop their capacities.

Keith Hopkins, West Englewood
Youth and Teen Center

Opposite: Camille Odeh,
Southwest Youth Collaborative

Alma Iris Montes was born in Mexico and raised in Chicago. By sixteen she was living on the streets. She is now twenty and the program coordinator for the Greater Lawn Community Youth Network.

It was a learning experience. I share this with a lot of people; I tell them that I have been to more funerals than graduations. It's a really rough experience, and I certainly don't wish for nobody, especially for a young woman, the experience that I had. I take that experience, and I try to teach others about the choices that I made, and try to get them to understand some of the issues that youth are dealing with in their communities, especially when there's not a lot of resources or a lot of places for them to go. I want them to feel they are a positive influence because that was an issue that my friends and I were dealing with. We felt like we were a problem, that the community, the adults, always looked at us as a problem—never as an asset to the community, but as a problem. So we became a big problem.

When I see my friends from back in the old days, the majority of them, half of them, have passed away, and some of the girls are pregnant with three kids by now. When they see me, they always ask, "How many kids do you have?" I have no kids—I work at a community center; I try to explain to them what I do, and they don't understand. Some of them do. Honestly, I feel like I would have been dead. Honestly. There was just a lot of violence around me. I am very lucky. I always say that—just this afternoon I said it to myself—I think somebody is watching over me.

Alma Iris Montes,
Greater Lawn Community Youth Network

Geoffrey Banks, age twenty-four, is an organizer for the Community Justice Initiative, where he works to build citywide action around the criminalization of youth.

The main thing about this year, this experience, is that it's given me more clarity in terms of the kinds of efforts that are necessary to really try to make any kind of fundamental changes. It's one thing to preach about how there should be changes, and up until this year a lot—not everything—but a lot of what I had done was sort of just philosophizing and intellectualizing in college—stuff like that. So it definitely was an opportunity to begin to try and put more theory into practice.

I come from a working-class background. My father grew up in the Englewood community on the South Side, but I had the opportunity to go to an elite, affluent private school because my mom was a teacher there. Growing up, I wasn't able to think about these issues of the differences between the haves and have-nots in an abstract way because I lived that discrepancy on a daily basis—having an ideal atmosphere in school and coming home and having problems, seeing folks who were close to me getting into trouble with the law and actually going through the juvenile court system.

That is one of the key things that drove me to look at ways I can contribute to the process of decreasing that kind of discrepancy between those quote-unquote haves and have-nots. Really, this experience has been significant in that it showed me how much real dedication and work and how much commitment it takes on the part of individuals to try and go about doing that. Not just talking about it, but going out and doing it.

Geoffrey Banks,
Community Justice Initiative

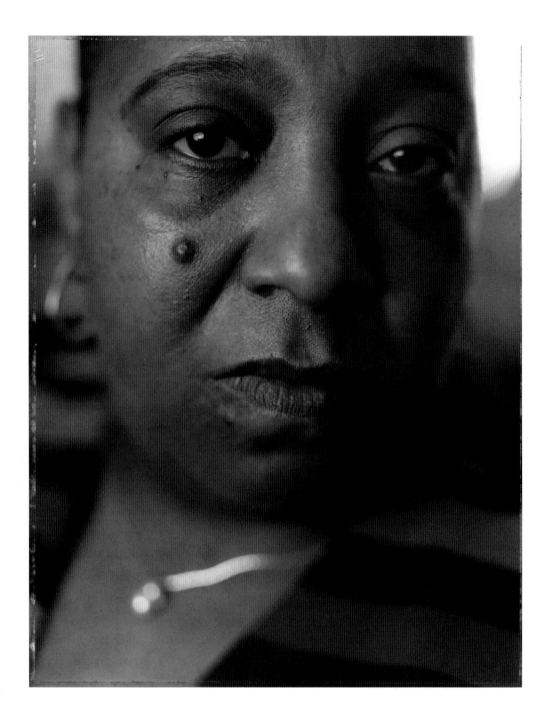

Barbara Echols, a self-described "recovering addict," spent six months in prison. She is the executive director of the Prison Action Committee.

Prison Action Committee is a way to make me stay clean because it helps me stay focused. It's fulfilling. I love what I'm doing. I love helping, and it's making me a better person. I got a letter just the other day from this young lady. She said, "Thank God there is someone out there that still cares about women." Women are the most forgotten population. Men, they stick together. They always have somebody fighting for them. The women, they just put them in prison and let everybody forget them. Society does not realize that the female population is the fastest-growing prison population there is today. When she told me that, when I hear stuff like that, that's when I know what I'm doing is really appreciated, and it makes me feel good when I get the little things. Not the big things, when you get on TV, and they say, "You've accomplished this," but those little things that really make me know that I'm doing the right thing.

Colette Rhodes, age twenty-one, an intern youth organizer with the Community Justice Initiative

It's been my dream to be a teacher. I know that's what I want to do, but working here has given me this initiative to always be involved in where I am and always be active. You can be living and working within your own city but really not be involved with what's happening in your city, the issues, the policies, the people who you live with, who you are surrounded by. I think this has given me an incentive to just constantly be at a grassroots level and really know what's happening around me with the people I'm with, the youth that I'm hopefully going to be teaching, the families they are coming from, some of the issues that we have to face.

I'm so impressed with the young people who I'm working with, how much they want to be involved in their communities and how much they want to organize and mobilize people that they know to create change.

Barbara Echols,
Prison Action Committee

Opposite: Colette Rhodes,
Community Justice Initiative

Raquel García II,
Community Justice
Initiative

Opposite: Héctor Rico,
Latino Organization
of the Southwest

Héctor Rico, outreach coordinator for the Southwest Youth Collaborative and executive director of the Latino Organization of the Southwest

When I came to the United States, back in the eighties, as an immigrant, I didn't feel connected with the new society. So, in order for me to have a sense of why I was here in this country, I got involved in small, different community projects. My first experience—and it happens to many of us immigrants who came to this country—was working with the community through a Catholic church in the south Chicago area. The church is named Our Lady of Guadalupe Church, which is the first Catholic church built by Mexican immigrants in the 1910s. By being part of the different community meetings and sessions that were happening at that particular church, that taught me to keep doing more for my community.

Before I actually got my first job as a community organizer, I used to work in a factory. And I remember in the factory when, after two hours or three hours of work, I was looking around and I only see Mexicans, or I only see immigrants, sweating. I saw a lot of pain in their eyes, I saw a lot of tiredness. Looking around, I realized that I have to do something to help those people.

That particular job wasn't for me, but I have to go out there and do something to help those particular individuals, those particular workers or laborers, to talk to them about their rights, to work in the community and improve their way of living. It really touched my heart, seeing the suffering, seeing the injustices, seeing those people working in this factory, putting in hours and hours of sweating, of painful work, just to make sometimes less than the minimum wage. By being part of that, by witnessing that, I felt some kind of angriness in myself. That anger inspired me to start working with my community.

See, what happened is that we were doing some block organizing in the community back in the middle of the eighties in this area. And we noticed—I was working with one of my coworkers—there were some posters, flyers, posted on the light posts of some areas. Those particular flyers were saying, "As a supreme order, keep this block white." So we took these flyers and threw them in the garbage. I kept one of those flyers as one of my souvenirs, my memorabilia. I can say I've witnessed that, I passed through, I sensed that. Those are the kind of things that shouldn't happen in our communities.

Now the community has changed totally. We are diverse. We're multicultural. You go on the streets in the southwest area, and in one corner you're hearing Arabic and in another corner you're hearing Spanish, and then you can see arguments among African Americans and Latinos or Arabs and Latinos. It's such a unique community and such a tremendous change. I'm very fortunate that I was part of the process. I put in my small contribution for that to happen.

Andrea Shields,
Community Justice Initiative

Andrea Shields, age eighteen and a member of Generation Y, the Southwest Youth Collaborative–sponsored effort to improve conditions for teens in southwest Chicago

Now being at the Collaborative, I know the meaning of community. I've made my own thing—common unity. It's not about your color. It's not about your age. It's not about what you do, or who you are inside. Sometimes those things can be very helpful playing a role in your life, but the fact that we are all here together supporting a cause—that's the main thing. I learned simply what it means to be a part of a community, part of people that can help you—people really liking you and respecting you. It shows you how to respect yourself. It's like I'm not so close-minded—I'm open-minded, and it's like I have changed from being a taking person to actually being a giving person.

I used to always think that black people want to fight me, black people want to laugh at me, turn their nose up at me, and then you get into this environment, it's like, no, not just black people, you know, any type of color, whatever age, it doesn't matter. People are people. People are going to act that way. And basically, I try to tell myself, I want to enable myself and others to become a productive member of society in any way possible, if I can do it. If I can come out and talk to people, or even share some things that are deep down in me that's personal, I would, to help people out.

I think you need to know your history. The more I know about my ancestors' struggles, the more I will teach it to the future generation—that's how I am. I want to be accountable. Everybody needs to do that. We need to set examples. I try to value diversity, and I try to know myself so everybody else, if they're related to me in terms of blackness, then I can help them. But if they're not, we have other programs that they can get into to try and learn something about their self, because if you don't know about where your past is, and where you been, and where you are now, where you're going—how can you know yourself? If you have no identity, no self-worth, you don't know nothing. But you are somebody.

Aron Hanson, age twenty-one, is part of a ten-month apprenticeship program called Public Allies. He works with kids in the Edgewater-Uptown area of Chicago as part of the Community Justice Initiative.

I'm a former gang member. I was convicted. I was also dealing drugs, and so I served almost a year in prison. I was convicted of felony possession of drugs twice. I have two felonies on my criminal record, which is on my adult record. My decision was to use my personal life story and turn it into a positive manner and use it as an example for the other youth out there that are going through similar situations.

I work well with the kids. Interaction is very good, and they just seem to look up to me. It's something that I never had, to look up to someone as an idol or a hero. I never had that feeling. When the kids look up to me, it makes me feel that I'm making a difference, or I'm teaching them something new. It might be something they know already. I just think it's something that I'm put here to do even though my past is my past.

Aron Hanson,
Community Justice Initiative

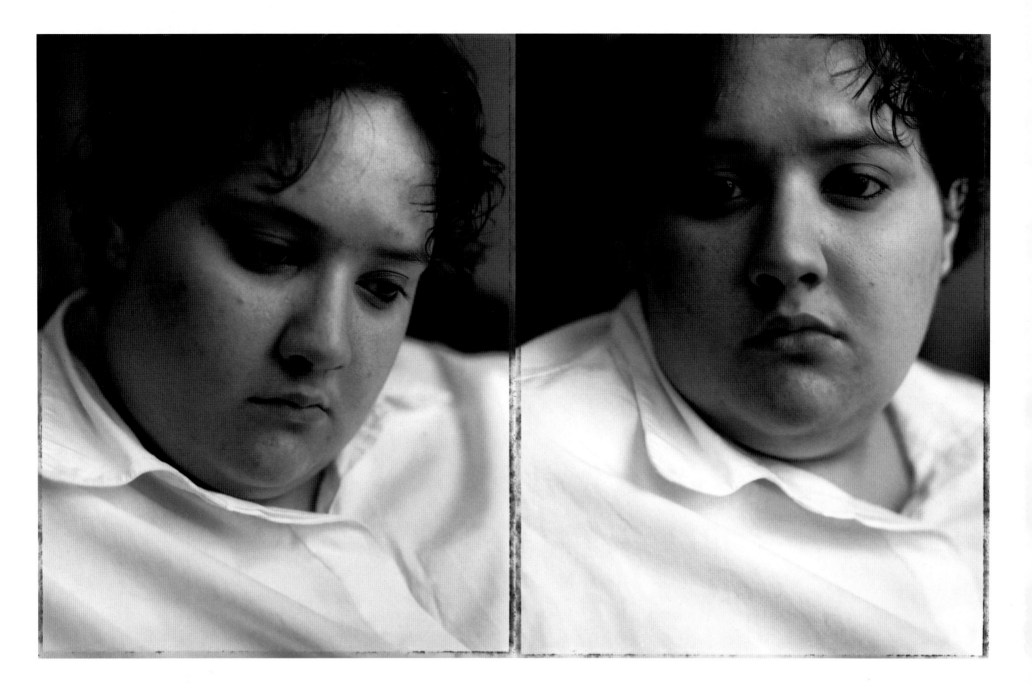

Janette Maldonado, age twenty-two and a former gang member, started working at the Collaborative in 1995 with the Community Justice Initiative. She is also one of the founding members of Generation Y.

I didn't feel comfortable. I was going to a school way out of my home district, and I felt like I was a loner there. People were looking at me like, "God, where is she from?" And other people would say, "Yeah, she's from over here and over there, so we should do this and do that." I got jumped on a couple of times. It's like, God, I need to help myself. I need to find somebody who can help me out because I don't want to be in this situation all the time. So because of my gang friends I felt like I was more powerful. Not more powerful, but I felt more safe. I knew that now that they know that I'm hanging with these people, they're not going to touch me. They're not going to say anything to me because they know I have these people as my family now.

I have great family support at home, but the Collaborative is like that second family that most people need. I feel like people need a second family. Whatever I can't discuss with my mom, there's somebody here that I can discuss it with. It is a second family, and we all are family in a way. We talk with each other. I mean most of us have been here for a long time now, so it's like we all know each other very well. We know when there's something wrong with another one. We know we can always go lay our head on their shoulders for any problem or anything. I feel really comfortable here, very comfortable.

Janette Maldonado,
Community Justice Initiative

Community Justice Initiative youth coordinator Sylvester Carrizales, age eighteen, talks with interviewer Dan Collison.

DC: Can you tell me about what happened to you yesterday?

SC: Yesterday? I got shot. By 18th and Morgan. I was just in the wrong place at the wrong time. I barely came from fishing and I was on the bike and I got shot because they were shooting at some other gang, gang rivals. Came out and started capping. Started shooting. I was going fast on the bike and I got shot and I fell to the floor. And that's about it.

DC: Where did you get hit?

SC: In the right buttocks.

DC: They took you to the hospital?

SC: Oh yeah. They took me to the hospital. The bullet is still in there. They can't do nothing about it. If it were to move a little, like if it were a little bit more closer to the spine, I would be paralyzed. So I was very lucky.

DC: And that was yesterday?

SC: Yeah. Yesterday around six o'clock in the afternoon.

DC: How do you feel now?

SC: I feel the pain, but at least I'm alive. At least I lived to tell about it.

DC: Is that pretty common in your neighborhood?

SC: Yeah. It's mostly pretty common. I've been shot before in the leg, and where I live you hear those gun shots going back and forth. It's a big problem there with gangs.

James Hollins, age twenty-two, has been with the Collaborative since he was fourteen years old, when he served as a youth board member.

One little kid . . . his name was Harold. He really wasn't in a gang or anything. He was only a young kid, but he wasn't in a gang. He just had a problem. It was like he was heading that way. You could tell if he didn't fix up soon he'd be another statistic. So I basically took him under my wing and really, to develop a relationship with him and try to find different things that he liked. Now we're just great friends. We both found that we like drums. I'm a drummer, and we both like to play drums. We both like basketball. So we just found a lot of common things, and those are the type of things that I like. I want to help the ones that have strayed away but I think it's also important to catch the ones before they get turned away

James Hollins,
West Englewood
Youth and Teen Center

Opposite:
Sylvester Carrizales,
Community Justice
Initiative

Adriana Bartow,
Greater Lawn Community
Youth Network

I come from a family of political activists. My father was a person from El Salvador, and he lived in exile for much of his life. He was kicked out of his country by a military dictatorship in the 1930s or 40s. I was very young when our father told us these stories, and I don't remember exactly when. But at the beginning of the 1950s, my father settled down in Guatemala, and it was in Guatemala where all of us, his children, were born. We grew up listening to my father talking about social justice and talking about the big responsibility that everybody who is a human being had towards other human beings. It wasn't a hard lesson to learn because we lived in poverty. We saw suffering around us. We were poor, but we didn't go hungry or face too much of a hardship.

Part of me belonged to this country, and I had to do something in this country to benefit the poor, the persecuted, the oppressed of the United States. Because living in this country, I discovered that all these ideas, this image that I had of the United States, wasn't real. That there was oppression in this country.

Whatever I did in this country, I wanted it to make a difference. I didn't want to do anything just to feel good. I didn't want to do anything that was charity. I wanted really to contribute to the transformation of society in the United States.

The Youth Network center is located in an area that historically has been entirely white. People from Lithuania, Poland, Russia, Italy have lived there. Because of the type of population we serve, which is mostly Latinos, we have had to face a lot of problems in the community. I would say that we have not been welcomed from the very beginning—since the center opened. There has been a lot of resistance on the part of the neighborhoods around the church where the center is located. We have gotten anonymous letters. The church has gotten anonymous letters,

threatening calls. The neighbors are constantly calling the police because of the teens that come to the center. And for a while, there was some police harassment. I would say that maybe in the last three years, we haven't had much of that, but before it was very tense.

The neighbors wanted us out of the church, and we just said, "No, we are here to stay." We opened the doors to Arabs, to African Americans, and Latinos. When I got there, the majority of the kids we were serving were white.

I will remember, in the first place, the racism of the community we work in. I will remember what happened when we opened the doors to children from all backgrounds: cultural, racial, religious, political, economic. I will remember the problems that even us as the staff had. I think one of the things that I will remember most is how I myself had to face the fact that I was a racist.

Not only racist, but also that I am prejudiced, that I have this prejudice against youth. And it's very hard for me to face that, but I have a responsibility to do that. When I am in the presence of youth, when I see how rebellious, how rude, how abusive sometimes they are—I want to use an adult as my authority. And sometimes it is very hard for me to really see where they are coming from. I struggle a little bit with that.

Children cannot defend themselves. I made my mission, wherever I am, doing whatever type of work with children, that I'm going to stand for the rights of those who cannot defend themselves. If I have to fight parents, I will fight them. If I have to fight institutions, I will fight them. If I have to fight the government ultimately responsible for children's safety and well-being, I'm going to fight them. Nothing, nothing, will stop me.

In prison for gang-related crimes, Carlos Vega began organizing prison-based educational and cultural programs for inmates. He is cofounder and assistant director of the Prison Action Committee, assisting former prisoners in their transition to employment and productive lives.

When I started organizing in prison and started uniting everybody, then I became a threat. I became a real threat. A real threat. Not because I was stabbing anybody or hitting somebody up side of the head with a pipe, but because I was uniting the brothers in the joint. I started realizing that there was a system here. That they wanted us to be divided. That they wanted us to sit away from each other. That they didn't want us to be educated. They didn't want us to have no culture. No history. And that really woke me up. That woke me up—it was so powerful. I said, "Wait a minute. What am I doing? Why is this like this?" I started questioning things—I didn't accept things no more as the way they were.

It happened to me when I was going to school because I didn't speak English. Right? I was already an oddball. I was a foreigner. You know. I was discriminated against, and that really made me feel worthless. Those are factors that contribute to the criminalization of youth. Once you start telling a young kid that he is worthless, he's going to believe that. He's going be a jailbird, he's going to believe that.

Wenona Thompson,
Prison Action Committee

Opposite: Carlos Vega,
Prison Action Committee

Jonathan Peck, a staff member of the Southwest Youth Collaborative and director of the Community Justice Initiative, was adopted and raised by mixed-race parents in Williams, Massachusetts. He credits his multiethnic background for his commitment to community work.

That's what it's about; it's having people who care about people, having those resources with them in those situations. A lot of these kids now don't have opportunities. They don't have the resources. The people that care about them are ending up in jail. And the people that care about them are under a lot of pressure by the system to perform, their mothers and fathers. A lot of these families are fragmented, and I think that coming from a strong family, coming from a strong community, coming from those opportunities and that privilege, combining that with my personal experiences with some horrific situations with people in terms of race and who I am, I think that I'm here because of that.

Jonathan Peck,
Community Justice Initiative

Opposite, left:
Vanessa Rodriguez,

A FOREST HOME

YAAK VALLEY FOREST COMMUNITY

YAAK VALLEY, MONTANA

In the far northwest corner of Montana, just below the Canadian border, there is a scattered settlement of under 150 families living in the woods of the Yaak Valley, often without electricity or even plumbing. Their private parcels of land make up only 2 to 3 percent of what is otherwise a vast national forest: 500,000 acres of federal land where large-scale logging has occupied the area for generations. As new paved roads and an expanding utility grid attract more retirees, second-home owners, and others who want wooded retreats but not to live off the land, Yaak and other historically small, unorganized rural districts of the Kootenai National Forest face a significant period of transition. Long dependent on the timber economy, Yaak community values and priorities are changing with the surrounding forest ecology they are a part of.

After decades of high-yield tree harvesting by international logging corporations, the pressure to address environmental recovery and sustainability is felt by vastly different constituencies, from Washington bureaucrats to fly fishermen. Any shift in thinking requires the insular Yaak Valley community to overcome divergent interests in search of consensus on the future. Harsh physical conditions, especially in the winter, mean "Yaakers" are tough, self-reliant, and deeply committed to their forest home. Many chose to move to this outland because of its isolation and privacy, making a public process and public scrutiny of that process particularly difficult.

Conflicts over logging, forest use and access, and the perpetual issue of people's relationship to nature, have hotly divided many

residents since the 1960s, when back-to-the-landers, hippies, and others with environmentalist leanings began to settle in this remote country. The newcomers' support of the protection of endangered species, moratoriums on road-building, and cut-and-run logging practices threatened the livelihood of some loggers and others who saw restrictions and regulation as the first steps toward the loss of their jobs, their land, and their freedom. In local meetings, the residents' debates were circumscribed by fear of two extreme points of view: those who want the area designated as wilderness by the federal government, and those who believe clear-cutting and unregulated logging offer both sound forest management and economic security.

The realization that these positions are in fact held by very few is one of many positive results of local participation in Forest Stewardship, a community pilot program of the U.S. Forest Service. The process of creating a community coalition to qualify for the program was a turbulent one, beginning with the formation of the Yaak Valley Forest Council. This activist group vocally supports ecological diversity and forest protection, particularly the last remaining roadless areas in the Yaak. Although their leadership was ultimately rejected by the larger community in informal votes, their role as a catalyst for dialogue and new approaches is widely acknowledged. The voices of the people that follow portray the issues and experiences of the valley and the struggle toward involving the community in government management of the land around them. Their differing perspectives reveal the value and "messiness" of democracy.   *T.W.S.*

Nancy Oar, a longtime local resident who works with her husband as a brain tanner, a traditional
leather-tanning technique

In the morning in the summer, when we get up, and Tom puts the coffee on and maybe I'll have a cup of tea, we go out on the deck, and he writes in his journal and has his coffee, and that's our *Good Morning America* right out there. You come see it in June. Come up and we'll sit on the deck and you can watch *Good Morning America* right out there. It's great.

Simone Ewing commutes monthly to the San Francisco Bay Area, where she is a landscape designer.

I love the purity and the fact that it's not our place to turn it into a golf course and put in our own airstrip. It really is home to the animals, and there's a deep thing in your subconscious about the fact that you know they come through your property, and this is where they live. I really like the fact that it belongs to them and it isn't something that you can turn into something else.

Rick Bass is an author who often writes about the Yaak Valley, where he has lived since 1987.
He is an impassioned advocate for wilderness protection.

You can really disappear in these woods. They're so thick and dense. They offer a lot of security for wildlife. It's not a traditional recreational wonderland. This is not a beautiful forest, a beautiful view. It's not a place to come play. There's places in the West that are, but this is a biological wilderness, not a recreational wilderness.

Recently settled in the Yaak Valley, Scott Daily provides part-time administrative support to the Yaak Valley
Forest Council and is a writer and caretaker.

People are realizing, hey man, we're just people. You're just a person, I'm just a person — we both love this place. Maybe our reasons are a little bit different, but overall we love the land. I don't think there's anybody who's up here that doesn't love the land, maybe in slightly different ways, but I don't know a whole lot of us up here — now that we've lived here and are becoming part of the rhythms of this place — that would be able to move back to the suburbs. I know I surely couldn't.

Opening image: Interior of Linda Stehlik's cabin

Opposite: View from Pete Creek Road

David Henderson taught at the Yaak School and is now principal of nearby Troy High School.

For the most part it's an unusually literate community. There are people up here who are some of the most prolific readers I've ever known in any university setting I've ever been in. I would put some of the minds and the range of knowledge of some of the people that very quietly live up here against some great university minds. Just brilliant people. And part of that is the product of the climate. When you've got a six-month winter and you don't have electricity, you better have something to do, and books become a very critical friend as well as your family. The four or five winters my wife and kids spent here drove us to communion between ourselves. You can't be locked in a little house for four or five months with very little access to anything outside of each other and not figure out ways to deal with that and build community—even within your own family.

Shirley and Crash Karuzas describe coming upon their future Yaak Valley home to Jens Lund. Crash is a self-employed, small-outfit logger, a "gyppo." Shirley is the business manager for the Yaak Valley School District.

SK: We had always wanted to live in the mountains and had this dream to be in the mountains, to live in a cabin in the woods—very idealistic. We thought (we were so naive) we'll go north, because it's cold there, and nobody will want to have land there, and it'll be cheaper! We spent a summer; we drove every highway in Lincoln; we drove every highway in western Wyoming, Idaho, and Montana; and we circled all the places on the map that we saw where we'd want to live. We were in Trego and I said, "You know, pal, we never drove on this little road right here," and he looked at it and said, "Well, that's not a road." And I said, "Yeah, it's black. It's a road." So we came over the Dodge Summit Road that next morning. We came over Dodge Summit into this country.

CK: I said, "We're wasting our time," because on the map it was obviously all national forest and the old Dodge Summit Road, at that time, was the only way to get into the Yaak from that end of the valley, from the east. It was just a glorified wagon road that hadn't changed much in about sixty years.

SK: It was cut right out of shelf rock.

CK: We came down at about three miles an hour. I had to walk the whole way, moving rocks and trees and stuff out of the way, just to get down.

SK: Oh, we met a log truck, and we met a skidder going the other way. I said to Crash, "This road wasn't marked 'one way' was it?" The road's only as wide as this table. You could walk up there today. It's nothing. Who'd ever seen a skidder? You know, "What's that? What was that thing?"

JL: "That was the biggest tow truck I'd ever seen."

CK: Yeah, yeah, that's why they were running together. The skidder was running ahead of the log truck to help him . . .

SK: . . . get over the top. We came down to Caribou Campground, and we camped there.

CK: At that point I was especially discouraged because, coming from Colorado, which is semiarid, we were in this thick forest. This seemed like the rain forest to me. I realized, "Good grief, I don't know anything about living in timber country." I was real discouraged at that point. I worried, "How am I going to make a living?"

SK: Oh, we were so naive, you know: how are we going to live?

JL: What year was this?

SK: 1977. We camped overnight, and we woke up the next morning and drove out of Caribou, and we came down this hill.

CK: As you come down Boyd Hill, this North Fork Valley opens up, and you can see everything, and we saw these old barns and the old homestead cabin and pulled in here, and I said, "Pal, someday I want a place that looks like this."

Martin Riedlinger, a longtime logger and Yaak Valley resident, has cut trees on contract for many large international logging corporations that harvest the forests, including St. Regis, Champion, and Plum Creek.

I was logging larch, white pine, spruce, lodge-pole, mixed. They call it Idaho Mix. I mostly logged Troy and the Yaak. I logged Fisher River. When I logged for St. Regis, I logged all over this country, wherever they bought a timber sale, that's where I went. Whenever they needed me.

The timber isn't going to be growing back when the other timber is gone. You've got to give it so many years, and they're just not doing that. Now they're working on some places we logged years ago—they're going back in and relogging it. They're cutting everything; they're slicking it up, all but a few little trees they're leaving stand, as though to say, "See, we're leaving something."

After years of seeing independent loggers largely ignored by the Forest Service, Crash Karuzas strongly supports a community stewardship initiative.

Surprisingly, the whole concept of forestry stewardship has been kicked around amongst loggers for easy ten years. One of our weekend neighbors, an old-time logger, from an old-time logging family, for years, while we've sat around the fire or something, he's said, "They ought to let you take that side of Wood Mountain, across the pasture and just do nothing but salvage on it." Even Martin Riedlinger, another old-time logger, one time said that they wouldn't have to build another road if they just turned everybody loose to salvage-log dead and down—they wouldn't have to build another road, and they could keep everybody who wanted to be a logger working. So, the concept has been around for a long time.

John McIntyre and Jeanette Nolan were people who were instrumental in the late sixties, early seventies, in stopping the huge two- and three-hundred-acre clear-cuts around here. They took an awful lot of flak for it from the logging community. Now everybody realizes that a hundred-acre clear-cut, "Yeah, that's kind of big." So, I'm logging now, enjoying it, learning how to be a skidder operator, instead of a timber faller. The concept of being able to have public input into what is going on with how a particular area is treated, as far as forest management practices go, is great.

A sustainable-forestry consultant, Steve Thompson, who lives in Whitefish, Montana, is working with the Yaak Valley Forest Council and the Forest Stewardship project to help inspect areas of the forest to be included in the pilot program.

When I first met Bob Love he was working for a big logging company. He helped make me realize that those caricatures of loggers are just fundamentally untrue, because there's a big difference between the timber mills, which are usually controlled by out-of-state interests and managed for quarterly dividends, and the loggers. I started to meet a lot of these loggers that have a very different perspective on things. They're in the community; they're in it for the long haul. As one of them described it, "On public lands, loggers are sort of stuck like peanut butter between the sandwich of the Forest Service and the timber industry." Most loggers are suspicious of the big companies and don't have any illusion that the big companies have their long-term interests in mind.

Crash Karuzas salvages logs.
JoAnn and Martin Riedlinger, loggers and early residents

Old clear-cut off of Vinal Lake Road

Tom Horelick of Libby, Montana, known locally as the "original environmental logger," specializes in low-impact logging.

I have more of an appreciation for the land and kind of see a big picture of things. What frustrates me to no end is I see a lot of opportunity for small loggers, and hearing this stewardship concept coming about . . . I feel like I'm in a no-man's land a lot of times. In the logging community I'm branded an environmentalist because I think just the low-key, low-impact logging can provide jobs that clean up the woods too. I think there's a lot of opportunity there.

I have a real simple definition of stewardship in my own mind—it's to concentrate on what you leave, not on what you take. That just says it all. Unfortunately, timber sales have been historically concentrated on what you take.

Reuben Kneller is a traditional logger and sawmill operator who was chosen by residents to serve on the Yaak Valley Forest Stewardship Steering Committee.

There's been a lot of timber harvested, but contrary to all the stories you hear—"There's no timber left" and "We're going to run out of timber" and that sort of thing—there's nothing to it. That's just somebody wants to make something out of it. I shouldn't say we'll never run out of timber, but if we harvest it sensibly, we can keep right on working.

Martin Riedlinger has worked in forest industries since the late 1930s.

We are still having the same damn problem with the environmentalists. They don't understand, in my estimation, a lot of things that they should. A lot of these stands of timber need working on really bad. They're not getting touched because they said, "There's too much old growth there. You can't go in there." I don't believe in saving quite all that old growth. I believe in saving some of it, you bet, but I don't believe we need to save it all. We need to go in there again and take some of it and get this country growing again. That's what it needs. It's not going to be any good to be dormant. It's no good for the game.

James "Seamus" Sedler is a writer who moved to the Yaak when he took a job with the Forest Service in 1968. His two sons were raised in the Valley and have remained, one working for the Forest Service, the other as a full-time horse logger.

We're not encouraged to encompass trees as living organisms—or the deer, the bear—as living organisms with actual rights to life. We're encouraged to believe that man is the absolute king. As long as people feel that way, that there's this hierarchy, and that we're the big boss and can do what we want because we have all the answers, then the real stewardship has not begun.

Dan Kelly, independent "gyppo" logger

Opposite: Reuben Kneller at his sawmill

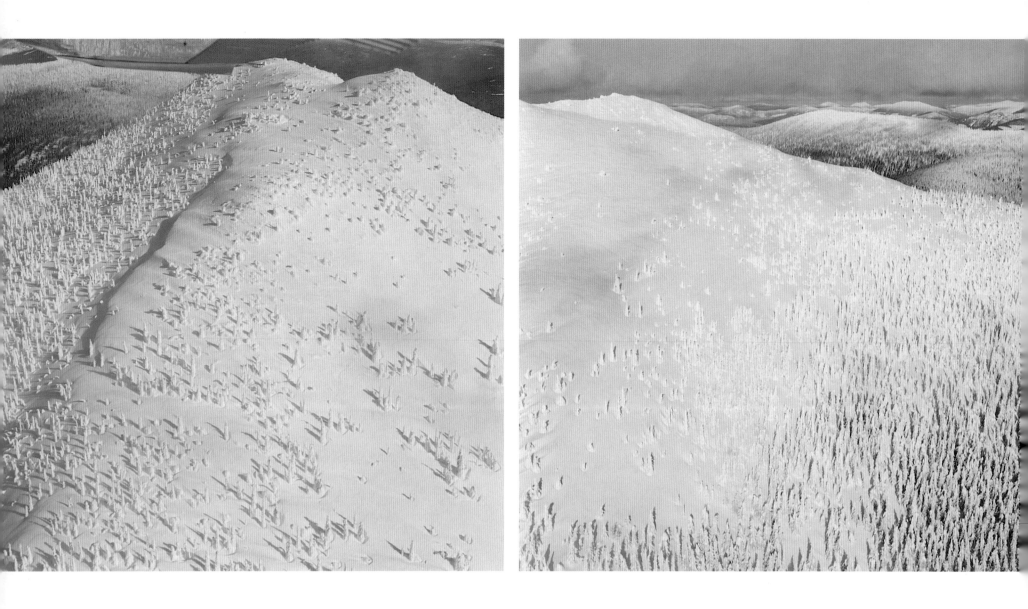

Aerial view of roadless area near Yaak Valley

Ted Schmidt, a retired naval officer, has been a landowner in the Yaak since 1988. Now a full-time resident, he is a member of the Yaak Valley Forest Council. He explains past controversies and why some "Yaakers" fear the government will establish the Yaak Valley as a corridor for providing safe passage for migrating animals.

It's not just forest use—it's development in general. Probably in the past, the bigger argument was development versus nondevelopment rather than logging and clear-cutting. The controversy back when I first got here was connected with a guy by the name of Don Vance, who, in conjunction with some attorneys in Missoula, started a lawsuit to stop logging because the mountain caribou was settled up here. That was the controversy then. He got his cabin burned down and actually left the area. There was no organization or anything, it was just individuals. The new road was a big controversy. When they fixed the road, most of the Valley didn't want the road, especially the younger people, but that was part of the logging, and getting a road would support the logging trucks. There were petitions going around for or against construction of the road, and there were constant arguments. Everybody had their own opinion.

Now the Yaak Forest Council has this big bad name to a lot of people that they're just green wackos who want to turn the whole place into wilderness. They think the government's going to come in and make us leave and kick us off our land and give it back to the grizzly bear. A lot of people up here, honest-to-God believe that the government is going to throw them out of here. They think if you start trying to preserve a roadless area, it just leads to wilderness, and wilderness leads to corridor stuff, which in turn is going to get us thrown off our property.

Suzanne Haggerty taught at the Yaak School before becoming proprietor of the local tavern and store.

Our community is nothing more than a little micropicture of the picture you see in our country at large. That's always been true of small-town America. Things show up a lot more clearly here because we are so small, but the issues really aren't that different. Some of us look at it and say, "You need to be putting this in the larger frame." Little by little we've had our personal freedoms whittled away and whittled away and whittled away. In our community now, our fear is that inviting these conservationist groups in, we're not getting just the roadless area. I don't think there are very many people in this valley who would put up that big a fuss if it just really were about the roadless area. But all of those groups bring with them gun control and people control. Those are the things that we are a lot more concerned with than just setting aside some roadless areas.

Mary Ellen Solem and her husband, John, who retired from managing a grocery-store meat department in Libby, have lived in Montana all their lives and permanently settled in the Yaak eleven years ago.

JS: I think the Forest Service, they know that they made mistakes and they're going back now and trying to cover their tracks.

MES: But you know we all make mistakes in the way we handle our resources, whatever resource it is. Through trial and error, they're learning. The one thing that I know the Forest Service does now, they do the environmental impact statements, and they get public input, and the squeaky wheel gets the grease. Those who yell and scream and complain they listen to. The people who are passive have no one to blame but themselves.

They started the Yaak Rod and Gun Club, and I ended up as secretary because there aren't that many people here year-round. I got to write all the letters, and it amazed me how important it is to write a letter. I was one of these passive people who said, "Well someone else can do it." But if you don't voice your own opinion, whether it's right or wrong, whether I agree with you or disagree with you, you have no one to blame but yourself. You need all the input from everyone to come to a general consensus of what is the right thing to do.

Lawrence "Larry" Dolezal of Troy served as Lincoln County commissioner from 1987 to 1999, representing the northern part of the county, which includes the Yaak Valley.

During the transitions of the late eighties and nineties, we lost over a thousand, probably over twelve hundred, basic industry jobs. Sitting in office as county commissioner, I'm wearing all these different hats, and all of a sudden I'm getting a real live taste of what happens, not only when industry leaves and jobs and people and families are impacted, but I also was sitting there watching our revenue sources drop off sharply. Our tax base went into a tailspin in the decline. During the same period of time, our harvest on our public lands continued to decline, and cumulatively it's had a devastating impact on our economy, our tax base, our people. It was a really tough decade to be county commissioner.

Robyn King is a founder of the Yaak Valley Forest Council and an advocate for both community dialogue and forest conservation.

It's real easy to sort of go along in your life and just let things happen when things are going good and the economy is good, and you get to go to your job every day like everybody does. Being in semi-isolation from everybody else around you can work to a certain extent. But, when you live in a place that is losing its way to support itself, you have to depend on each other. You have to reach out to the other human beings in the community. This is such an incredible opportunity to not only do that but also to do it in ways that create something new, that create new ways of talking and communicating and disagreeing.

Writer and resident Rick Bass on the community's involvement in the U.S. Forest Service stewardship program

What everybody is excited about—and they should be—is the paradigm shift on taking what the forest has to give, not what you want. It means taking the weak, sick, diseased trees and leaving the healthy stock, focusing on restoration. That's all great and can really change the Forest Service's direction and image. But all along I've said that what I think the real sleeper value of stewardship forestry is that it can force a community to get people together who otherwise had refused to get together and cooperate in a project. It has that potential. It can get people sitting down at a table finding out what they have in common when they look at a stand, a unit, a forest, a grove, whatever you want to call it. Even though they may differ philosophically in many respects, it can become a common currency, a common language, a common denominator where they can agree on specifics, rather than these abstractions that are so destructive and fear-filled and hate-filled. The abstractions are what are keeping us from prospering as a community.

Robyn King and Jimmy Martin, at home
Zeita Mae Romeiko, thirty-year Yaak resident
Opposite: Jesse Sedler horse logging

A seventies "back-to-the-lander," Barbara Lindsay settled in the Yaak area and raised two children with her husband, John, a tree planter in the Kootenai Collusion, a local cooperative. Now the whole family conducts species-stand exams for the U.S. Forest Service.

Ten years ago there was the loggers and there was the environmentalists. Now I see this sort of thing happening where the loggers and the environmentalists see that they're dealing with the same problems really, and there's beginning to be not "I hate you, I hate you" on both sides, but "OK, we've all got problems and maybe we could handle these problems by talking about them." Ten years ago, the twain didn't meet.

James "Seamus" Sedler on the bitter arguments between residents over the future of the forest

There's an enormous difference between pulling someone out of the ditch and having a community meeting where no one is really taking the time to listen to what the other person has to say. We've so prejudged each other that we can't even hear what someone else has to say. There's an enormous difference between pulling someone out of the ditch and that sense of respecting each other. That's personal responsibility. Whether you think it's a good reason or a bad reason, whether you think it's to save the forest or to save your own backside, you can't jam your feelings down someone else's throat and expect them to share them with you in a community.

Left: Horse logger Jesse Sedler with his father, Seamus
Right: Scott Daily, a local environmental activist
Opposite: Logged area near Yaak Valley

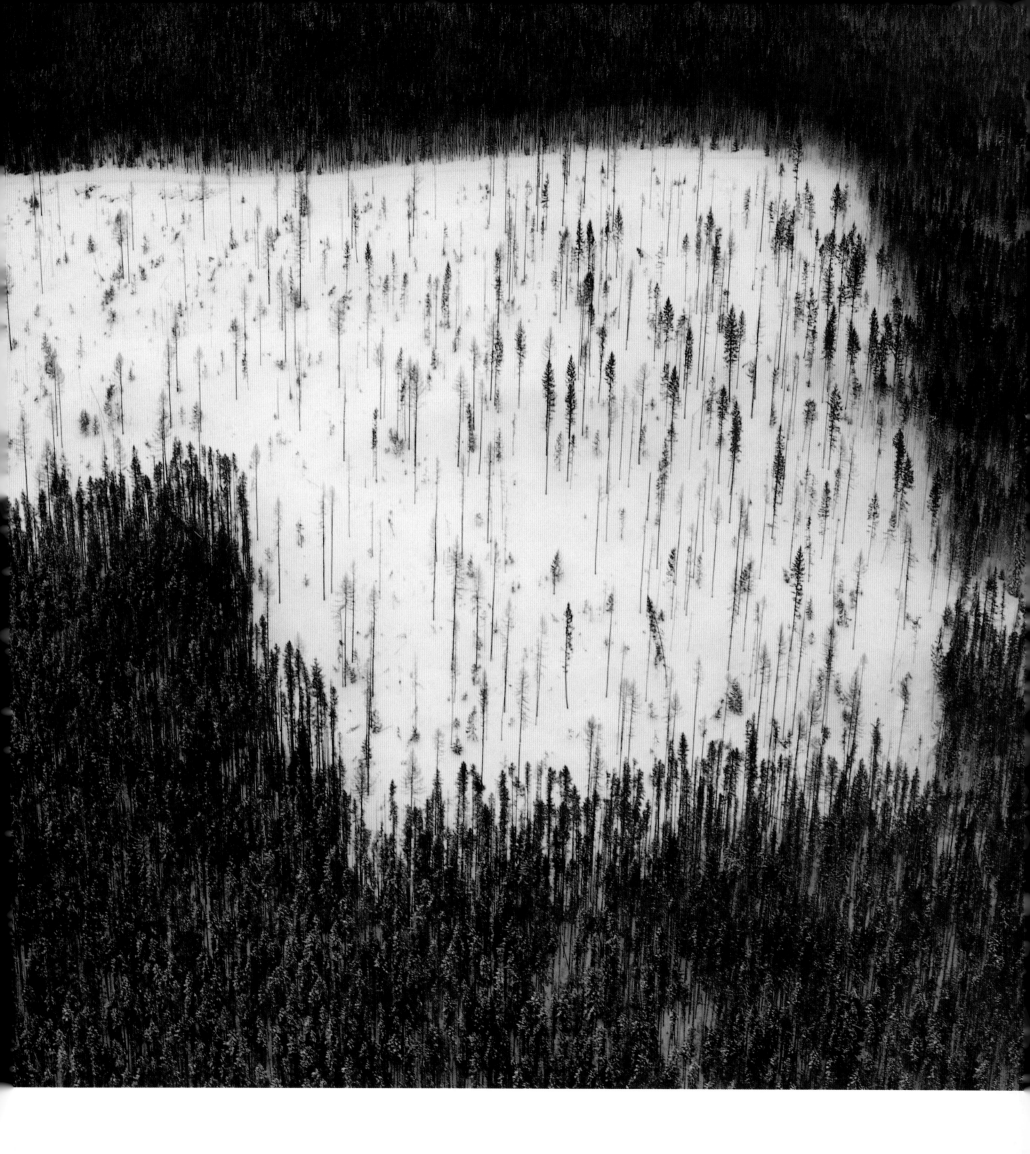

Artie Wright works construction and does maintenance and groundskeeping at a Yaak Valley hunting and fishing lodge.

I'm kind of more of a listener. I got to worry about a lot of stuff that's more personal, like a truck payment or a land payment, that's important to me. I see a lot of people with attitudes that are almost like born-again Christians. You know, "It's all right to have your beliefs as long as you believe the way I do." I'd just as soon keep my beliefs to myself, and, if it comes to a vote, I'll vote. As soon as you open your mouth, there's somebody trying to convince you that there's a better way.

Tim Linehan is a hunting and fishing guide and outfitter who has a related television show, *Trout Unlimited Television*, on ESPN2. He is the only Yaak Valley Forest Council member who also serves on the Yaak Valley Steering Committee, which is charged with developing forest management projects with the U.S. Forest Service.

The process by which we arrived at certain points was maybe the most important thing that went on. That was the only reason that some of us continued to come to the table each time. If it was some other process, it probably wouldn't have worked. It almost didn't work, so I think that we learned more about each other during the process than we will ever learn implementing the actual project. Yes, implementing the project will be as much a process, but getting here was huge, and getting here opened many, many eyes with wonder and surprise regarding how we can better work together and be neighbors within resource-based communities.

David Henderson, an educator and sometime Yaak mediator, recalls what he said to a group struggling to resolve differences of opinion and make progress.

Do any of you sitting here think that our disagreements, our controversies, are even remotely as severe as the same disagreements and controversies that existed between the southern colonies and the middle colonies and the northern colonies when they gathered in Philadelphia trying to create a constitution? Their disagreements were monumental. They were enormous — and the democracy that they were trying to create was huge. It was a mess. It was absolutely a mess. It was so ugly, and the process was so fraught with disaster, but it happened, and it can happen in any community.

Robyn King is a small-business systems manager and community activist.

It was so beautiful when we took the vote during the first Yaak Valley Forest Steering Committee meeting. It just happened, people were raising their hands, and we had an absolute representation of a cross-section of this community. It was beautiful how it happened. The most exciting thing I saw was all of this high emotion and all of this energy going on in the room beforehand and after the meeting was over. People were talking loudly, but not loudly in anger. They were so excited — even the people who had many, many questions about what was going on and what was really happening. What you saw was excitement, excitement about something new happening, excitement about potential, excitement about being empowered.

No matter where it goes, we were in this process of how our country works, and it was just really great to see.

Opposite: Aaron Karuzas

For the most part, the story of Yaak's forest is a story of codominance, which seems to me to be a good metaphor for the community. We have significant diversity in our community, and no one view, no one person, no one group, should run the show, nor do they run the show. The real challenge that we're facing as a community is how to keep that community vibrant and engaged with the issues, just as we're trying to keep this wonderful, multispecies forest intact and functioning, rather than overmanaged, overmanipulated, overharmed, overinjured, overcontrolled. The community gives off the same kind of vibrance, the same kind of help. There's windstorms and ice storms in the woods and we have those kinds of flurries of activities in our community, but a healthy community cannot only withstand those stresses but bends and sways and develops a strength as a result of those stresses, if there's a commitment to do that.

In the forest, that kind of commitment is called life. The trees have to do it to survive. The forest has to do it to survive. In a community, it's called democracy.

Rick Bass

I believe the landscape helps sculpt us and shape us, and we also carry our internal psyches into a landscape, and we seek out—certain bunker types like myself and the other folks up here—seek out dark, secretive, secluded places. So we carry that with us. The landscape certainly doesn't encourage us to be otherwise. We go to seed up here, which is what we came here to do. It's a lovely experience to give yourself over to the landscape in that manner and to the community. We all know each other's weaknesses. We know how to make fun of each other. It can be a real wonderful integration. We are all like little owls, peering out at the great, bright world beyond, but we like it back in here where it's cool and shady.

At the Clam and Oyster Feed, the annual school fundraiser given by the Yaak River Tavern

Opposite: View across the Yaak Valley from Pete Creek Road

Shirley Karuzas, a Yaak resident since 1978

It's a whole different community than it used to be. Work is not the issue anymore. The people who live here now don't need to work or don't work in traditional ways. It's not resource-based, so it is a real different community.

Mary Ellen Solem has known the Yaak since childhood. Her grandfather was one of the last original homesteaders.

It scares me because so many homesteads are so chopped up, and it's like wall-to-wall people in some places. You'll find, especially down at 14 Mile, across the river, one of the first developments. I don't know what it's called, Yaak Meadows, or something like that. Those parcels are less than an acre. Very few people live year-round—maybe four families at the very most, maybe five. In the summertime it's vacation people. I don't know where the Yaak really is going to go. It's not going to be what I see now. It's going to change.

Dario Scarabosio is a Yaak landowner and retired RV dealer from Oregon. He has organized the opposition to efforts to provide permanent protection for remaining roadless areas in the Yaak Valley.

I don't want to be booted out of here. Someday I won't be healthy enough to stay, but to be booted out of here because somebody has the wild vision that this should be a preserve for who knows what, so you could drive through here like a tourist. I don't understand it.

At the Clam and Oyster Feed benefit
for the Yaak School

Opposite: Top of Hensley Hill

Jeanne Higgins works for the U.S. Forest Service and was formerly the district ranger working with the Yaak community.

If the communities can resolve issues, there's a lot better chance of us being successful than if the lawmakers are the ones trying to resolve the issues.

Steve Thompson, a sustainable-forestry consultant in northwest Montana

The American people have put the hammer down and said, "We are going to protect endangered species. We're not going to wipe out all these species—the spotted owl, the Canadian lynx, or the grizzly bear." So, part of it has been imposed by the American people. But, part of it has also been internalized by the world community that says, "Hey, we care about our native trout fisheries." Aesthetics isn't necessarily the issue for them. It is for some, but I think more are saying, "We have some pride in our place. By gosh, my parents use to catch beautiful cutthroat, and now we can't catch that beautiful cutthroat trout anymore. Why is that?" And they care about that.

I'm seeing some great transitions. The Yaak is really beginning a transition towards this whole notion of sustainability and stewardship and community vision.

PHOTOGRAPHS BY **JOAN LIFTIN** · INTERVIEWS BY **MERLE AUGUSTIN**

CITIZENS ON WATCH

HAITIAN CITIZENS POLICE ACADEMY AND ROVING PATROL · MAD DADS STREET PATROL

DELRAY BEACH, FLORIDA

When great numbers of immigrants settle in a new place in a short period of time, they often challenge community stability. Older residents may express impatience with these newcomers and nearly always penalize them for their intrusion on territory that is "not theirs." Delray Beach and Palm Beach County, Florida, for example, were unprepared for the huge influx of Haitians who arrived there after leaving their island home in search of greater political freedom and the better life that America promised. Their dream—like that of many immigrants—led many to risk their lives to make the trip, traveling in unsafe boats, with some literally swimming ashore. This influx of immigrants has changed Delray forever, with close to 17,000 Haitians now making it their home—nearly 33 percent of the city's population.

Delray Beach has never been the kind of high-rent, elite resort that Palm Beach or Boca Raton is. Instead, it has been home to many white and black families whose livelihoods depended on work in the white-sand resorts of the Florida coast. Haitians, finding Delray a likable and prosperous place to get a start, blended in easily with the African American community, moving into rented homes and eagerly taking service jobs. At first, many whites were insensitive to the differences between Haitians and African Americans, but Haitian immigrants often ignored housing taboos, crossing invisible lines of racial separation as the community spread throughout Delray Beach. At the same time, crime was on the rise in Delray, and by the 1990s the downtown area had declined quickly, fed by a combination of fear, racism, and the realities of drug-induced crime.

For police and other officials charged with maintaining safety and interacting with local residents, the challenges to effective communication were exacerbated by this wave of immigration. Many newly arrived Haitian residents had little or no understanding of local police practices and American laws. Haitian newcomers faced language and cultural barriers and were quickly stereotyped and victimized. For Delray to embrace its new residents and grow to build partnerships involving all sectors of the community, the city had to build bridges of understanding between ordinary people and law enforcement agencies.

The Delray Beach Police Department, with other organizations, saw the need to build trust and communicate with this new population. The department embraced the concept of community policing, with law enforcement officers serving as advocates for local people as well as patrollers for safety, and with police officers providing a regular presence in the neighborhoods. The police department initiated programs that reached out to groups throughout the city and brought local people into the work of policing. Two key groups that came out of this process are the Haitian Citizens Police Academy and Roving Patrol and MAD DADS, an African American community policing effort aimed at reducing drug-related crime in Delray. These two volunteer organizations are powerful examples of a city's ability to change and grow. Delray Beach has seen a remarkable improvement in cultural understanding and in relations between citizens and city officials, and the neighborhood streets are now safer places for all of Delray Beach's people.   *T.R.*

Lamousse Valcena works for the City of Delray Beach in partnership with MAD DADS.

Lula Butler, director of community improvement, has lived in Delray Beach for twenty-eight years.

The Haitian community has crossed boundaries—that's the interesting thing about immigrant populations—they don't really know where the lines are drawn. They don't come to your town understanding that there's a line—they just live wherever they find housing. So some of the neighborhoods that were traditionally white are now predominantly Haitian. I mean they automatically integrate.

I don't think I was working for the city at that time when we were having an immigrant population coming into Delray. On Southwest Tenth Street there was that one big house, and all of a sudden there was just a huge number of people there. That's when I first heard, "Oh, God, we've got Haitians coming." I remember the newspaper articles in the city, talking about how we've got to get these people out of there. There must have been a hundred of them in there. I remember that and I remember the conversations when they started to live in the southeast section—because that was crossing the line—they had crossed Swinton.

We really need to decide what we want for our kids, not let someone else decide for us. We know what we want. But as I said, Haiti is different. When they were in Haiti, they were not in this kind of environment. The environment here is new. Since it's new, we have to learn how to adjust to the new environment and take advantage of that environment, and also blend into the American society.

We want to keep Haitian culture because there is a lot of value in the culture. But, since we are in America, we have to learn the system, how everything functions. The only way they can be successful is to learn the way.

I'm proud to be Haitian because my people, when they understand, know what they want. They are, I would say, a people with incentive. They know where they want to go. The only problems we have are language barriers. Also people have taken advantage of them because in Haiti—I don't want to be offensive, but let me put it this way—ignorance is a way of exploitation, so some people tried to keep them in the darkness. My job is to make sure that they understand everything. I tell them how to take advantage of all the programs in this community, and in this way they can really move forward and be what they want to be.

Opening image: Haitian church outing

Above: Robert Augustin and his sister

Opposite: Islande Chery, wife of Renold Chery, Haitian patrol sergeant

Lamousse Valcena has a radio program about parenting on a local Haitian radio station.

My job is to encourage the Haitians to be involved in whatever is going on in the neighborhood. What I try to do is help them understand that the neighborhood belongs to them, and nobody will come from somewhere else to do something for them unless they are involved, unless they are concerned.

Daniella Henry, director of the Haitian American Community Council, moved to Delray Beach from New York City in 1990. Her own immigrant experience led to her work as an advocate in the Haitian community.

It was hard for me when I first came because there were only a handful of Haitian kids here. We didn't have the opportunity to have bilingual teachers or language specialists. Nobody could understand us. It was very difficult. We were just sitting in a classroom. I never understood nor heard what the teacher was saying. Then in 1979 the refugees started coming. I was still young but the stereotype of the Haitian boat people was just like a curse. When I started mingling with the other kids, they said, "You're Haitian," and they were cursing that I was Haitian.

So when the Haitians came by boat, it was worse because now we became the image that was being displayed. They were thinking everybody was coming illegally by boat, and it was difficult in school for us. Every time you go to school they say that's the way you came—by boat—your family came by boat. It was like a curse, but, hopefully, that has helped me to do something with myself. We had Haitians come in 1991 after the coup, and I wanted to help them not to go through the same problems that I went through when I first came to the United States. I wanted them to have somebody be an activist or be on their side when it came to some problem, to help and direct them. That's when I became interested in working in Palm Beach County, especially Delray Beach.

You have to be willing and wanting to do something. It was a dream. I needed to put myself into helping the people. With another friend, I started the Haitian American Community Council. It was a willingness—I stayed two years before getting paid—but that was what I wanted to do. After two years we started getting funding. Once you believe in something you put yourself into doing it. People watching, they see that you have a willingness—you have the good will to do something positive—and you are going to help.

A daughter of one of the dancers
rehearsing for the Haitian Flag Day
ceremonies at Our Lady of
Perpetual Help Catholic Church

Fremiaud Basse holds a photo
of his fiancée, Guerline Joseph,
believed to have drowned off
Florida in March 1999. Two boats
with at least forty Haitians aboard
capsized twelve miles from shore.
All but three drowned. Relatives
and friends brought photographs
to the Haitian American

Father Roland Desormeaux is parish priest of Our Lady of Perpetual Help Catholic Church, which has a largely
Haitian congregation with 956 registered families.

The suffering, the poverty in Haiti is not new. It's very difficult. It's an impossible life. I don't know how people do it.
Therefore, they have to leave Haiti looking for a better life. When people are suffering, they are out there looking for
something better. As a result, they go to the boat, to the Bahamas, hoping to come here.

    You cannot tell people not to come, not to find a way out of Haiti. It's a way to tell you that things are so hard
in Haiti that people have to find a way to get out. It doesn't matter how many people died. They will tell them, "Don't
go because so many people die." But, they will always think, "Well, they will die and they've been dying, but it's not
me. I won't die!"

Skip Brown, police officer and volunteer coordinator, is concerned about the risks Haitian immigrants take to travel to south Florida by boat.

My thing to the Haitians guys—to my guys out there—is I try to go around the backdoor and tell them, "Look, it's not the money, folks, it's not the money. It's not the nine thousand dollars that one of your Haitian compadres out here is making on these people. You put twenty on there, that's a hundred and some odd thousand dollars that someone's making. It's not the money. It's the two, three bodies that come washing up on the shore. There's no amount of money worth your brother, your sister, your cousin, washing up on the beach because some captain of some illegal ship shoved them off the boat a hundred yards from shore and they can't swim." I say, "Come on, folks. Give me a break on this, give your families a break." I say, "We've had three or four funerals already in the past two years right here in Delray Beach just for the same stuff. It's not worth it. There's a way to come into a country, and there's a way not to." I say, "If I can't appeal to you on the legal part of it, let me appeal to you on the humane part of it."

Marie Elmon and her nephew at
her brother's storefront church

Wilner Athouriste is a longtime member of the Haitian
Roving Patrol.

When you live in a different country, you have to learn the
culture of the country where you live before you can give
your children your own culture. It is really hard. As a Haitian,
I cannot bring my Haitian culture into my kid's head. No.
That's really hard.

The child was born in a different country from yours.
Where I was born, there's many hundred different things I
did that I cannot do here. It's not even available to children
here, to do it here. In Haiti, you used to go to the little river
to get the water for your grandma. Here, who's going to go
get the water for grandma? Right there, that's a different
thing. Little boys, the first day they're born, the first thing
you see in front of them is a television, a refrigerator, and
everything right inside the house. In my country, nothing is
inside the house. You see what I mean? It's a different place.

What I do for my kids, especially my five-year-old who
is here with me, is take him on vacation almost every year
to Haiti. I show him his grandfather, his grandma, his
uncle, and where I grew up, where I was going to school. I
make him meet my teachers in Haiti and all the other kids
and see how they live. I talk to him and tell him what it is,
but that doesn't mean I can bring that culture inside his
head. No. I have to learn this country's culture and help my
son to understand my culture. But I cannot take my culture
inside his head here. We can never do that, never.

Richard Overman became Delray chief of police in 1991, at a time when the police department was held in low esteem by minority communities.

We had to overcome a serious perception and image problem. Frankly, my approach was very simple. One, I'm never going to lie to you. Two, if you are depending upon the police to change your circumstances and your situation down here in your neighborhoods, if you're depending on the police alone to do that, it will not happen. It won't happen under me. It won't happen under the next five chiefs to come. If you don't get involved, if you don't work with us, if we can't have partnership, if we can't put a team together here to deal with these issues, it won't happen. I'm not a miracle worker.

What I promised was: I will give you attention. I will be there. I will work with you. I will sit at the table with you and discuss these issues. We can develop plans of action. But, the long and short of it is, if we don't do it together, it won't happen. It's real simple. It's a team sport here. We've got to do this together.

Wilner Athouriste, Haitian patrol volunteer

BREAKFAST
$ 5.00
SALT FISH
MORRUE
5.00
LIVER
FIE
6.00
FISH
P ISSON
5.00
GRITS
MAIS
PLANTAIN
LUNCH
8.00
POISSON
700
FISH
LAMBI
$ 6.00
CONCH
CABRIT
499
GOAT
POULET
4.99
CHICKEN
PINTADE
499
GUINEA HEN
LEGUME
499
VEGETABLE
FEUILLE
$ 4.99
SPINACH
GRIOT
JUICE
$ 2.00
GRENADIA
2 00
ANN SEET SOUP
2.00
PAPAYA
2 00
PEACH
2 00
SOURSOP
1 00
LEMONADE
0.50
SODA

Wilner Athouriste has lived for sixteen years in Delray Beach, where he is an irrigation technician.

Today, you can feel you're living as brothers and sisters. In most of the neighborhood, there is a Haitian house, then maybe an American house, a Haitian house, an American house. Even the Caribbean food Haitians eat is mixed together now—the Haitian eats American food; the American eats Haitian food. When my son graduates in the next few weeks, we're going to cook Haitian food to bring to his graduation party, and it's not only us. There are some other Haitian kids' parents who are going to bring Haitian flavor to that party. This is the American way. See what I mean? Everything is getting together. This neighborhood really lives like brothers and sisters now.

At a Saturday night dance

Opposite: Restaurant Chez Zette

Skip Brown coordinates over a thousand volunteers in ten different programs for the police department, one of which is the Haitian Roving Patrol.

This is 1999. In 1995 we were just getting into what they call community policing—that's where you see a police officer ride by in the car and that's the last time you see him until the next day. Community policing involves the police officers getting off their butts, getting out of their cars, and getting into the neighborhoods and saying, "Hi. My name's Officer Brown. What problems do you have here? How can I help you?"

   Along with community policing came volunteerism. Volunteerism is probably the purest form of community policing that you can get because it's the community actually doing the policing, helping and keeping an eye not only on their own neighborhoods but also their assigned neighborhoods. They work side by side with the police officers. When they call something in, the dispatcher says, "Oh, boy. OK. They must have something out there. We're going to send an officer right out." It's instantaneous response. Not only do the citizens see police now, but they see a faction of the community helping to make their community a safer place to live.

We were looking at the amount of victimization that the Haitians were experiencing out in the neighborhoods. What we were seeing was that a lot of Haitians were not even calling the police, because there was no trust there to begin with. They didn't want to compound an already major situation for them by calling the police. Today we have probably sixteen, seventeen thousand Haitians that live in the city of Delray Beach, and as a police officer, I haven't got a clue about what is going on in the Haitian neighborhood. That's a little scary. You take seventeen thousand people in a fifty-five-thousand-person city, that's a big chunk of people. A big chunk of population that I have not got a clue about what's going on out there.

We decided—and when I say we, the city government, the police department—we took a hard look at a lot of things: the victimization of the Haitians, the effect of so many living here and coming on our beaches illegally. It was a wake-up call to say, "Hey, something really should be done by this community to reach out to them." Somewhere along the line they had chosen Delray Beach to come and live, and it would probably be very foolish for a government to turn away and not really care what's going on with these people.

There was a need for us to reach out and say to them, "You are a part of this community. Now come on board and give us a hand running this." Very seldom, even to this day, do I see any Haitians at all at city hall for the commission meetings. They stay away. To this day, they still don't trust government. They still don't trust a lot of the city authorities. So it's still an ongoing problem.

Fear of the police is deep-seated in many Haitians. It's visible in how people react when patrol members show up. It's obvious that the person is afraid and not quite themselves. That's why it was very difficult for the police department to gain our trust. These guys were our enemies. From our perspective, the authorities have never been our friends. Thinking back, I realize that I was my own worst enemy because the police are there to provide safety, to protect us. They are there to enforce the law, and they are there to set things right. But from what I knew then, I only saw them as a punishing force and not as upholders of justice. It was very, very difficult.

The Haitian Roving Patrol wouldn't have happened without the police academy class. I wouldn't have been part of it without these classes. Through the academy, we learned about the law and how it works, and now all the Haitian community says the patrol does a good job and they look up to us.

Sergeant Renold Chery talks to a possible recruit for the volunteer patrol.

Cell, Palm Beach County Stockade Correctional Facility

Opposite: The Haitian Roving Patrol

Chuck Ridley was raised in Delray Beach in a close-knit African American community. After years of drug use, he has reformed and was a key player in starting MAD DADS.

They were going to sell that same poison to my children that destroyed my life, and I wasn't going to have it. That was absolutely unacceptable. I didn't want to hear anymore about slavery; I didn't want to hear anymore about oppression; I didn't want to hear anymore about these systemic changes; I didn't want to hear anything from an academic mind-set. "Damn it, get these drug dealers from in front of my house or shut up!"

I was just angry, I was very, very angry that no one seemed to get it. The police department, in my mind, was saying, "It's not my problem; it's your problem." The neighborhood organizations were saying, "It's not our problem; it's the police's problem." The government was saying, "It's not our problem; it's the neighborhood organizations and the police." And I'm thinking, "You know, they're going to sell poison to my

children. Don't you get it? They're going to shoot each other in front of my house. Don't you get it? Those bullets fly by my windows. Don't you get it? I have to show my family how to lie on the floor when the drive-bys start. Don't you get it?" No one really seemed to get it until I made that call to MAD DADS in Ocala.

Here is what they say they did: a group of local men began to walk in the most difficult and most troubled spots, and they stood there. They weren't vigilantes, and they weren't aggressive. They just stood there and observed and occasionally would talk. They began to talk to these young people, saying, "Look, now, we're not going to tolerate you selling drugs, but we're not here to hurt you, either. We're here to strengthen our community."

From there, just having the courage to walk in places where the police department wouldn't come, unarmed, and willing to stand there as a symbol of something different and new, as men, they unleashed a kind of energy that began to transform their community. They not only saw crime reduced over 19 percent in their neighborhood, they began to see resources line up to strengthen the fabric of the neighborhood and help the youth develop. They also saw a dramatic improvement in race relations as people began to understand the true impact of what happens when human beings get together and love. It made sense to me. Can't tell you why it made sense to me, but it did.

Interior, home of preacher Adner Elmon and his wife, Helene Elmon

Opposite: Member of Adner Elmon's congregation

Skip Brown telling a story about his relationship with Alfred Etienne

1997, August, I got a call; I got beeped at home. I was out cutting the grass; it was a Saturday, and it was Alfred. I called him back, and he said, "I need to see you. I need to see you right now." So I said, "OK." I dropped what I was doing, went up to the police department and met him there, and we went up to the chief's conference room. I sat him down and figured, this guy's going to quit me, or something's happened, because he's not looking very happy. I said, "Alfred, here I am. What's going on? Tell me what's happening here." He reaches over and grabs both of my hands in his, and I look at him and tears are running down his face, and he says, "Officer Skip," he says, "you give me life." I had to put his hands down and get the hell out of the room because I wasn't prepared for that. I understand exactly what he was trying to say—that our friendship meant a lot to him, the program meant a lot to him, being associated with the police and opening up opportunities for him meant that much. Here I have a forty-four-year-old guy sitting there, crying like a baby, telling me this stuff, and this is something that the old American tough cop isn't ready for. It was an educational experience, to say the least, but that was probably the first time that I really took a good look at Alfred. Alfred's my mainstay for the Haitian patrol. He's the one. If I didn't have him, I wouldn't be faring so well. He runs interference for me; sometimes he explains to me how Haitians think and how they feel. He guides me through this program and all the people that surround it. I'm very happy to have him. I can really truly say that I love him like a brother.

The drug dealers wouldn't sell while they looked at us. For whatever reason, we symbolized something that challenged them. They didn't say, "No, we're not going to sell," but they called us "snitches." It was, "How dare you?" You know, "Ben, you snorted up, a whole block, and Chuck smoked up half the community, so how dare you guys be out there? If the truth be told, you all told us how to sell drugs when you all used to sell drugs." They were a little angry.

What was interesting was some of the neighborhood members would say, "Psst, psst. Come here, come here. We want to tell you something. See the house over there? It's a crack house. But don't tell anybody I told you." They wouldn't want to be seen talking to us. Pretty soon they didn't mind being seen talking to us while they were walking the street, and pretty soon they started walking the street. Then, pretty soon, the people who were on drugs started telling us stuff, and they would be seen talking to us. Soon we got them in treatment, and then they became the nucleus of the street patrol.

MAD DADS is an anointed concept, and it starts with men walking in the street. Street patrol is the most powerful. It's the only thing that MAD DADS does well, having the courage to stand in the gap for this neighborhood where it hurts the most. And out of that real miracles have happened.

When I first entered the community, being a product of the sixties, going through school back then, being an idealist, I first went into the neighborhood with this fix-it attitude. It took me a while to be humbled and realize that I was not going into a neighborhood looking for what I needed to fix. I discovered that what needed the most fixing was myself, my perspective. I don't have the answers. You really have to try to meet people where they're at, and then they're more open and likely to accept you where you're at, and together we find solutions.

The solutions are always different and they can be creative, but there's no right answer. When outsiders, so-called do-gooders, come in and don't respect the community they're entering, I've taken a perspective of defense for those people who have become my friends in the neighborhood. If you're going to someone's house that you've just met and trying to rearrange all the furniture to suit you instead of learning what they're about, you're not meeting them where they're at. After you're there a while, you learn to love the way the furniture's arranged in the room. You learn that it didn't need to be fixed, but maybe just needed to be understood, as you needed to be understood as well.

MAD DADS, an antidrug and volunteer
street-patrol group, on patrol

The two pillars of society no matter where you live, whether it's inner-city Delray or any other city in the United States, are health and education. If you don't have a physically healthy community, you cannot do anything. We need that first, but what comes hand in hand to support that is the educational pillar. Without education, we will not know where the opportunities are or to take advantage of what is out there for us. We need to educate our population so that they have opportunities, or doors of choice open up to them.

We work in programs where we say that literacy doesn't solve all the problems. It's not going to guarantee you success, but without the literacy skills you need, you're almost doomed to failure in our society because you don't have the tools you need to make choices. Through literacy or an education, you learn that there are other ways to resolve issues in your life. When social problems do arise, where do you turn to for help? Through education, we know that there are people out there and how to access the services that are already in place. We do not need to reinvent the wheel. What we need to do is to educate the population to tap into those resources.

I believe that MAD DADS is bringing to the community the two pillars of health and education. They now need to build upon that foundation. The structure needs to be erected, and we have to go out there and start putting those building blocks in place.

At the Fourth of July outing organized by Father Roland Desormeaux, parish priest of Our Lady of Perpetual Help Catholic Church

Mother and daughter at the
Fourth of July picnic

Do we have a voice? Yes. Is it as strong as we want? No. But it's a far cry from where it was. Is the community completely aware? No. But the awareness has risen to a level that we haven't ever had in this community. We've developed an infrastructure. Is it culturally diverse? Yes. Are the three ethnic groups working closely together? No. We're working together, though, and building relationships.

We fight, oh, we fight and argue, but we're fighting and arguing among ourselves and in such a way that we won't get up from the table and leave. We hold each other accountable. We're moving to a point where we like the neighborhood we live in, where on some days we have the audacity to love the neighborhood we live in. That hasn't happened in this neighborhood in a long time. A symbol of hope has replaced despair.

The key word is partnership. See, if you don't have the partnership, you cannot build a network. The best source of information are people who are in the community. What I perceive as a problem may come strictly from a police officer's point of view, and that in itself is a bias. Unless you live in the community, unless you are subject to whatever happens in the community, you cannot really pinpoint the problems. That's why you have this partnership with different organizations like MAD DADS and Roving Patrol. You build that network and get a better understanding of what needs to happen.

A father and son in their
backyard on Sunday morning

Opposite: The beach at night

PHOTOGRAPHS BY **LYNN DAVIS** · INTERVIEWS BY **JENS LUND**

SEA CULTURE

ALASKAN FISHING COMMUNITIES

NORTH PACIFIC COAST, ALASKA

Often identified as America's last wilderness, the state of Alaska includes over thirty thousand miles of shoreline—nearly half of all the shoreline in the United States. No place in America is more connected to or dependent on the sea. Here, both the fish populations and the communities of commercial fishermen thrive on the Gulf of Alaska and Bering Sea fisheries. These waters provide over 50 percent of all U.S. domestic landings of fish while the fishing industry in Alaska is the state's largest private sector employer. As many of the world's fishing waters are now depleted by overfishing and poor resource management, Alaskan coastal waters have become increasingly attractive to the world's fishing fleet. This competition for fish puts huge pressure on Alaska's maritime habitats and threatens a range of species. Additionally, bycatch, the catching and killing of fish not targeted or not marketable, has decimated fish populations.

In 1993 coastal residents and others dependent on marine resources for their livelihood organized the Alaska Marine Conservation Council (AMCC) to educate and collaborate with a variety of business, environmental, and regulatory groups and local communities throughout the state to protect and restore marine habitat. A consortium of fishermen, environmentalists, scientists, and educators, the AMCC is a community of individuals who are connected through their occupation, their ties to the environment, and their proximity to the sea. Collectively, this community supports a commitment to sustaining fish habitats through greater local stewardship of the sea's resources and to making fundamental changes in fishing practices.

The organization's work to manage the sea's resources is visible throughout Alaska's fishing industry. Among other accomplishments, the AMCC led the statewide, grassroots effort to win passage of the federal law to set limits and curtail overfishing. Smaller, independent fishermen now have a voice in resource-management discussions, thanks to the Alaska Marine Conservation Council. AMCC's advocacy on behalf of Alaskan native communities and their rights to subsistence fishing practices helps preserve native people's traditions. The AMCC also negotiated an agreement to limit bottom trawling around Kodiak Island and in the Bering Sea in order to protect marine habitat, showing how well it builds consensus that leads to change.

No typical group of environmental organizers, AMCC members have come to their understanding of ecology through living in and off the natural world, and they act on the belief that the best solutions to complex ecological problems are driven by local people. The AMCC seeks solutions that consider the needs of the ecosystem and the cultural and economic needs of fishing families and their communities, that sustain Alaska's sea culture and preserve a deeply held way of life.

T.R.

Bill Foster, originally from the Lower 48, is a charter boat captain who lives in Sitka.

The old joke is that if you go to the Anchorage airport, within an hour you will see two, three people that you know. That's kind of the hub for traveling all over the state. Sometimes, if you miss somebody and you know they're leaving town, you know you can catch them at the Sitka airport. You can take care of a lot of business right there at the airport. Just like the post office here. At one time everybody in Sitka had a post office box, and every day, in the late afternoon, you knew that you could find at least one representative from every family in town at the post office, gathering that day's mail.

Carolyn Servid, with her husband, Dorik Mechau, runs the nonprofit Island Institute in Sitka, whose mission is to mediate resource protection and the needs of human communities.

There are a lot of questions that are about human values. It's not necessarily about saving the wilderness. It's about how people live well in places. The environmental movement is starting to recognize that they need to address that question more than they have, and that the kind of advocacy that has created these deep divisions is not necessarily productive. There are better ways to go about it. It's interesting to me that the question of people living well on the earth has to be classified in such a negative way from a lot of people's standpoints, when where else do we go—except maybe to a space station or something? The fact is, everything that we need and use comes from this planet. We are tied to it in inextricable ways, and we can't deny that fact. We need to pay attention to that fact because it's not an inexhaustible resource.

I tend to want to just throw out that language and the baggage around the environmental movement versus the development movement and acknowledge the reality of our dependence on the planet, on the resources. We can't stop using them, but we have to figure out better ways to use them. There are far too many people now for this planet to be able to sustain us in the way we've been accustomed to using things in the past. It can't happen. It won't. Something is going to break down. We might as well try and figure out—before it happens—how we can change things, how we can be more responsible.

Opening image:
Mount Edgecumbe from
Eric Jordan's boat, Sitka

Above: Holy Ascension of Our
Lord Russian Orthodox Cathedral,
Unalaska, Aleutians

Opposite: Raven totem, Sitka

Walter Tellman, a small-scale commercial fisherman who carries on his family's fishing tradition, is an Alaska Marine Conservation Council board member.

I was born across from Anchorage, across the inlet, in a village called Knik. Then we moved even farther out from there shortly after I was born. When I was a year old, we moved up the Susitna River a few miles, and my father homesteaded that area in the late fifties. He was a commercial fisherman, and so was my mother. They fished on open skiffs, twenty-foot-long skiffs over here across the inlet doing set nets for salmon fishing. My mother, she's Indian. My father was a non-Indian. He was from the U.S., from Missouri. But he came up in the late forties, so he had been around for a little while. Raised dogs. He was a trapper and fisherman. He lived a traditional life up here.

My mother's family, they were fishermen, fishing families living here on the Cook Inlet. They put up fish mostly for subsistence purposes, for food and for trade. As commercial fishing became an occupation, they started commercial fishing. They had a place on Fire Island just a few miles out of Anchorage. As a lot of natives did, they set nets off of Fire Island. Well, it was in the sixties, and a lot of our salmon were getting intercepted by the more modern fishing fleet down there at south Cook Inlet. Seiners and drift-gill-netter-type fisheries, and a very few fish got up our way.

So when I was about ten years, we had to sell out. It wasn't worth fishing anymore. We sold out, and my father he took the few thousand he got out of his fishing sites and small boats, and he built a bigger boat that I still use today. He built it in '69. I grew up fishing with him for salmon and for halibut all up through school years. Kind of went to school here and down the peninsula, the Kenai Peninsula. Then shortly after high school in about '79 I moved out to Unalaska.

I still do a little fishing out there. I built small skiffs and fished out of them for a few years. Did some small-time salmon fishing just for food and trade, and also crab and halibut. I do a little bit of halibut fishing for commercial, but not enough to really speak about. Mostly my days are for personal-use fisheries. It's sort of like an industry for local folks. They put it up, smoke it, jar it, salt it, freeze it, what have you, and then we trade and barter. For instance, we trade with my wife's cousins who live in the Pribilof Islands, and we trade for seal. We trade with folks up here like my relatives on the mainland for some moose and smoked fish.

I recently traded for some sheep fish and caribou from a fellow in Kotzebue just a month ago or so. Then we take that and pass it around the community and we do local trading around there. A kind of a traditional thing.

In my time, we're making dry fish, smoked fish, salted for winter. We do that for all these years, and I'm still doing it. I've been on the beach almost sixty years. I was taught fishing on the beach, when I was eight or ten years old. I'm seventy-three years old. I can't do nothing much now. I'm blind. I still see enough to go around—as far as I can go, walking. I don't work anymore. I used to drink, smoke. I quit smoking. I quit drinking about twenty-five years ago. But I can't leave my Copenhagen. I'm still chewing Copenhagen.

Well, everybody around here working all summer long, but them people they're not living no more. All dying off. Lot of fun, good weather, warm weather, people. Big table outside and making baskets, talking. Somebody drying and cooking fish. No more nowadays. It's like our fun is all gone ever since the Fish and Game come around. But he wouldn't stop mine—I go fishing off the beach. I could make a fire off the beach and cook me fish, if I want to. They pretty poor for all the natives in Alaska. All got limit. Way before, no limit. But look, that many fish go up to the creek every year—spawning every year. You can't even cut across when the fish start spawning. Fish and Game holler at me, one time I cut across. Said I stepped on fish eggs. I just laugh at it. I don't know what the hell he's talking about when he told me he didn't want me to cut across.

When I was younger, the boats would go out and bring two hundred fish in, and all the old ladies would sit at the beach in front of the village downtown, because there was only downtown, and they would sit there and the boats would go out and bring all this fish in, and all the women would be splitting fish there. I don't see a lot of that anymore. They were silvers, and pinks, and it would just be a really neat community thing. All the old ladies, like my grandma and her friends, some of them would have *ulus* [fish knives], and they'd all be splitting fish down there together. They did that every fall, and they just quit doing it over the last ten years.

I've got a lot of smoked salmon. I'm on my last bag of dried halibut. I've got a lot of ground deer. I've got a lot of ground elk. I've still got some ducks, frozen in water. I'm set. You're always eating something that you caught. You know? I've been eating fried halibut for a while.

I'd say at least one of your meals a day is going to be something you caught or shot. For me, anyway. A lot of people don't do it—lot of that stuff is given to them. I gave a big bunch of dried halibut to Phyllis because it's that time of the year. I'm going to start drying halibut again.

It's not a custom, it's just the way. You start with your family members. Then your friends. Then your neighbors. Pretty much everyone here is related.

House of a subsistence fisherman, Kogwonton Street, Sitka

Leslie Fields is the author of *The Entangling Net: Alaska's Commercial Fishing Women Tell Their Lives* and has been fishing for twenty-two years.

Commercial fishing really brings up the whole subject of risk and how people deal with risk. Most people who fish know what the risks are, walk into it with their eyes wide open. I find this one of the interesting paradoxes of fishing if you really analyze what motivates people to do it. One of the greatest motivators is a sense of independence and freedom. Yet when you look at commercial fishing you realize—as you look at that boat out in the ocean, and you look at that little skiff out on the open ocean—you realize there are incredible layers and layers of rules and constrictions and restrictions on these people, especially if you're a deckhand.

You are under the absolute authority of the skipper. Your life is in his hands. He may be safety conscious; he may be fanatical and want only to fill the hold; and you might fish in any weather. Doesn't matter. You're on this tiny little vessel. Doesn't matter how big the vessel is. When you're out in the open ocean, it's tiny. You are totally at the mercy of the forces of the wind and the water. You are completely under the authority of Fish and Game and their flags: stop, go, stop, go. But the interesting thing is that, in spite of all of that, most people experience a sense of freedom and independence, and they feel control. They feel like they're in control—even though they're in the riskiest profession in the country and they're out there on that water, they still retain a sense of control.

Prayer for fishermen, their families, and the Coast Guard by Reverend Todd Putney at the Memorial Service for Fishermen Lost at Sea, Crab Festival, Kodiak, May 1999

Lord of the sea and all good fish,

We look to you now for your presence,

For your comfort during this service this afternoon.

Lord, thank you for the good work that you provide,

For all the fish,

And for what it provides for our community here in Kodiak.

Yes, today Lord we remember those

Who have lost their lives in the doing of this good work.

And we pray that you'll keep them and their families

As you comfort them and give them your peace.

We pray that you'll help the families

Who are struggling with the losses of loved ones

To find their way in the new circumstances that they find themselves in.

And we ask that you will protect those who are out fishing even today,

Who will be out again soon.

Protect them and their families.

And we ask that you continue to be with the Coast Guard

In their efforts to help protect those

Who are out fishing from our community.

Lord, in Christ's name we pray. Amen.

Opposite: Little Priest Rock, Sitka

Stosh Anderson, founding board member of the Alaska Marine Conservation Council, fishes with his family out of Kodiak.

A definition of "bycatch": ocean creatures that are caught incidental to the target species. If you are out catching pollack, you want to catch pollack and sell pollack. If you catch other species accidentally, that's bycatch. Some of it is marketable. Most of it is not. Why is it so important? A sustainable ecosystem is, I guess, an objective that I think is worthy. It doesn't necessarily mean that each species within that ecosystem is going to have the same relative or stock size at any one point in time. There's going to be changes in the balance. We, as man, are harvesting food for our populations and, as individuals, to earn a living, and if we damage the ecosystem by either eliminating a species or doing mechanical damage so a species can't propagate because it needs that type of habitat, then we're doing a disservice to our ability to have sustainability.

Joe Macinko is a commercial fisherman and an Alaska Marine Conservation Council board member.

The more I've educated myself on it, the more I understand bycatch isn't the biggest problem. It's habitat damage. That is something you don't see. If that isn't there, it's like clearcutting. I hate to use that analogy, but it's like farming. When you clear the land, plow the field, you create a monoculture. Intensive bottom trawling—whether it is in the Barents Sea, off of Australia, or on the East Coast of the U.S.—creates an environment that certain flatfish species thrive in, ones that can deal with silt and constant disturbances. Sure, maybe there flatfishing is pretty good, but your species diversity decreases, and some species just completely disappear. They want to believe that dragging is no worse than other things, but they are saying that in the face of other evidence.

Every fishery in Alaska is overcapitalized. There is no fishery up here where fish will go unharvested, where we don't have the power or the capacity to harvest these fish. What we're doing is sort of playing "screw your buddy." I get a faster, bigger, boat than you so I can pack more, or fish rougher waters, or get there first.

Opposite: Tramp steamer, Unalaska, Aleutians

Julia Suzanne Schmidt works as a fisheries and processing plant observer.

Mary Jo McNally, a member of the Halibut Task Force, fishes with her husband.

No one likes dragging because it is an easy thing to point fingers at and there is always going to be animosity between different types of fishermen. It's the basic fishermen mentality: "Every fish out there is mine." Any type of competition, whether it's a different vessel type, a different gear type, a different boat operator, it's going to be seen as competition—thus bad. There are some really, really dirty seiners out there too. There are really, really dirty longliners, and there are really phenomenal clean fishermen as well. For the most part, the fishermen are very good. They are very conscientious. But, it's like anything; you can go to the restaurant and eat a bad meal. You're going to tell ten people how terrible it was. If you eat a good meal, you'll tell one. The stories of the bad ones are the ones that are being brought up. So, it all depends on who you talk to and what their personal take is.

If you walk through a field of wildflowers, you're going to have lots of different wildflowers. You're not going to have just the wild irises. It's an ecosystem. Everything feeds off each other. There is no way of having a selective net. All fishing is dirty. Some are just dirtier than others. That's the bottom line. All fishing is dirty.

My husband caught one—I think it was 320 pounds. That was before I ever knew him and before he ever really realized the value of what a fish like that is. I don't want a fish that big. I don't want it in my boat, and that's what a lot of the charter boaters say now. They don't want them in their boats. They're dangerous. You've got to tie 'em up. We shoot our fish. I remember the first time somebody told me they shoot their fish, and I went, "Oh, yeah, right!" It's true. We shoot our fish. We want them dead. I want them dead before they come in my boat. I'll just take my fifty- to eighty-pounder, take a couple of those, and I'll only take what I need. I don't need to go out and kill all these things. That's the mentality of the people that come here on a charter boat, come to conquer. "Let's kill a grizzly bear. Let's kill these things," and I'm not a tree-hugger necessarily, but if you don't need it, why do you need to kill it? If I can't eat it, I don't need them stuffed on my walls.

Large Marge's dog, World War II bunker, Dutch Harbor, Aleutians

Opposite: Halibut, Sitka

Triptych: Bob Storrs and his house, Unalaska, Aleutians

It seemed like the draggers have an awful lot of control, or they have in the past, over the cod fishery and most all the ground fish. I still don't understand it—why the draggers get to fish so much more time than the small-boat longliner. How we got kind of squeezed out, and how did the draggers keep prospering through these last ten years or so?

I started fishing because of my love for fishing, and I like it small, simple, and close. That's my way—I enjoy life—being independent and fishing my small boat, when you're actually catching the fish, instead of working as a crew member. I have no desire to work on a great big dragger. I couldn't. I wouldn't like myself at all if I would do that—just to see all the bycatch that gets thrown over the side. I've seen the bycatch they throw over, and in fact, I get a lot of it at the cannery, for bait, just totes and totes and totes of bycatch, and you can find everything in their bycatch. You can find king salmon, halibut—this is the bycatch that makes it to the canneries, that accidentally slips into the hold, as they're sorting the fish, and so that's only a small part of the bycatch.

Stosh Anderson, Kodiak fisherman

You have to have respect for other people. If you can't respect other people, then you have trouble trying to respect any decisions you make with them. If you're trying to negotiate with somebody, you have to respect that they have integrity and that they're forthcoming with their thoughts and ideas. It's the same in the community. Different people are going to have different views, and there are some pretty colored discussions from time to time when people are trying to deal with allocation and deal with who is catching what where, and "I used to catch it, and you can't have it." There's a certain amount of greed in all of us. But it's an island community, and hopefully you can live and let live. There's a time and place to try to vent your frustrations, and there's a time and place to try to work things out. The further the decision gets away from home, the more potential everyone has of being a loser.

Fishermen are the last of the hunter-gatherers. There's no more buffalo and there are no more hunters. We are hunting a wild resource and bringing them to harvest and to market and providing food for a very large portion of the world population. I don't like seeing any fishery eliminated. I don't think that's a good goal or objective. What I would like to see is fisheries that may have to make some changes and transitions so that they can provide for a sustainable ecology, an environment, an ecosystem that will support the ability of the communities to have a sustainable economy.

Eric Jordan, a commercial fisherman and Alaska Marine Conservation Council outreach education coordinator, chairs the Halibut Task Force.

The harvest of natural resources can't be just driven by market demand, or we'll damage the ecosystems that produce them. There needs to be a balance, and almost a reverence, a spiritual humbleness, when you're working with natural resources such as the forest and fishing. In my experience, the small-time players, the small operators—for example the farmer who loves his land, the woodlot owner who manages those trees, and the logger who's out there in the woods, and especially the fishermen who are running their own boats—they're in tune with the environment around them. To be the best fisherman, you really have to have a sense of what species of bird is where and what's happening with the tides. You have to be in tune. You have to develop those predatory senses.

Jay Stinson, president of the American Draggers Association, is concerned about the survival of the independent fisherman.

It's a very complex thing. Maybe the demand will increase as the need for world food supplies also increases, but the conservation groups and the politics of the nation are changing. It's much more difficult to operate as I know it, as a small-boat operator, in Alaska. My paperwork requirements have increased five-, tenfold in the last ten years. My observer costs probably equal one crew member. I fish with myself and two other crew members usually. I am required to carry an observer 30 percent of the time. My observer costs this year were between 250 and 300 dollars a day for every day that I carried an observer on the boat.

There's a very large economic burden being placed on the individual fishermen of Alaska. Larger corporate structures might be able to absorb the paperwork burden and the observer costs and adapt better to government regulation than individual fishermen. Individual fishermen working in the federal fisheries are being severely stressed economically, and I don't see any end to that.

Opposite: Theo Grutter, Sitka

The fact that we were able to come to an agreement is almost as remarkable as the agreement itself. There were times when we met that I never would have believed that we would get anywhere, but when we started that whole project, we had a goal. We had a problem statement, and we developed a goal. Through the tough times in our negotiations, things were really falling apart, but we had something to go back to. We had our goals to go back to. We were able to take a break, cool down a little, and sit back down and start over by using our goals and our means of getting to them. It took reasonable people—there weren't any radicals. We were able to work through the difficult times with that goal in mind—providing an area locally for local residents to have a reasonable chance of going out and catching a halibut to eat.

Everything that we did was by consensus. It took everyone's agreement to move on.

In Sitka, and often in other communities in Alaska, a lot of that common ground is the fact that people absolutely love this place. They're here because of the place, and the irony to me is that we can't use that shared love of place to bring us together to solve the problems, the conflicts that have come up. If you love a place, then you have some obligation to live well in it and to protect it as much as you would anything else that you love. So part of our work is to get people to acknowledge that. You can't do that very directly. To get people to talk publicly about love is not an easy thing to do.

As far as the habitat of the Bering Sea or the North Pacific goes, that just comes out of strong concern for the future of the fisheries. If we don't take care of the Bering Sea, it's going to look just like the North Atlantic, and cod stocks are going to go the same way, and everything else too. So we're at an interesting point in time here. We have benefited, I hope, from a mass amount of information that we've been able to gather as human beings in the end of this century, based on the disasters and mistakes of other people in other places. This is one of our last chances to take a relatively unscrewed-up ocean and employ some of the things that we're supposedly learning in order to prevent the same thing from happening to the Bering Sea that's happened to so many other of the world's oceans.

Opposite: USS *Northwestern*
(bombed in World War II), Dutch Harbor, Aleutians

I look at history and say, "Show me an ocean in the world where there has been industrial fishing, and it hasn't been changed and it hasn't been altered to the point that ships are going all over the world to look for new places to fish." Boats are having to leave their own borders and fish in other people's waters. Now we have the two-hundred-mile fishing zones to protect what we have because people want to come halfway around the world to take ours because theirs is gone. Still, we deny that we're having any effect on the fisheries of the world. You can watch and see the changes. I don't know what the solution is. There are a lot of good people that don't need to be thrown out of work, but we have to find another way, a way to throttle back on this so it's not just gone in a few years with a handful of people with massive gear taking it all. We want lots of people being able to feed themselves and take care of their family needs on what's there—and make it last.

Some of the major green groups, Sierra Club or whatever, will just drive around in their Porsches and then say, "You all have to stop what you're doing and you can't do it anymore and you can starve to death." I don't appreciate that kind of approach. The Alaska Marine Conservation Council is taking a really good approach that puts the fishermen in with the endangered species and realizes they are part of the whole thing, and there is a culture here.

Joe Shaishnikoff, Dutch Harbor, Aleutians

William "Buzz" Lekanoff, Dutch Harbor, Aleutians

Opposite: Theo Grutter's son, Ivan, Sitka

I'm a champion of the little guy. I want everybody to make a living, and the rest of it's cream. You don't get cream until everybody is fed. That's community. There are ways to do that. This town should be fed and happy and thriving, and it would be if we were looking at the real picture and if we were not fighting over some international game and if all our canneries weren't owned by international megacorporations who could close them down for a while or give you pennies on the dollar.

There's a lot of fear out there about the future of fishing, and I don't think it's groundless. There's reason to be scared. I'm scared personally. I'm a troller. I troll salmon, and king salmon in the Northwest are being listed as endangered species. The answer I have is you need to be proactive on this issue. You need to be very aware of what the issues are. You need to develop your own conservation consciousness. You need to be proactive within your fishing groups. Instead of reacting to conservation issues imposed on you by other people, you need to be proactive about taking a conservation lead on the issues that you know best about.

Halibut, Sitka

Opposite: Seafood processing
plant worker, Sitka

PHOTOGRAPHS BY **LAUREN GREENFIELD** · INTERVIEWS BY **GEORGE KING**

YOUTHLINE

COMMUNITIES IN HARMONY ADVOCATING FOR LEARNING AND KIDS (CHALK)

SAN FRANCISCO, CALIFORNIA

The pressures on American youth are often talked about and analyzed, but how do young people actually find their way through the situations that mark their passage into adulthood? As they face choices, they often need support and information. Families, relationships, sex, school, faith, self-image, entertainment, income are just a few of the categories that define their experience. In a major American metropolitan center like the Bay Area, there are hundreds of organizations, programs, and services available to younger residents, a network of resources that can be elusive to the lone teenager struggling with a problem. To whom that searching youth will reach out, and how, are questions that Communities in Harmony Advocating for Learning and Kids (CHALK) addresses.

Only three years old, CHALK 's Youthline is a toll-free phone service offering noon-to-midnight access to "listeners," young staff trained to direct callers to help and information through an enormous database and the Internet. Listeners support their peers with conversation and encouragement, empowering callers to identify all their tools, personal and public, and use them to improve and enjoy their lives. Youth-to-youth communication is a central premise of Youthline, as is allowing young staff to supervise and operate the running of the phone service, reporting to adult directors. Coming from diverse backgrounds, the staff reflects the complex demographics of the cities and counties they serve.

CHALK employs youth who are from sixteen to twenty-two years old, pays them hourly, and gives them a minimum of eighty hours of training in social work and communication skills. They increase their knowledge and sensitivity to such serious issues as AIDS awareness and sexually transmitted diseases, drug and alcohol abuse, gang codes and violence, child abuse and rape, eating disorders, and suicide prevention. They are carefully prepared for crisis calls, and supervisors are available to talk them through difficult encounters with the most desperate callers. All calls are confidential. Emotional topics range from youth questioning their sexual identity to classic struggles between parents and children, between teachers and students, and between friends. But CHALK staff members are quick to point out that Youthline is a gateway to youth services and information of all kinds. Callers can request horoscopes, local movie times, or job listings; they can find out where to get free geometry tutoring, join a chess club, or buy a new bike.

As the Internet aggressively forms new communities without borders, the telephone remains (and with the cell phone becomes increasingly) the most prevalent and accessible means of remote interaction. Youthline was conceived and championed by Bay Area technology experts, who saw the potential of computers and telephones working together to reach the greatest number of area youth.

Youth helping youth, creating their own virtual community of support and a bridge from isolation to connection, offers a potent charge to those who work at Youthline. Their valuable training and impressively developed communication and technology skills are exceeded by the experience of extending themselves to their peers, feeling the power of making a difference in the lives of others. *T.W.S.*

Charles Earnest, media and community liaison for the Microsoft northern California district, worked with CHALK cofounders David Glickman and Jason Singer on initial corporate funding support.

They were very clear in their vision. They were able to divine for me how, by using technology, they were going to reach into this community of youth. And how, through the database they were developing and through the tools they were providing the Youthline listeners, they could actually help these youth make changes in their lives: provide them opportunities to get out of gangs or help their friends get off drugs or find a tutor. This is a groundbreaking nonprofit. They have taken on working with city government, working with corporations, working with the incredible bureaucracies of education. They've been able to navigate and really make a difference with the youth listener line. They're a unique program, and I hope to see it grow and replicate throughout the country.

They had a vision and were able to deliver on it. It was very risky for them. This is not something that is easily done without the passion that they both carry.

JS: We put ourselves out there in the community and got some good press, and we demonstrated how technology could be used. It was really successful. The mayor was very close at hand, and he became infatuated with what he calls the "CHALK boys." He really liked what we did and had his Office of Children, Youth, and Families contact us and ask us to come in and talk to them. They had a couple of projects that they were trying to get going—primarily they wanted to put Youthline online. They wanted to put it on the Web and have this database of programs and services that people could access on the Internet, but we looked at that and came back and said, "You know what? We don't want to put it on the Internet. We do want to build a phone service." That's how we got involved with Youthline.

GK: Why did you decide to use telephone as opposed to computer?

JS: Even today, even though it's a huge buzz and more people are going on the Web every day, two or three years ago no one was on the Web. It was a very small percentage of people and households that were on the Web. Recent stories in the papers have stated that right now minorities can't afford to adopt technology to the extent that others can. It didn't make sense. No one would have used it.

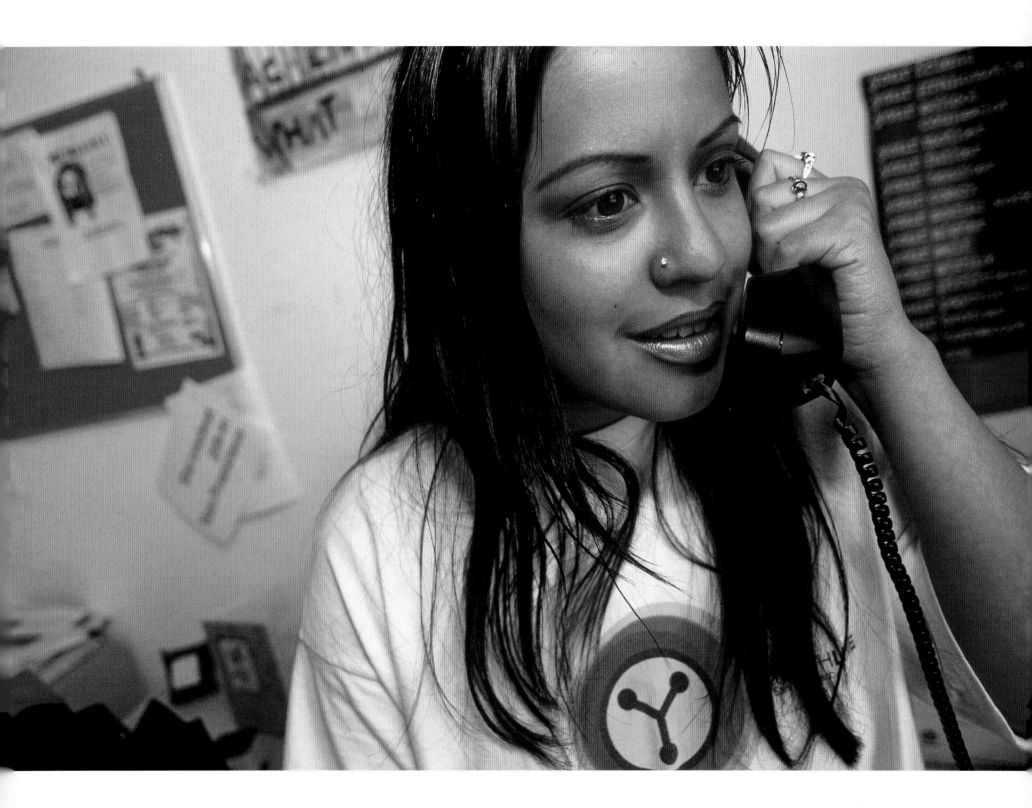

Youthline supervisor and listener Asante Matthews, age twenty-one, has since left CHALK to attend college in Atlanta.

It's not just a job because I love helping the community and working in a family atmosphere like CHALK. At first it was—OK, well I'm just going to go there for the job—but it turned into more. It's love now. I love my work, so it's not really work. It's love for my community and for uplifting and educating myself, and helping other people. Being a listener, being able to understand and feel what the caller is talking about, just being there for the caller. With communication skills, I am now able to relate to other people who are not quote-unquote like me.

Opening image: Youthline listener Ayana Matthews talks to her sister on the phone outside their apartment in Bayview–Hunters Point.

Above: CHALK development coordinator Ruth Barajas talks to her boyfriend during her shift.

Opposite: CHALK and Youthline founders Jason Singer and David Glickman talk to San Francisco mayor Willie Brown at the opening of a new Blockbuster store that is part of an effort to bring business to the inner city.

Ruth Barajas, age eighteen, is a CHALK development coordinator and a Youthline listener.

It's important that I'm a young person. Young people are always going to need someone to talk to about what is going on in their lives. Youth is harder than other times of life because we deal with a lot of issues that we can't talk about with just anybody. A teenage girl who thinks she might be pregnant can't talk to her mom and maybe can't talk to her boyfriend because she doesn't know how he'll feel about it. She can't talk to her friends because she knows that her friends don't like him. It leaves her alone, but she needs someone to talk to, and that's where Youthline can come in. We're there to talk to them, nonjudgmentally, confidentially, and we won't give them any advice. We are not an advice line. We provide support.

When you go through these rewarding, rewarding calls, it's obvious we're making a difference, being that link between organizations and agencies for young people, and knowing about what's out there. We are the middleman. You know, before I came here, I didn't know anything about what was out there. Now when people call, they're in the same state I was in, and I have this information—I'm the key to unlock this door.

Suemyra Shah, age seventeen, is a Youthline supervisor and student at the University of California–Berkeley.

I love it. I like talking on the phone anyway, but combining talking on the phone, getting to know somebody, and providing somebody with a service was the ultimate thing. It's fun. It's also really emotional and powerful when you're on a support call. It puts a voice to what's going on out there. It's moving to know that you are able to help somebody out who doesn't have somebody to talk to, or who has never had a parent there, or has no clue what to do, or is stuck in a totally isolated situation and feels completely alone, someone who picks up the phone and hears your voice and hears somebody willing to listen and talk. It makes them feel a lot better, and you can hear it in their voice. And it makes you feel good that you were able to make a small difference or make one person happy.

Jennifer Berman, CHALK outreach director

Street Outreach is a really important part of what we're doing because listeners actually have one-on-one contact with the young people on the streets. They can talk to them about the program, talk about issues that are going on in their lives, and then let them know that this is a service that they can use. It builds a personal connection around the service—it's not just the logo, it's not just the phone number, it's not just Youthline. There's a face behind that.

CHALK is an incredible youth employment organization. This is more than a job for a lot of the young people that work here. It's a transformative experience for a lot of those people who come in here thinking they're going to have a part-time job and come out of it so much richer and with such a wealth of knowledge that it changes them and changes their perspective on different things in their lives. It's really incredible actually to see the transformation.

William Walker eats Cheetos during a Youthline meeting.

Opposite, top: Listener Aya Cash takes a support call.

Opposite, bottom: Ruth Barajas role-plays a "support" telephone call with a student during a community outreach event.

Ruth Barajas, in an outreach meeting at Youthline

Karma Bret Sweet, former Youthline listener and outreach coordinator, left CHALK to concentrate on college and find new challenges.

I came into this organization with a very numb feeling about the world. There was a core of people who cared about me, but outside of that ring, everyone else was out to get me. Why should I care about them? That made most of my life very numb and cold, very sociopathic, kind of "Oh, great," you know? That kind of sarcasm.

You can't live your life like that where you say, "If I don't get my hopes up, then I'll never get disappointed." Because if you don't get your hopes up, you won't taste anything, you won't see anything. If you don't feel, you won't feel. All your meals will start to taste the same. Everything will look the same. You will get bored. You will get unhappy with yourself because you're not trying.

I broke out of this very dangerous pattern I was in, in my own head. I really thought I had a lot figured out, and it was hard for me to be intimate and open with people. I had this holier-than-thou attitude. I had seen it all. I had worked for mine, and you can't tell me nothing. The interactions with youth humbled me a lot. It made me realize that we're all going through it and that I do have something to give, and that I am important to the process. I am somebody and I can change things. I have as much power as anybody else.

Janice Crotty is a computer consultant and Youthline volunteer.

There is something about introducing to a young person the idea that they are just fine. They're just fine—that's the magic piece. If you can get a young person to accept themselves for who they are, they become less angry, less defensive. They start to feel that they have some power in their own life. Any program that can actually get to a kid and make that shift happen, that's worth any money in the world.

Seventeen-year-old Aya Cash, Youthline listener and aspiring actress, was fourth in the National Shakespeare Competition in New York in 1998.

Mostly I'm an insecure person—but I don't know where that came from. I think it's just being a teen. I think the more I'm at Youthline, the more I really relate to being a teen and being insecure. You get these girls calling up, "Oh, my boyfriend, I think he's cheating on me," even when she hears him saying, "I love you. I love you." It really makes you feel, "No, you know what? I'm fine. I'm normal. I'm just angsty because I'm sixteen."

Joanna Kramer, Youthline director, coordinates the extensive training CHALK listeners receive before they can answer the phones.

One of the hardest things to get across, and to get people to internalize, is that you do not have the answers for somebody else. You may have experienced something very similar. You may have read about it and think you know the answer, but you don't. That's the philosophical approach we try to emphasize here: you know what's best for you, but we can help you come up with the answers by asking you some really good questions and giving you some options for resources that might help. It's very hard not to give advice, very hard.

Active listening is trying to understand the underlying meaning of what somebody is saying; what's really going on and what the feelings are behind that. It is trying to get a sense of what this person is experiencing in their world, focusing completely on them and leaving your experience out. It doesn't happen that often. I look at it as a real gift to sit down and listen to somebody. I'm very aware when that happens to me, when I'm talking with somebody, and they are truly trying to understand my experience. It takes time to do that, and most people don't take that time. We talk at a very surface-y level: "Oh, yeah, I hear what you're saying, I hear you, I hear you." Active listening takes a lot of effort. It can be exhausting—every call becomes very intense because you're using all these skills. When somebody calls and says, "I don't get along with my parents at all; they don't understand me," you take that one sentence and ask things like, "Well, when you say your parents don't understand you, what do you mean by that? Can you give me an example? What's that like for you? How does that make you feel?" To understand this person's full experience of their parents' not understanding them and then validating, that is what active listening is.

Listener Ed King at a barbecue with his close friends in a San Francisco suburb. They throw lighter fluid on the barbecue to raise the flames higher.

Opposite, top: Karen Cortez gets her brow pierced at Body Manipulations. She went to the piercing studio planning on a tongue-pierce but after being told that her tongue is the wrong shape, she ends up getting her brow pierced.

Opposite, bottom: A Youthline listener begins to tag "THE CIA SELLS CRACK" on a San Francisco wall until a woman shouts from a second-story window and a man on the street responds by chasing the listener's vehicle.

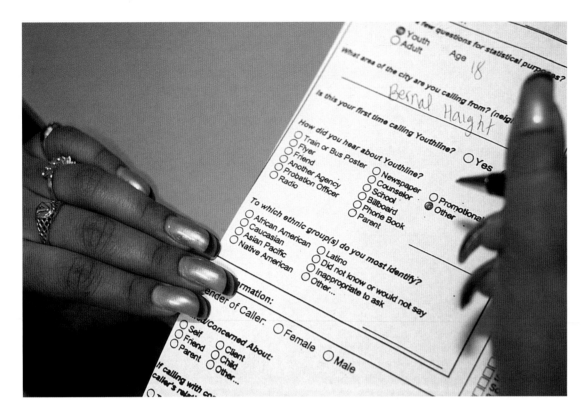

Nineteen-year-old William Walker, a Youthline outreach coordinator, talks with George King.

GK: Not everybody in the world is concerned about the world around them, how people are treated, empowerment, these kinds of issues. What influenced your life to lead you in that direction?

WW: A lot of it comes from being: one, young; two, of color; and, three, somewhat economically disadvantaged. I wasn't middle class. My family couldn't afford to live in San Francisco, but we made it. Those three things kind of put me at a disadvantage coming into this world. Because of that, I had a lot of grassroots already in me, feeling that I had to make change in order to survive in this world.

My mom was also an activist. We lived in an apartment complex, and she was an advocate for low-income housing. Her mother marched in Washington in 1963 with Martin Luther King. So it comes from a long line of activism in my family, as well as just that fire in me, because I want to be different, I want to make it.

Having those values instilled in me, as well as that personal desire to do better for my people and for myself, drives me in my activism on a daily basis.

Bertha Canty, William Walker's mother

It's important to me, because I raised him with activities that were going on in the city for the betterment of the community. I guess he picked up some of my speed, but he took it and went a little higher and a little deeper than I did.

Listener Violeta Perez fills out a questionnaire during a call. Callers remain anonymous but get asked a standard set of informational questions.

Opposite: Youthline listeners pose for a group portrait at Expressly Portraits at the Stonestown Galleria shopping mall. Many listeners socialize together, and two who are leaving wanted a picture of their Youthline friends to take with them.

GK: What in your life experience formed you as somebody who was interested in social change or wanted to challenge the order that existed, to try and leave the world a better place?

JS: I had powerful role models and people who meant a lot to me whom I looked up to. I also had some really powerful experiences. My mom was always involved in and dedicated to the community. One of the strong tenets of both Jewish culture and the Jewish faith is a commitment to community and a commitment to *tzedavah*, which is charity, or *tikkum olam*, which is making the world a better place. I don't think it was until I was an adult that I ever learned those terms and put two and two together. But the expectations were always there in my family to give back, be participatory, to volunteer. My mom, in the sixties, went to sit-ins in Oklahoma to lunch counters and different places. She was involved in the civil rights movement. That was a really important element.

Growing up, my dad ran a steel business and he was very much a businessman. He is the most brilliant businessman I've ever met. He never, I don't think, truly understood his employees and their daily lives, but he was insistent that my brother and I work there. We worked there every summer and worked with everybody. We had to learn how to do every job in the steel business. Part of that became a real appreciation for the differences between my life experience, which was privileged, and the folks that worked for my dad who really struggled with a lot of things like health care and more immediate needs in terms of what they could afford to do for their family and what they couldn't. I remember being the voice that always tried to bring my dad back to the center; make him more empathetic and understanding and clearer about what he could do to bridge that gap in his own business.

One of the most powerful experiences in my life was meeting Elie Wiesel, who lived through Auschwitz and Buchenwald when he was thirteen years old. I remember that he spoke at my temple and I met him afterwards. I just remember that he was not bitter at all about the experience and didn't come back with a sense of entitlement. He came back with a sense of what can we do to continue—to make sure that this doesn't happen again, to educate, to commit ourselves to communities so that we're building communities that don't allow these types of things to happen, where everybody is treated with the same amount of respect and value. I just remember that being a really powerful moment. I have vivid memories of it.

Former Youthline listener and outreach coordinator Karma Bret Sweet talks with George King.

GK: You mentioned that you were "biracial, multiracial." What do you identify with?

KBS: It's an evolving and changing process, as these identifications are. The more I study and learn the history of this country and the history of how race has been used, I understand that the culture makes you who you are, but it doesn't define you. I have a serious problem with having been assigned accountability and responsibility, that is, having to answer for what the color of my skin is.

Usually when people ask me what I am, I introduce myself and say, "That's my name. That's who I am. And you'll find out the rest later." I grew up being too light sometimes to play with the dark kids and too dark to play with the white kids. I also recognize that as I get older, culturally I'm open to all sorts of things. I don't think it's positive or healthy to stay in one realm and be, "This is just black. This is all I deal with. The only things are the black things." It's not healthy to be just white, you know? I studied Chinese martial arts for six years, through high school. I wasn't Chinese, but it was very good for me.

It's very hard because there's a lot of history put into race. People have tried to put this cultural, ethnic, biological, genetic IQ, humane, humanity, gender concept all together in one word: "Race." The Eskimos have seventy-seven words for snow, and they see a lot of snow. We've got one word. You have to be very careful defining with that.

When I was around twelve, thirteen, I was rebelling a lot, like most kids do. I would run away from home and go hang out around Telegraph Avenue and stay in squats for a couple of nights. Most of my friends were runaways or had got kicked out of their houses. There was definitely a lot of tension in that period of my life, in my family, but I outgrew that. I was sort of idealistic, antisociety, anti any sort of rules. I didn't want to accept the fact that my parents were trying to have rules, and I hated school and didn't like kids my own age. I feel like I just grew up fast, and I feel like I've seen a lot more than I should have seen.

Seth Katzman, a social worker, is Molly Katzman's father.

It wouldn't surprise me if she spent a night or two there, but typically what would happen is she would hang around on Telegraph with a group of squatters and punks, fairly heavy-duty punks, people who certainly didn't have regular domiciles. We'd see her up there sometimes because we'd kind of clandestinely check. I remember one time driving up Telegraph with my wife, and Molly was in the center of a group of punks that were walking down the street shouting a song, and she was sort of aglow. I mean you could tell there was something really thrilling to her to be in the midst of this kind of rebellion. We were mixed about it. She looked so happy that we thought, OK, we've just got to keep an eye on her. We figured that if we tried to squash her, she was going to do more severe things, and mostly we were worried that she would run away because she talked about it, and we wanted to keep her close by. So we let her, for example, stay out till eleven on Telegraph, as long as we could pick her up, and we would have to pick her up on the side street, on Haste, right near Moe's at around eleven. She was always there, always on time.

George King talks with Mamie Matthews, Asante's and Ayana's mother.

MM: When we die and leave here, we'll leave something of value that'll carry on the torch of helping others and doing the right thing. If we can just help one, it was worth it all.

GK: Is that something you taught your children, or do they just see it by observing?

MM: Well, I've taught them. We talk about it, and we live it. We live it.

Asante Matthews tells George King about her neighborhood.

AM: It's a low-income neighborhood. Most people think that it's a bad neighborhood. Since I've been living there, I've been able to show people that positive people are living in Bay View–Hunters Point. My sisters and I, we're positive people in the community. I feel that it is a positive place, even though the media makes us look negative. They don't show the positive that I would show to be a positive role model.

GK: In what ways are you involved in the community?

AM: My sister and I both are working on neighborhood beautification. We go into the community and try to get people to stop writing on homes and other property in the neighborhood. We paint and hold different functions, like barbecues, to get the community together. I'm also involved in a program called Project Shine, and I help tutor elderly citizens. Well, they're not citizens fully, but they're trying to take their citizenship exam. They're from China and Japan and places like that. I basically do that and help whoever in my community that I can.

GK: Where do you get this interest in helping people?

AM: Basically from my mother. Everyone knows that my mother, Mamie Matthews, is always lending a helping hand, trying to help someone who is in need. She's just there for the community and there for others. That's where I get it from.

Listener Molly Katzman with her father in their Berkeley home. Molly's father was not pleased when she and her sister got matching tattoos. Tattoos are forbidden by the Jewish religion. He speaks about it now with humor and says that their tattoos are featured on a Web site called "Tattoo Jew."

Opposite, top: On her eighteenth birthday, Youthline listener Karen Cortez prays with her grandmother and Rafael Gonzales, a friend from her grandmother's church. Her grandmother will have a serious operation in several days, and they pray for her health together. Karen was raised by her grandmother and her father. Her mother went back to El Salvador when she was a child.

Opposite, bottom: Listener Asante Matthews does her mother's hair as the family prepares for church on Sunday. Asante's mother, Mamie, has seven children of her own and four foster children. Ayana and Asante help care for the younger children but will be leaving for college in Atlanta in the fall, the first in their large family to attend a four-year college.

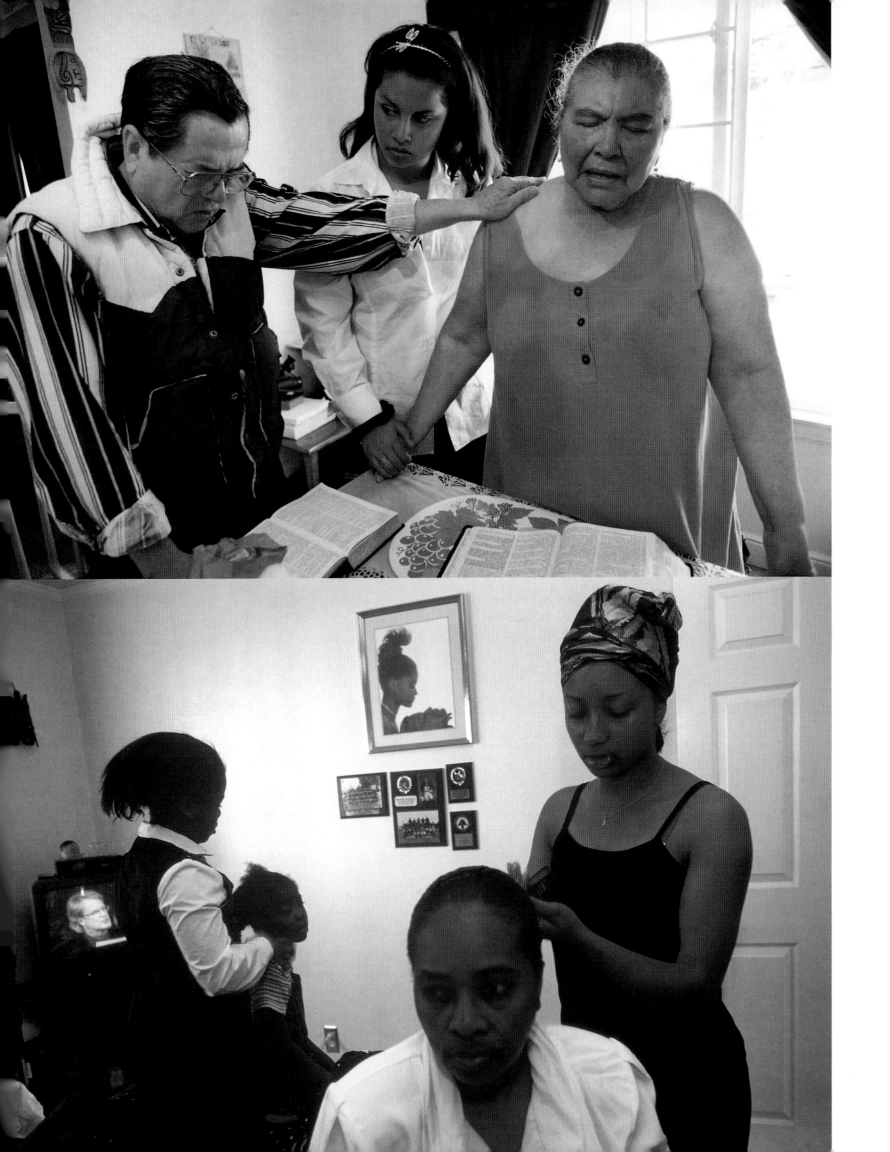

Listener Violeta Perez kisses her boyfriend who has been in a wheelchair since he was shot in an incident of gang violence.

Opposite: Drug transactions take place constantly outside Ayana and Asante's impeccably clean apartment in Bayview–Hunters Point, one of the poorest neighborhoods in San Francisco. Mamie Matthews, their mother, has always been active in the community, and out of respect for her and her family, drug dealers do not loiter directly in front of their building.

Ain't nobody in the U.S.A. consider it war right now, but I got a few hundred friends out on Twenty-fourth Street that are at war with people five blocks away from them—for nothing. You know what I'm saying? People getting raped, killed, and why? To me, there is no hell. This is hell right here.

We don't give advice. We give options. Like, if you were to say, "Oh, I got into a fight with her, but it was just a verbal argument. And now she's standing outside my door hollering about this and that. I feel like going out there and physically hitting her." If I were to give you advice, I'd ask, "Well, what is she saying?" If you said, "Well, she called my mama a bitch." Personally, I'd be like, "If somebody called my mama a bitch, I'd want to hit her." I'd probably be like, "Go out and hit her." Then you go out and hit her and the police officer's standing right there, and you get arrested, you blame me, right?

But, if I told you, "What would happen if you thought about going out there and asking her, 'Why do you talk to me like this?'" You think about that for a second, right? That's your option now. You have the option of doing what you want to do or thinking about what you want to do mentally. You know what I'm saying? To know you helped somebody, like you help one of your friends when they're stressed out or something? You know that feeling you get? I understand that feeling. It just feels good. It's like one of the best things.

I almost hate to profit off the Columbine thing, but it draws a good example. When a thirteen-year-old kid calls up to say that their best friend totally doesn't talk to them anymore, and they're really upset about it, that little seed is something that, if he or she doesn't have someone to talk to, can really blow up into something a whole lot bigger. It doesn't for everybody, but for a lot of young people it does. They find another social group to hang around that may be positive or negative. So the listening component of Youthline is a huge component. About 35 percent of the calls we get are listening calls. I'm a firm believer that a community needs a Youthline as much or more than it needs a symphony.

Aya Cash in her basement room of the house she shares with her mother, a poet. Getting ready for school, she looks for books and other necessities under her piles of clothes.

Opposite, top: Karen Cortez holds her fourteen-year-old cousin's new baby in the apartment she shares with her father, brother, and grandmother. Her other cousin, Jessica Ramos, talks on the phone with her boyfriend.

Opposite, bottom: Violeta Perez talks on her cell phone during a shopping spree at the Stonestown Galleria shopping mall.

Joanna Kramer, Youthline director and social worker

A really incredible lesson that I've learned is to come in here and offer what I know and also value what other people have to say and their experiences, no matter where they're coming from. That's changed me. Working with teens you have to be able to say, "You know what, I don't know the answer to that. What do you think it is? What do you think would work in this situation? What's your opinion on this?"

Karma Bret Sweet, a former Youthline listener and outreach coordinator, is a student at San Francisco State University.

One of the main shortcomings is this is a new organization, so it's trial and error no matter what. There is no "Youthline, this is how you do it." Nobody has written a book and told CHALK how to do anything. We're all making up the rules as we go along. You have to be very honest about that. Some things don't work. Some things are going to piss you off. Some things are going to offend you. But you have to speak to them and work through them, because there's no handbook.

Beyond the work we do, we are educating the older people here, and bringing them up on our issues, and they are educating us. We're developing them culturally; they are developing us professionally. It's a nice trade-off.

Suemyra Shah, a college student majoring in ethnic studies and anthropology, is a Youthline supervisor.

Knowing and not doing anything about it—knowing that the government targets minorities and targets young people and locks them up and is building more prisons than schools and is putting the money into all these crazy places and doing all the messed up stuff that it does—if I knew that information and didn't do anything about it, I would feel like a totally worthless, guilty human being. I couldn't be content with myself sitting there on a couch reading a paper, just sitting back and thinking about it. If nobody is going to lead or get involved, I don't see anything positive happening.

Suemyra Shah protests cuts in the ethnic studies department at Santa Clara University. She was one of the leaders of the successful UC-Berkeley protests on the same issue, where the students went on hunger strikes and mounted tent cities.

Opposite: Listener Josh Farr (center) questions CHALK founders Jason Singer and David Glickman (right) about why they have decided to leave their jobs as coexecutive directors. He is concerned that their replacement may not have the

Karen Cortez on her graduation day from Balboa High School. She has been admitted to UC–Santa Barbara on a scholarship and will be the first person in her family to attend a four-year college.

Listener Josh Farr and his mother, Rosa Robinson, at the San Francisco airport before he leaves on a trip. Rosa says she always cries when he leaves. He is an only child, and she is a single mother. Soon he will be going away to college, and his imminent departure fills both with trepidation. He has received a full scholarship to the University of Wisconsin and will be the only African American in his program.

youth at CHALK.

It's frustrating. It seems sometimes like the underlying comment is, "If you want to get ahead, you've got to get over on people." But those of us who don't want to get over it, we're just supposed to get the shaft of the stick, you know? If you don't enjoy hustling other people, stealing, taking, lying, being a bad person, being morally against living off other people like a vampire, then you get a penalty for it: you're poor. Great. Or you get to do this, you know what I mean? We're not going to elevate you. There's something wrong with that.

I consider myself spiritual. I have a soul, you know? And I believe this universe was created by a sense, a creator, a most-high being that holds justice in their heart, that holds right, order, fairness, propriety, a sense of righteousness. Look at the human condition. We've got opposable thumbs; we've got speech; we spend all this time differentiating ourselves from beast and animal. What is it for, if not to affect and make better, if not to build, if not to create, if not to synthesize something stronger each time? Anyone can destroy. It's very easy to kill and hurt. Now, let's talk about healing. That's the hard part. That's the reward.

Love is the most important and enduring thing in this world. When you live in this world without sharing that love, something dies. Something dies in you, and you kill something outside of yourself. The most important thing that you can do while you're here is affect. Leave it a better place than you find it. What's better for me may not be better for other people, but I've come into enough contact with sufferers, with the wretched people who live in the blues. I think it was one of the Delta blues musicians who said, "The blues ain't nuttin' more than a good man feelin' bad."

Success is being able to sleep at night, to look in the mirror, to be happy with yourself, to have dignity and to be able to smile when you walk down the street. It's not waiting up at night, looking at the wall and thinking, "What did I not get done today?" or "Oh, man, I wish I hadn't. . . ." Success is not having regrets, not being eaten by your own regrets, and not letting the external negative forces just chew away at you. It's being happy with what you do and bringing a sense of positivity to anyone you touch.

Molly Katzman is currently considering a career in social work.

I can't see myself living a life that's about me. I really don't see the point in having a job or a career that is so self-centered. I guess I've always wanted to work with other people, and that is really my main goal in life, to try to make at least one little piece of this world a bit better.

Karen Cortez will soon leave Youthline to attend college.

It's weird to think that I'm going to Santa Barbara. Everybody is so proud of me and making such a big deal about it, but I don't see it as such a big deal because I knew I could do it, from the beginning. It's not a hard job. You've got to keep your mind straight and be careful. I mean, you can have fun during your high school years, but you have to be careful not to fall into the trap of needing to be socially accepted. It's really hard, especially being young, because we all want to fit in. I know I did. I really did want to fit in. But at the same time, sometimes it's

PHOTOGRAPHS BY **BILL BURKE** · INTERVIEWS BY **JOE WOOD**

LOCAL MONEY

ALTERNATIVES FEDERAL CREDIT UNION

ITHACA, NEW YORK

Every city in America can be described by its geography, the size and makeup of its population, its sources of income, and its popular characteristics—from landmarks to sports teams to favorite sons and daughters. Ithaca, a picturesque lakeside college town of thirty thousand that endures long, icy winters in upstate New York, is like any other place in that regard, but it has long had a reputation that sets it apart, a reputation that is decidedly "alternative." Ithaca's particular combination of qualities has led it to cultivate a disproportionate number of progressive businesses, organizations, and initiatives that challenge the mainstream.

Alternatives Federal Credit Union is a nexus for this remarkable array of nonprofits and microenterprises, and even an innovative local currency called the Ithaca Hour. Working within federally controlled standards for credit unions, the programs and policies of member-owned Alternatives are shaped by a commitment to social change and local investment. This mission is rare in the banking world, but after twenty years, this unusual credit union has earned its legitimacy, paving the way for local opportunity and setting an example for community development credit unions around the country.

The voices of Ithaca's citizens delineate the larger community that spawned Alternatives, representing a place controversially dubbed "America's Most Enlightened City." Many of the individuals interviewed here either work at Alternatives or have been touched by its services. Others have no connection to it but experience the economic realities that motivate its work. Some confront the obstacles of low-income survival firsthand, while others sympathize but are themselves distanced from actual need. Together they form an alliance of credit union members—individuals and small businesses looking for a chance in an atmosphere of fairness and person-to-person service, and Ithacans who want to support the potential represented by that chance, choosing to invest locally at a grassroots level.

Ithaca proper is nestled in a valley, with two hilltop institutions of higher learning, Cornell University and Ithaca College. The former attracts international students and faculty and brings affluence, sophistication, and privilege to a town surrounded by a large, depressed, and underserved rural countryside, the northern end of Appalachia. The population of greater Ithaca, while remarkably diverse, is still polarized by race, class, lifestyle, education, and splits between town versus gown, country versus city, business interests versus environmental concerns, and other categories of difference that challenge progress in many American communities.

Ithaca's large and influential alternative population, which typically rejects establishment structures and conventional lifestyles, evolved from roots in the 1960s. The credit union officially bears one name associated with this era, "Alternatives," and unofficially another, with its nickname, "the hippie bank." Stories about how it evolved and how the public's perception of it has developed over time are revealing and engaging. But its impact on community development and individual opportunity is the real deal. Inventive credit union programs and products that provide low-income and "high-risk" members with such fundamental financial tools as mortgages, small business start-up loans, personal savings incentives, fee-free banking services, lines of credit, and fiscal education are bankable evidence of homegrown Ithacan enlightenment.   *T.W.S.*

Opening page portraits of Ithacans associated with Alternatives,
top to bottom, left to right: Black Peter Donovan, Karen Nguyen,
Bill Myers, LaBerta McGruder, Tim Brown, Amber Boyd, Emme Edmunds,
Paul Glover, Leslie Muhlhahn, Jeff Furman, Camila Vargas, Kenneth Broadwell

Above: The Alternatives-financed Long Point Winery building under construction

Jeff Furman has advised socially progressive enterprises locally and nationally, including Ben & Jerry's.

It's basically taking an institution and turning it on its head. It's taking the institution of business, which is the most powerful institution on the planet right now, and making it very values-driven, instead of just economically driven. It's somewhat anti-institutional to create this very staid, business-suit kind of thing and give it real progressive values.

Alternatives is a bank whose focus is to provide some economic support for people who live here. It tries to come up with creative ways of doing that while still maintaining its economic mission of being a viable credit union that is able to pay its bills and meet all the national tests for a credit union. Within that structure, it's trying to do the same thing that a lot of different institutions here in Ithaca are trying to do.

You really can do institutions differently, and the best way to do them differently is to start them yourself rather than stand outside and yell at them or throw stones at them or try to work within them.

Leni Hochman began working for Alternatives as a teller in 1982; she is now assistant manager and marketing director.

When I came here I wasn't interested in being a teller, I wasn't really interested in banking—but I thought that the philosophy of the credit union as a place where we could have an excuse to gather funds and then redistribute them the way we thought they should be redistributed as loans was a great idea. It just seemed like a very grown-up thing to do.

The major philosophy now is to say, "Everybody who has anything to do with the credit union starts out somewhere on what we call the credit path—the spectrum of transactor to owner." We want to help people move along the path to gain assets, because those assets really can change people's lives.

Bill Myers is considered the economic visionary behind Alternatives philosophy and practice.

One of the things we understand very well is how to motivate people, in a grassroots not a corporate sense, and how to organize them, how to speak to peoples' hopes, and how to describe their self-interest to them in a way that would help them. That was the ideal skill for us to have—the financial skills were secondary. One of the things we've always said about ourselves is we don't want to be professional bankers. We want to be passionate amateurs or experienced amateurs or people who have skills from other areas who can bring them into the fairly dead world of banking.

Although bankers perform a crucial role of gatekeeping, you can also look at that role as the gatekeepers of the old guard, keeping the world the way it is. Is it possible to put somebody else at the gate and change the world?

Bill Myers is the manager of Alternatives Federal Credit Union and one of its founders.

I don't think I'm here on earth just to earn money. Obviously you have to take care of your family, but beyond that, I'm here to develop myself. I'm here to extend myself, to learn what I can do, to see how things work, and to make the place better.

Alan J. Cohen, mayor of Ithaca

We as human beings underestimate our potential. We have the power to effect great change. If we only believe enough in ourselves and our ability to do so, as individuals and as communities, things would be a hell of a lot better than they are now.

Paul Glover is a local activist and inventor of the Ithaca Hour, a new community currency.

Even though Ithaca got the distinction a couple years ago from the *Utne Reader* as "America's Most Enlightened City," I would not pretend by any means that we are. We don't levitate. We fight and gripe. Yet, there is within these communities a willingness to challenge ourselves and each other to explore better directions.

A lot of people are proud of Ithaca and feel responsible for it, and a lot of people feel hope here. That's pretty unusual. Look at the number and variety of grassroots organizations which consider themselves to be not merely patching and mending the mess, but striking into new territory.

With her partner, Inge Alexander, Zan Gerrity built an alternative-energy house with a loan from Alternatives.

We're connected to people who are making a day-to-day impact on the people in the community. We hadn't wanted to take a mortgage. I know it's hard to believe, but we're human. We really didn't want to do it. Though in the process, it came to me that I really like the idea that Alternatives would hold this mortgage. So, it's our way of giving back to the community. I don't look at it as Alternatives taking our money. If you have to have a mortgage, it's really a bonus. It's not pie in the sky—we're giving it. I know Alternatives will use it for the other people in the community. So, in a way, it's a forced charity, and it's great.

A former air force sergeant and used-car salesman, Steven E. Valloney is now a yoga instructor and Alternatives member.

What appealed to me was that the money stayed local. Of course Alternatives has to run at a profit, otherwise it's going to fail. I understand that. But they don't have to answer to stockholders—not that stockholders are a bad thing—as to why the profit isn't higher. They really seemed to be interested in helping people whose wish is to be part of the dream of owning their own property. They're also ecologically minded, which is very, very important to me. So if you buy a new car and it gets better than x amount of miles per gallon, then you pay less interest, which is neat. You get a bonus if you get a car that's more efficient, that will pollute less and use less fuel.

Paul Carubia owns a commercial waterfront building in Ithaca and rents space to several small businesses that also are Alternatives members. He is an environmental consultant.

I was drawn into Alternatives by the people. I'm glad it has grown, I like the idea of them as a bank. I tried to get a house mortgage in Norwich at a commercial bank, and they jerked me around. They didn't like my style. They didn't like the fact that I owned my own business. They were willing to give loans to people who could get laid off tomorrow from some factory in town that was posting losses every year. They'd still write loans to that guy, because he had a factory job with a big corporation. I was a little corporation. Even though Alternatives is a "bank," they have treated me with a person-to-person respect and faith.

Home of Zan Gerrity and Inge Alexander outside Ithaca in Slaterville Springs

Opposite: Rick Dobson, owner of Danby Motors, an Alternatives business account

Jonathan Kline, Alternatives member and owner of Black Ash Baskets

Opposite: Raina White at RIBS, a community bicycle repair shop that is a business member of the credit union

Patrice Jennings, general manager of GreenStar Cooperative Market, a grocery store that is one of Ithaca's best-known alternative businesses, along with the Moosewood Restaurant and Alternatives Federal Credit Union

A local currency is very good, because when you spend a dollar at a fast-food chain, seventy-five cents leaves the community and twenty-five cents stays. When you spend an Ithaca Hour, it all stays. That's why cooperatives like GreenStar and banks like AFCU are really important, because we are local. We're locally owned. We reinvest locally. Nothing leaves the community when you buy from us.

Raina White, assistant program coordinator of Recycle Ithaca's Bicycles (RIBS), talks to Joe Wood about their cooperative program. She is a work-study student at Cornell University, where she majors in engineering.

RW: Instead of dealing with money, we deal with volunteer hours. Everything we have is priced in hours. If someone wants a new wheel, it's three hours. So they volunteer for three hours and they get a free wheel.

JW: Do you only strictly pay in terms of bikes or pieces of bikes?

RW: Yeah. Or full bikes.

JW: People can work for a full bike?

RW: Yeah. We have a whole shed full of them. Any bike that we fix up that obviously doesn't belong to someone who came in to get his bike fixed up is a donation. So we fix it up. We have one of the shop managers do a safety check on the bike, and if it passes the safety check, it gets assigned a number of hours and put out in our shed. Then if anyone wants a bike, and they've volunteered enough hours, they'll say, "I want to go get a bike," and they can look through our bikes. They range in hours from about eight for a kid's bike to about thirty-five or forty for a nice mountain bike.

Alan J. Cohen was an Ithaca restaurateur before becoming mayor.

I describe Ithaca Hours as a glorified barter system that has a currency which facilitates multiparty trades. Instead of you and me being limited to trading between us—you might weave baskets and I might make tattoos. I want one of your baskets, but you don't want a tattoo, then I can't get my basket. But now, I can get my basket from you—I can give you an Ithaca Hour, and you can go talk to Susie, who gives massages, and get a massage because you want that, and you can give her the Ithaca Hour. And Susie's going to go talk to Jorge, who gives piano lessons, because that's what she wants, and Jorge happens to want a tattoo, so he's going to come to me.

It's that barter system which creates community. It links more people together. It has enabled people who have had fledgling businesses to find outlets and opportunities for people to utilize their services or to patronize and buy their goods. It has served to raise the wage scale in some senses because of this arbitrary fixing of an Hour being worth ten dollars. And most important, from my perspective as mayor, it forces the recirculation of money into the local economy.

Rosalind Smith is a daycare provider and mother of six adopted children. Her dream is to attend law school.

When I heard about the IDA program, I said, "Three to one? You mean if I put five hundred dollars in and they give me fifteen hundred dollars, then in four years, I get eight thousand?" That's what I need to go to school, so I tried to see if it could help me come up with that five thousand dollars in three years.

It taught me how to save and not miss the money. It comes right off the top, that forty dollars, as soon as I get paid. That first year rolled around so quickly. Every month when I looked at my statement, it kept going up and up. It's like instant gratification. I said, "This is the best thing since peanut butter and jelly."

Audrey Cooper is a local Native American community activist.

If you don't have enough money to stay ahead on your bills, how can you get a mortgage, how can it be approved? If you can't prove that you are upper-lower income, if you don't make that much money, you're not eligible for a loan. It's a catch-22 situation.

Alternatives does have some new program initiatives, which I think are really good. But whereas somebody could, if they had twenty dollars extra each month, be able to put it into a savings account, the hard-core reality is there are people who absolutely cannot afford to put twenty dollars a month into savings. They're trying to figure out how they're going to stretch their paycheck to take care of medical bills, food, buy the children clothing, and do all of that. There's nothing left to play with. It's paycheck to hand every week.

Gloria Molina, a preschool teacher and Brooklyn transplant, is an Alternatives member and is considering opening an IDA account.

I've never had a checking account. I would cash my check when I got paid for my jobs and keep it at home. I decided that I need a checking account, and Alternatives was the easiest and the cheapest. You cannot open a checking account in some banks unless you have a certain amount of money, or a savings account. When I came, I had a couple of dollars in my pocket, and that's all I needed to start dealing with Alternatives.

Ed Ryan is a VISTA worker and the Individual Development Accounts (IDA) coordinator at Alternatives.

Individual Development Accounts are special, restricted, matched savings accounts. They are designed to help low-income people save for and invest in assets. The IDAs that we have are limited to people at or below 150 percent of the federal poverty level if they are saving for small business or postsecondary education. For home ownership, they can have income of up to 200 percent of poverty level. They make their monthly deposits into their account and up to five hundred dollars each year will be matched three to one. It's a nice way for them to get a nice chunk of money towards those goals. Meanwhile, they get money management training. In those classes we cover the basics of how to make a spending plan all the way up through getting a larger macroeconomic picture of economic indicators, such as, how they each play a part in the economy, how the economy affects them, and how to see if their community is doing well. We're trying to give them the idea that no matter how much money you have, you play a part. It's all about choices: your financial choices and every other choice.

Deirdre Silverman is director of Community Programs at Alternatives, where she writes grant applications.

We're part of this national demonstration of different Individual Development Account programs. A lot of the programs were having problems recruiting participants. You would think, you're going to give people money—they get two dollars back or three dollars back for every dollar they put in the bank—people would be beating down your doors. But all over the country the programs were having trouble recruiting people. A big part of it was that a lot of these people had not had any dealings with banks, or their contact with banks had been very negative. They had been rejected, or they had failed in their financial dealings. So, suddenly, if somebody comes to you and says, "Hey put your money in this bank and we'll give you back three dollars for every dollar you put in," you know, you're not going to believe them. Part of the reason we didn't have that problem is that it's such a small town. If we screw around with your money we can't hide; you're going to see us on the street.

Opposite: Bathroom of Don Ruff and Barbara Brazill's owner-built, Alternatives-financed home

Raina White, a Cornell University undergraduate who works at RIBS, a community bicycle repair shop,
talks with Joe Wood.

JW: What is the attitude of your friends up at Cornell about Ithaca?

RW: It definitely varies. Some of the rich people never really leave campus and College Town, and are just clueless about what goes on in the rest of the community. It's two entirely different worlds. If I didn't work here at RIBS, I'd get off campus very little, excluding College Town (that's a strip of stores and places to eat right next to campus that is all overpriced and very different from downtown Ithaca and the Commons).

There are some students who are involved in community service or who are more aware. That tends to be the hippie-type crowd, who are involved with the Ithaca sense of community. But there are a lot of rich people who are oblivious.

Leni Hochman, Alternatives assistant manager and marketing director

There are people who still say we're the "hippie bank." That's all we'll ever be—even when you say, "We're famous and we're known nationally." When I go off to conferences, especially in the community development financial institution field, we're a model, we're well known. People know our programs and think we're doing good stuff, and we are very quick to share with them. We want people to replicate what we do. So I know that this recognition exists out there. But in Ithaca, for the business people and the conservative people, we'll always be the "hippie bank."

Alternatives business member Dennis Montgomery owns Cayuga Wooden Boatworks,
a boat-building and restoration business.

I came to Alternatives and found that they were much more friendly. For instance, any check under five thousand dollars is immediately good with them. That's something very unusual in the banking business. I was looking for financing. When I went into Alternatives and started talking to them about it, they were more than just mildly interested in what I was doing. They were extremely interested in the nature of my work and what I was bringing to Ithaca. I was going to be hiring people from Ithaca, which has a pretty good talent pool, so they were really receptive and interested in helping me. We worked it out, and here I am.

Justin Armstrong,
a Cayuga Wooden
Boatworks employee

Sisay Sisouphone, proprietor of the Sticky Rice restaurant
and catering service, is a beneficiary of the Community
Enterprise Opportunities program at Alternatives.

Inger Giuffrida directs Community Enterprise Opportunities (CEO), an Alternatives-backed business development program that teaches budding entrepreneurs how to start their own businesses.

The greatest benefit for the people that go through the CEO class is that they get to learn from the other twenty-five people in the class with them. There is so much sharing and brainstorming. They run ideas by this large group, "Is this a good name for my business?" or "What do you think of this product?"

I honestly believe people start businesses not because of the CEO program or any other program. Hopefully, we provide additional tools to make it happen faster, or a little bit more efficiently. But, really, it's the individual that makes it happen, not the program. It is really important to say that, because so often organizations and programs want to claim successes that really aren't theirs alone.

Jeff Furman, an Alternatives Community Enterprise Opportunities counselor, describes how Da' Spot, a hip clothing store run mostly by young mothers, was conceived as a way to help revitalize the downtown pedestrian mall, Ithaca Commons. Da' Spot was financed by Alternatives.

I'd been asked to sit in on these meetings of businesspeople who were trying to do something for the Commons. You can go and talk about it at ten meetings a week, but let's try to do one thing that's real, instead of a lot of things that are not real or are impossible or are grandiose. I said this clothing store would be my contribution to try to get downtown up and running and also provide some good working opportunities for young single mothers, so we built the structure of the store around the fact that there were single parents, and they had kids to care for. We would know that up front and try to make arrangements for all of life's necessities for somebody who is trying to be a good parent. So, we tried to come up with this thing—it's a store that's struggling along, and it has a lot of issues, and we are trying to make it work.

Leslie Muhlhahn, a pastry chef and owner of her own small business, Just Desserts

They're less of a bank. I mean, they're a bank, and they're professional, but they're less of a bank. They'll try to find a way to work with you. My credit is not good because I've been a single mom for years, which means that things don't always get paid on time. I'm not a good credit risk when a regular bank looks at me, and yet Alternatives was willing to take a chance on my business because I'm in their community and because they know me.

Alternatives member
James Spiers working at
Stiehl's Body Modification Station

If you decide you want to start your own business, you can't let people, or doubt, or anything, stand in your way. Just go for it. Do what you've got to do. That's the only way you're going to make it. You've got to be strong.

We actually didn't even get a loan. I worked day in and day out, and my cousin, he worked, and we basically just saved up money. We really didn't want to start off with loans or grants or whatever, even though there was money out there available for us. We chose not to do that because we wanted to see just exactly what we could do on our own.

It's not just a barbershop. Our barbershop has been a ministry. Our barbershop has been a place where you can come and just relax. It's like a home away from home where you just want to forget about everything you do. Just come here and sit down and take a nap. Get away from your kids and everything else.

That's what the barbershop was for, and people on the outside looking in didn't see that. They just saw a bunch of black people together, and they started getting nervous.

I think that racism in the United States still exists. We should not let that happen. My customers—black, white, yellow—are still my customers. I'm not talking about politics. The black community or Asian communities have to work harder. I haven't seen one black president in the United States. I hope one day we have one, and that we will change the face of the United States. It makes me think—is this just for white communities, or does anybody have the right to be president? I hope one day it will happen. Different skin colors for the president of the United States. Then I will see the United States, the government, change to some good sense.

It was a good thing that the community went through what I would call an educational process—and even I did, too. During the two public hearings that we had, I learned about the role the barbershop played in the black community. To me a barbershop is a place where you go to get a haircut. In the black community, the barbershop is a social gathering place. It was a place where young people went to get mentored by older people. The community at large didn't have an understanding of that and how the black community felt about the events that led up to the temporary closing of the barbershop. It's important that issues are raised rather than sweeping them under the rug, which a lot of people prefer to do in this community.

We're one of the most hypocritical communities around. It's laughable that Ithaca got the *Utne Reader* "Most Enlightened City" designation a couple of years ago. We're enlightened to the extent that we're aware, but do we follow through? A lot of times, no. The people who are the most guilty of that are the so-called open-minded liberals, who talk a good game, but when it comes to what impacts their own lives, it's their way or no way.

Joe "Pops" McKnight gives customer
David Richardson a trim at his barbershop

Rob Root, Dave Engasser, and
Matt Lee of Cascadilla Tree Care,
an Alternatives business member

Anna Sims Bartel is a Cornell graduate student in comparative literature and works in a local restaurant.

I'm a believer in all sorts of reasons for communities. What bums me out is when the bigger reasons—economics or race or religion—are the reasons for dividers. But I think that's hopelessly naive. Those dividers are fundamentally there, especially in America.

Rosalind Smith has experienced racial inequities in Ithaca firsthand. She is an Alternatives member.

Ithaca's is one of the best high schools in the state, but you've got to fight to get that education if you're Latino and African American, so we did. That's the community that we live in, but I feel it's everywhere. You just learn to live in the community that you're in. "We shall overcome" is real.

Credit union manager Bill Myers on Alternatives' role in aggressively raising the bar on morally responsible banking practices through the Community Reinvestment Act (CRA), a federal law that requires banks to invest in their lower-income communities

Four years ago, one of the banks was merging. We organized a huge CRA protest against the bank, and a series of very embarrassing negotiations about what they were and weren't doing. We exposed these nice little colored maps showing, "Here's the white areas, here's the black areas, and here's this overlay of where you lend and where you don't lend."

We had a negotiation with a local bank in Binghamton, where we had a huge cake at the beginning. We invited the politicians to come to the meeting too, and the bank officials were sitting at the table, and the woman who was dividing the cake divides it up and cuts pieces that are totally uneven. There was this teeny, teeny little slice, and she goes, "What we're going to do today is what you've done to us. This is the slice of your assets that you've taken from this community that you've reinvested in the community." It was a piece of cake that was one-eighth of a cupcake. Then she said, "I'm going to do what you guys get to do every single day—take a quarter piece of the cake and eat it myself."

The principles behind our founding are that we, as an institution, are serving a market that's not served well by banks, and we reserve the right to criticize the banks for not picking up their fair share. In fact, these banks take money from the whole community and then reallocate it to the top end. That's not right.

Alternatives manager Bill Myers was a Cornell student in the sixties.

The part of the sixties that resonated with me was a moral currency, that is, knowing what's right and wrong. It was drawing out of a moral currency that had deep roots, and the good thing about the sixties was that it fed on those deep roots. The bad thing about it was they were unconnected to "how are we going to change things?"

Some of the policies that we adopted early on internally were specifically designed to promote us as a community institution, and one of them was hiring at the bottom. We always hire tellers. We found that if we try to hire in the middle—there are a lot of bankers floating around because so many banks have merged—you get somebody that doesn't have the Alternatives philosophy. You never get a community person. You never get a minority person. You've got to be willing to hire people from those groups. You've got to treat them right, which means pay livable wages, and then they'll talk to their friends about it. We're going to pay them more from the start. We're going to hire from within at other positions too, so they have some upward mobility. They're not going to be the cashier at a megastore who's a cashier at the same megastore ten years from now, earning twenty-five cents more an hour. It's going to be a real opportunity for advancement.

Bill Myers guides Alternatives' lending policies, programs, and strategies.

We're very market-driven. It's a contradiction about us, but we are absolutely market-driven. We use market pricing for almost everything. A lot of small funds across the country say, "Oh, we're doing microenterprise loans. We're going to charge these people 3 percent or 6 percent." We look at it and say, "Naw, we want to charge a market rate of interest." They're fairly risky loans. The amount of money that they're borrowing is small enough so that it's not going to be an additional burden for them, and we have to support ourselves to make this thing go. We're not a social service agency in the sense we can afford to give it away. Any banker would understand that. We've got to make money—we've got to continue the operation.

Opposite: Alternatives member Steven E. Valloney and Charlotte Rosen at the Sunrise Yoga Center, which Valloney owns

Metalsmith and blacksmith Durand Van Doren
owns Durand's Forge and is an Alternatives
business member.

Alternatives' CEO program counselor Jen Furman set up "Youth Scoops," a nonprofit, youth-run Ben & Jerry's franchise in Ithaca (the first of its kind) that teaches kids how to run a business by doing it themselves.

One of the problems in the educational system is they don't teach people anything about how business works in the real world. No one's given an opportunity to see how it functions. I try to incorporate that by giving people a hands-on opportunity to learn while doing, as if to say, "This is how a business runs." They experience some of the things that work, some of the things that don't, some of the things that are hard—so that they can learn by doing. I also work mostly with at-risk or low-income kids because they're never given the thought that they might become job creators, not just job seekers. Everybody says, "Hey, you want to be a job seeker? Don't forget to dress well, come on time," and all that stuff. But we say, "Well, a few of you are going to have some passions and excitements, and we'll provide you with the concept that you can create something too." Creation is a lot of fun, a lot of excitement, a lot of challenges. It's not meant only for a certain group of people in the world. Everybody should have that chance.

Inger Giuffrida is director of the CEO program, Alternatives' small-business training and support initiative.

My true love is the economic literacy and money management side of it. I think economics is this gigantically powerful force. People don't understand it but they make up the system. Increasing people's economic literacy is central to everything. That's one of the reasons educational programs got started at the credit union. I think it should be in schools from the time children start, and adults who didn't have the opportunity to learn about the economy in practical terms, and what money really is, and how to use it, should have the opportunity now.

PHOTOGRAPHS BY **DEBBIE FLEMING CAFFERY** · INTERVIEWS BY **JEFF WHETSTONE**

SMALL TOWN REVIVAL

HANDMADE IN AMERICA · SMALL TOWN REVITALIZATION PROJECT

WESTERN NORTH CAROLINA

Throughout America small rural towns are struggling to survive and maintain their character, economy, and way of life. In the last thirty years the proliferation of megastores and franchise restaurants, along with the building of roads designed to avoid the centers of small towns, has depopulated the once vibrant courthouse squares and main streets of America. Rural town centers were once trading places for local goods and havens for small independent businesses. As businesses and chain stores moved to shopping malls on the highway bypasses, towns began to die. This is especially true in the rural South, as agriculture and small manufacturing jobs are supplanted by more centralized industrial and service employment and people do their shopping in malls located strategically to attract commuter traffic.

In western North Carolina, HandMade in America, a nonprofit serving twenty-three counties, works to restore life to local economies and small communities. HandMade in America was founded in 1994 to assist mountain communities as they embarked on environmentally and culturally sensitive economic planning. While the State of North Carolina has grown with spirited industrial and business recruiting, the results have not necessarily been good for small towns in the western mountains. The topography of the area, moreover, resists usual approaches to economic development. What the mountains need, argues HandMade's executive director, Becky Anderson, is a "more creative approach," one that couples recognition of the unique characteristics of the region with an understanding of the qualities of the past. With its "more creative

approach" HandMade works from the premise that handmade objects can build a strong and diverse economic base. The tradition of mountain people making utilitarian objects and tools, building their own furniture, making clothing, blankets, and quilts, reflects the isolation of these hard-to-reach communities. HandMade has turned to this mountain culture for solutions, as has its spinoff, the Small Town Revitalization Project. Small Town Revitalization works with seven towns and focuses on each town's unique cultural and economic assets. The project looks not so much to new marketing fads but rather in the region's own backyard, seeking to build creatively on the past.

Marshall, the county seat of Madison County, is one such small town. In the last years of the 1700s, Marshall became a stopover along the French Broad River for livestock drovers; it then evolved into a stagecoach settlement and, by the end of the 1800s, a railroad town. Marshall became a major trading center where people came to conduct business at the courthouse and purchase supplies. By the early 1960s, however, a highway bypass, coupled with the passing of railroad travel, began the town's gradual economic decline.

The Small Town Revitalization Project develops ideas for preservation of a viable small town using Marshall's own history. These ideas—of how to promote and handle tourism, develop small businesses, and maintain existing commerce—have emerged from many community conversations. The citizens of Marshall are building the future while preserving the character of their town and their cultural legacy.   *T.R.*

Pug Shelton, a tobacco farmer, talks with Jeff Whetstone.

JW: How would you describe the mountain culture?

PS: Well, it's about gone now. It's just about gone. Used to be you'd have your gatherings on Sundays, maybe back there in what they call the Garden. Back in there, I've seen as high as thirty or forty back in there cooking and eating dinner and everything. Maybe some weekends you'd run into twenty-five or thirty camping out back in the mountains. Now you don't see that.

JW: People just getting together?

PS: Yeah, just getting together, but as I say now, you don't see nobody back in these mountains camping out hardly. We kind of have a family reunion and go once, or sometimes twice a year and go back summers on the mountain.

JW: How many show up for that?

PS: Well, anywhere from fifteen to twenty-five.

JW: Why do you think people don't get together?

PS: Times are too fast, too fast. You can run down here and run out to a movie theater or something, run out to a fast-food restaurant and get something to eat. I don't know. It's living too fast.

JW: Do you think since people aren't having these get-togethers, you say you think it hurts the entire mountain culture?

PS: Oh, yeah. I've got neighbors less than a mile from me that I've not seen in a year. Used to be we was together at least twice a week.

JW: Doing what?

Jerry Plemmons grew up in Marshall and works as a community advisor for the French Broad Electric Cooperative, a utility company.

Before 1960, when the Marshall bypass was completed, the traffic all went through downtown Marshall. Particularly in the summer, traffic in Marshall was unbelievable. It was not uncommon to take thirty minutes or more to get from one end of the town to the other because of the semis and all the tourist traffic. At that time there were service stations open twenty-four hours a day. There were three restaurants open twenty-four hours a day, seven days a week in downtown Marshall. Quite a change, then to now. Of course, when the traffic moved to Interstate 40, that certainly diminished a lot of the traffic on 25/70. The other thing that happened about the same time frame was that so many folk started getting jobs in manufacturing and in the service industry and in government. In the beginning, a lot of folk who had been growing tobacco continued to grow some tobacco in the afternoons and on the weekends, but as years passed and they felt more secure with the jobs off the farm, they didn't pay as much attention to the farm. This is particularly true of the second generation, the generation that had not been in farming. The children of the farmers didn't want to maintain those operations, so more and more of the small farms that were used for second incomes kind of diminished. Now we have very few farm operations in the county and very few full-time farmers. I was looking at some numbers not too long ago. As late as 1959, just about 50 percent of the labor force in Madison County was farm-related. Now that number would be somewhere between 1 and 2 percent, I suppose.

Opening image: Marshall police chief Denny Goforth and Justin Jones

Above, left: Davitus Gosnell with a large cabbage. Davitus says he is offered $150,000 every week for his land to be turned into a gated community.

Above, right: Boy jumping from the deep water trestle off a railroad bridge across the French Broad River, Hot Springs

Opposite: Outside Bakersville

Joe Penland Jr. initiated the HandMade in America movement in the town of Marshall.

Joe Penland Jr.

I think it was 1962, the French Broad Electric Co-Op finally provided power to everybody in Madison County who desired it. During that time we were introduced to electricity, telephones, and that led to having televisions and more communication with the outside world. For some reason, the government picked out this place to come here and send people and have documentaries on television to tell us how poor we were and how uneducated we were and how we were just living right on the edge of some hellacious lack of civilization, the end of the world. At that time I remember folks here didn't, perhaps, have a lot of money, but we did have a lot of exchange. It wasn't with United States currency. We all had plenty to eat and we shared that with one another, whether it be by barter or trade or sale or whatever. We understood that things had to last a long time, not like the stories of my grandfather who said he got one pair of shoes a year and he only wore them when he walked thirty-five miles to school one way or whatever that story was that he told. We were conservative and all of our clothes, no matter if we were town kids or farm kids, had patches. But they were all clean. We had pride in who we were as a culture, as a mountain culture. Then we became introduced to how the other world lives and not only were introduced to all the glamour of other societies on television, which was a magic thing where you could see how people get along, we also were introduced to how little we had and it was pointed out to us not only by the media, but the government who actually sent people here to tell us that and to set up little charity kinds of things. At first it was surplus food. You'd hear this was going on in a foreign country, but it was happening here also. And then there were medical services and some things that were actually good. But the idea was that if you weren't poor, you needed to maintain the appearance of being poor and ignorant because the poorer and more ignorant you were, the more you got for nothing. That changed a lot. That changed people's pride. People who used to raise huge one- or two-acre gardens and can and put up food suddenly quit doing that. I've had folks say to me, "Why should I do that because I can go to the grocery store and spend three hundred dollars a month?" Well, three hundred dollars was just an astronomical sum to these families who had been cash-starved forever, but rich in so many other things. That changed our society. I don't think that was a good change, and we're still suffering from it.

When Becky Anderson appeared, she started talking about HandMade in America and what they've done for small towns. I quickly bought into her vision as a much more important one. What she seems to have been able to do is to help people come to some sort of consensus—not for Joe Penland to come in here and say, "OK, we're going to buy all of these buildings and we're going to change everything. We're going to remodel and renovate and this town is going to be a period town and we're going to encourage this kind of business or that kind of business." What Becky is trying to do, and the thing that is so appealing to me, is to gather together a diverse group of folks who can come and talk about lots and lots of visions, and put together several scenarios to take back to the people who live here and live around here, and let them buy into it so that it becomes everyone's dream. It may just be a brick in the sidewalk that was a particular person's idea, but they share it, they own it. That's the culture here, to be able to say, "This is what we have done together as a community." Just the way it used to be when the churches and the communities made sure that no child went without food, no child went without clothing. They're going to make sure that our culture and our towns, which have been so important to us, survive.

It's the process of community helping community, internally within that community and externally with other communities in the region. I guess some of the things that intrigue people most about what we do is that we ask our communities to covenant with each other. We take the old biblical sense of covenant, meaning trust, and we ask them to covenant with each other in sharing their knowledge, sharing their resources—they literally will give each other their money if there's a need. This was unheard of five years ago. When Bakersville suffered a devastating flood a few years ago, the other little towns jumped in to help, offering money, equipment, and people for assistance. They painted, cleaned up, and in a single day, literally did a facelift of the whole town because it was a neighbor. These are the things they covenant with each other. Each small community can select a town that they think is similar to them or has done something unique that they would like to do and we get them there and the exchange is incredible. What you really get are not just organizations that are bound to each other, but you get people that are very bound to each other. It becomes very personal and, in the end, that's all that it is, personal.

Opposite: The Carolina movie theater for sale, Spruce Pine

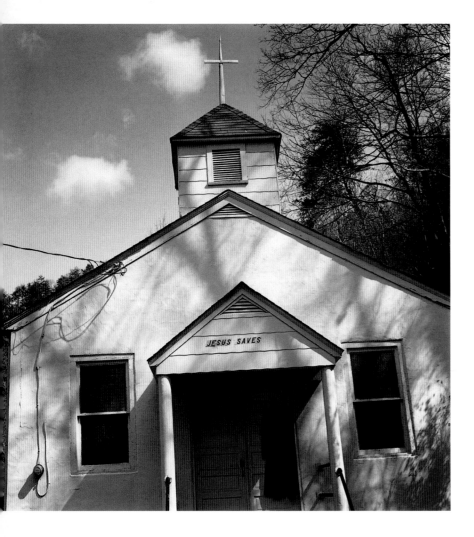

Up until the mid-sixties there was basically no in-migration into the county. The people that lived out in this county had very deep roots in the community. Everybody knew everybody. In the sixties, folks started moving in. They were sometimes referred to as the hippies, the alternative lifestylers, the back-to-the-landers, people who were moving back with a very romanticized view of living a self-sufficient lifestyle. Many came in with very unrealistic expectations. They expected to be able to live off the land, have a very fulfilling life with little or no money. Many of those folk froze out pretty quickly. The folk that followed after that were more realistic. They either came with more money, came with a nice trust fund, or in some way had a means of making money while living back in the mountains. At the same time, many of the families here had children who moved north to manufacturing operations. In some cases, the older couples left behind had no children or grandchildren close by. The folk who moved in quickly realized that they had a wealth of knowledge about how to farm, how to get along in the mountains. So the people moving in started talking to them about different ways to do things and different crops to grow, like how to take care of bees and how to grow sorghum molasses. I remember one elderly lady telling me one time, "You know, I just can't believe it. These people come in here and say they've got all this education. They've been to college and everything. Here I am. I barely went to school and they're asking me everything. They don't know nothing about growing crops and living in the mountains. They have to come to me for everything."

You could sense that that lady had a tremendously improved sense of self-worth. For all these years she had heard in the media, in the newspapers, and on television, about mountain people and how little they had to contribute and how little they knew, and here these folk were drawing on her wealth of knowledge about living in the mountains. She was so pleased and so excited that she had something valuable to give to somebody else.

People were genuinely concerned about preserving those things about the character of this community that they wanted to preserve, and were certainly not turning their backs on change. That's not the point. They wanted to be clear about what they wanted to preserve, and the character of the development as it occurred, so that we could control it.

See, you're still in a small town, with the traditional value system that's associated with small-town life, where people feel a sense of ownership in this community. I mean, you can talk to the mayor, you can talk to the board of aldermen, you can talk to the town manager. You just know everybody in this community, and you know them on a first-name basis. And so when people say, "We need you," it's just part of their tradition. It's just who you are. It's just part of the nature of small-town life. You need help, I'll be over to help.

We're very conscious about the fact that many of us choose to live in this community because it is a small community. The rural values that are very near and dear to us, and a strong sense of community that's part of this—we don't want that simply bulldozed over in the process. We want to preserve those values. So how we do that is striking that delicate balance between integrating the kind of growth we want and preserving the small-town character of this community—the balance—so that those bulldozers that are down there don't plow up our values and the small-town community that we have here.

You say, what are some of those values? Well, we have a police chief that calls about twelve or fourteen elderly folks who live at home by themselves, calls them every morning just to make sure they made it through the night all right. And if they have any needs we see if we can take care of them. Those are the kinds of things we don't want to lose, the face-to-face way we do business. When somebody wants to be concerned about traffic out here, they want to be able to talk to somebody, not get a faceless voice on the telephone or put on voice mail. They want somebody that they can talk with who will listen to them.

And of course they want someone who's responsive, and I think on the local level, in the small-town government, we're not dealing with bureaucracies, we're dealing with people. It's a very face-to-face kind of existence.

Everette Boone's Church,
Ponders Chapel, Marshall

Opposite: Amerady Cantrell and Fred Shelton
with hummingbird beans, Shelton Laurel

Davitus Gosnell, an avid gardener, is a ninety-year-old tobacco farmer from Marshall.

It is a good little town. You take everybody down there, they're just as nice as they can be. They accommodate one another. If one ain't got the money and he wants something, he just goes to the store there and gets it and pays for it whenever he wants to. That's the way George Penland and them is by people. People they know, why, they'll let them have anything on earth they've got. That's the way they live. You take them other stores down there, they're just like that. If I didn't have a penny in the world, I can go down there, and if I wanted five thousand dollars' worth of stuff, I can get it, no trouble. And the banks work right with the people, too. Yes, sir, they're just as good to the poor people as anything on earth can be.

That little old town is mighty good to one another. That's the reason I like to stay here. I just don't never want to get away. These old mountains are hard to beat. You can take a man out of these mountains, but, I'll tell you, he'll want to get back. He can't get that blood out of him. It's just like an old chicken, you know, at roosting time, why, he'll get around pretty close to the roost, you see, and before it gets dark, he's going to fly up. So, that's kind of a little way people live: you get away, but you want to get back directly. No place like home—that's that old song, isn't it?

Jeff Whetstone talks with Davitus Gosnell.

DG: Now, if we'd treat that flag right, everybody'd live right, we'd have a better place to live, wouldn't we?

But I tell you, our country is a-going. That's according to the Bible, you know? Bible says it'll get from bad to worse, bad to worse, and that's the way it's going. But now, we needn't to look at that. What we need to do is just be ready to go, and then whenever you pace out of this life, you've got a home. And that's the way I'm trying to live it, too, and I'm going to.

JW: Have you lived in these mountains, right around here, all your life?

DG: Oh, yeah, I was, I was raised right here in these mountains. And I've been all over the country, but I've never found no place like these mountains.

JW: What do you like about them so much?

DG: Well, it's just one of the most beautiful places that there is in the United States to live in. And your land is good. You just can't beat it—no way. I don't care where you go. And I've been over a lot of country in my life, but I've never seen nothing to beat these mountains.

July 4, 1999, Madison County
Courthouse, Marshall

Opposite: Davitus Gosnell

In small towns civic life replaces social life. You generally eat a lot of meals together. Our folks do. They seem to find a great excuse to eat together all the time, and I think that's great. On their day off, they're together building something, doing something somewhere. In my mind, their civic life and their social life have become intertwined. As we've discovered in our work, people don't look to Washington to resolve it, or to Raleigh, the state capital, to resolve problems. They know that the only thing that's going to be resolved is right there where they are.

All politics is local to most people. They don't look for a political solution anymore, and I think there was a period in this country when we did. There was a time when we believed the government would really resolve issues for us, but I don't see that anywhere in the towns we work. I see local people using politics a little bit to get some things they might want or need, but I don't think they look at it as what's going to resolve their problems at all.

Becky Anderson

I think Marshall still needs to retain its major focus, which has always been the governmental center of the county. The courthouse is there. It's a fantastic building. They restored it, and it's still the centerpiece of the town. There's talk of putting governmental services up in the industrial park or off a bypass. They need to retrofit some of the buildings or build some new buildings in downtown Marshall. They need to retain governmental services in downtown Marshall.

They're going to have some things leaving their Main Street, so they need to begin to think about what fills that space, and the economic restructuring team will do some surveys.

The goal is for the citizens of Marshall to determine what they want their town to be. What is it they want right now in the history of the county? What should it be ten, fifteen years from now in the history of the county? What should they preserve about it that's theirs, that's sacred to them? What should they add new to it that makes life easier for citizens or just keeps the town vibrant and alive?

The dreaded door, Madison County Courthouse, Marshall

Opposite: Madison County Courthouse, Marshall

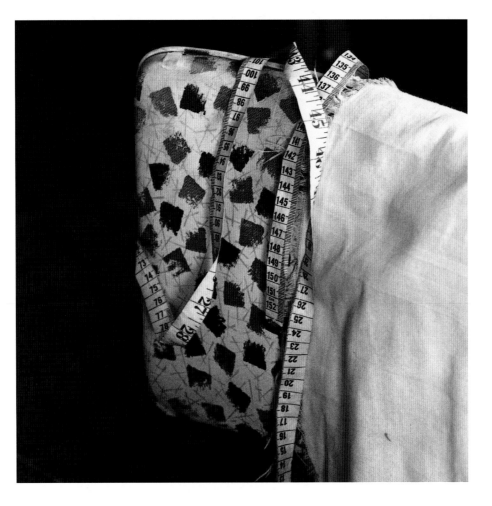

I don't know of any other places around here that sell fresh fruits and vegetables along with undergarments for ladies. Over the years they've done things, from having a seamstress, selling cloth, selling tobacco supplies, selling seeds for your garden. Because all of the little grocery stores closed up in town, they have fresh vegetables and they, of course, sell cigarettes and chewing gum and other things that take on the flavor of a pawn shop at times. If you'd like to buy an engagement ring for your beloved, you can find that there. Or, if you'd like to find some way to put your beloved out of misery, you can find that here also. Or you can trade for a car, or you can just sit down and not trade for anything at all. Everyone who comes is welcome.

Everyone's gone except George. There used to be about three or four dry-goods stores on Main Street in Marshall, but Penland's the only one's left. You can't go buy no groceries unless you can go to a dry-goods store, and that's Penland's. There ain't no grocery store or nothing left in downtown Marshall. When Penland and Son's is gone, nobody will take up that store. It'll just be another empty building.

Used to be when I was young, you'd go down there and the streets of Marshall on Saturday evening were full. You'd have people running over people just to have a place to go. Now when you go down Saturday evening, that's a desert. It's deserted. Ain't nothing left there on Saturday.

We try to treat people fair and honest, and we go out of our way to treat a customer as good as we can. We know all of our customers. We call them by their names as they walk through the door and that means a whole lot. We know their grand-young'uns and their great-grand-young'uns. We have a lot of people come in here, and they sit down and they trade with us, and they'll tell us some big tall tales, and most of them are anywhere from eighty to ninety, ninety-one or -two years old. They come in every day or two, just to have a place to go. They do trade with us.

A lot of these people growed up about the time that I did. Some of the families had anywhere from twelve to twenty in the household. They'd come and get them all the clothes at one time. Sometimes, the ones that had six, seven young'uns, they'd measure the foot by breaking off a stick and they'd bring the stick in here with them and I'd measure up some shoes and go from there. Had pretty good luck; none of them ever brought the shoes back. They'd have string for the pant size, and I'd go by that. We'd always manage to come out all right.

Above and opposite: Penland and
Son's dry-goods store, Marshall

Tourism can build community. I'm firmly convinced of it. It can also quickly divide community. It can destroy community. But when you look at the fact that 67 percent of all the handmade objects in this region are bought by visitors, that's the market, that's how people earn a living. How do you enrich that? How do you expand on that? How do you make that purchase more knowledgeable for the visitor and how can it have a more personal meaning to them? We've found that visitors have got to meet the person making the objects. That's the sacred part. It's between the maker and the person who's buying it. I firmly believe, if it comes from the outside, if it's designed by an outside developer, that's tourism in the cause of making a fast buck. People resent that. But, if the local people design it, if they have a part in it, if it fits their community, it's the best possible experience for a visitor. Why would you want to go where you're not wanted? Why wouldn't you want to go where people have already said, "This is what we want to share with you. This is what we want to show off. This is who we are. Come see us."

A. J. Bridges and J. D. Rollin
dancing at the Depot, Marshall

Opposite: Stella Riddles with fourteen
four-leaf clovers, outside Marshall

While we're moving into a twenty-first century of leadership, it's also a restoration of the old eighteenth- and nineteenth-century notion of barn-raising, of neighbor helping neighbor. That's why I think we're just blessed to live here in western North Carolina where that ethos, that value system, still is intact. You can draw upon that to get a number of initiatives done in the town, in the county, or among the towns in the county and the region.

The worst-case scenario would be that we'd let our guard down and not continue the planning that we're doing with our zoning efforts and some of the other initiatives for traffic control so that we would simply be overrun by development that we don't want. I mean, we are very conscious about the fact that we do not want to become another gas station stop on Interstate 26. The people we want to attract off of I-26 we hope are discriminating, in the sense of interested in cultural heritage tourism, interested, for example, in this town where the hooked rug industry really had its beginnings, people who would want to come in and buy a quality craft, as an example. In essence, we will try to attract a more discriminating tourist. We don't want to be overrun with gas stations, fast-food restaurants, and ticky-tacky tourist kind of rubber tomahawk stands. We're just not interested in that, and we'll work to discourage that kind of development.

Joe Penland Jr., a building contractor for the past fifteen years, was born and raised in Marshall.

Marshall may never be the town of my youth, but it can be something full and rich. We have things to offer here for folks. We hope that we can offer some things not unlike the State of Washington that used to say, "Please come and visit, but then please leave." Perhaps that's what we need. The topography here is not such that we can accommodate a lot of big homes or big industries. But we have wonderful arts and crafts, and brilliant philosophers who just sit on the street and will be glad to tell you about life. We have that to share with folks. My vision is that we will be able to create a town that is not a T-shirt town, not an amusement park, but a place where people can come and see the goodness and fullness of this place.

Berke Landrum is the minister of the Marshall Presbyterian Church and chairman of Marshall's HandMade in America committee.

People are easily seduced by talking about what was and how great it has been. That's true, and that's wonderful, and I'm thankful we have that memory. I'd also like to make it our vision because I think there's a lot of neat stuff that Marshall can do. I'm hoping that this HandMade in America conversation, this listening team, will be an opportunity for us to hear and to open the door to people's dreams and hopes. I think sometimes it's safer to talk about what was because that's concrete. I think if you stick your hopes out there, it can be a little scary. To talk about the future, to talk about our hopes when perhaps they've been dashed, can be a little more threatening and a little more scary. I hope our HandMade in America conversation will be an opportunity for people to safely share their hopes, and to begin to look with new eyes at this town—not just where it has been, but where it can be.

Evelyn Clay at a cakewalk at the Depot, Marshall

Opposite: Rodeo clown Randy Wilson and the American flag, Marshall

Joe Penland Jr. says the prayer at the end of a HandMade in America meeting.

Anne Davidson, who is with the University of North Carolina's Institute of Government in Chapel Hill, speaks at the biannual meeting of the towns involved in HandMade. The institute provides training, advisory services, and research for North Carolina's local and state government officials.

We're so thankful for this time to come together and express our own opinions and our diversities, but it's all through the good of this town that you've given us, Lord, and we're so grateful. What a wonderful place you've given us and you've appointed us to be the stewards. We ask only that you show us your way and your wisdom and your will and we ask it in the name of those who have gone before us and been stewards. Amen.

You all already are teachers in your communities. You're models. You're examples, and you are teachers for each other. You are teachers for new communities that will be coming on. You have two big roles: teach other people in your town, and since a lot of you are graduating and going on, you will be helping these new towns.

There are some little tips here for you to think about as you begin to take on this new mentoring or teaching role. Remember that other people need to make their own mistakes. Your role as a mentor is not to be doing work for people, but to be guiding them, sharing what you did well—your successes and failures—sharing everything that you know, and then helping them from a distance. It's not about doing things for them. It's about letting them learn those lessons, your being there to advise and help.

The other important tip here is: Spend some time with the individuals in your community whom you're going to mentor. If you're one of those teachers who's helping new towns get started, spend some time at the beginning to talk a little bit about what that's going to be like. This is a chance for a whole new set of friendships.

Left: Stacy Lee Wilson, volunteer fireman, Marshall

Right: Donald Shook working at a Christmas tree farm between Marshall and Mars Hill

Opposite: Prayer before bull-riding

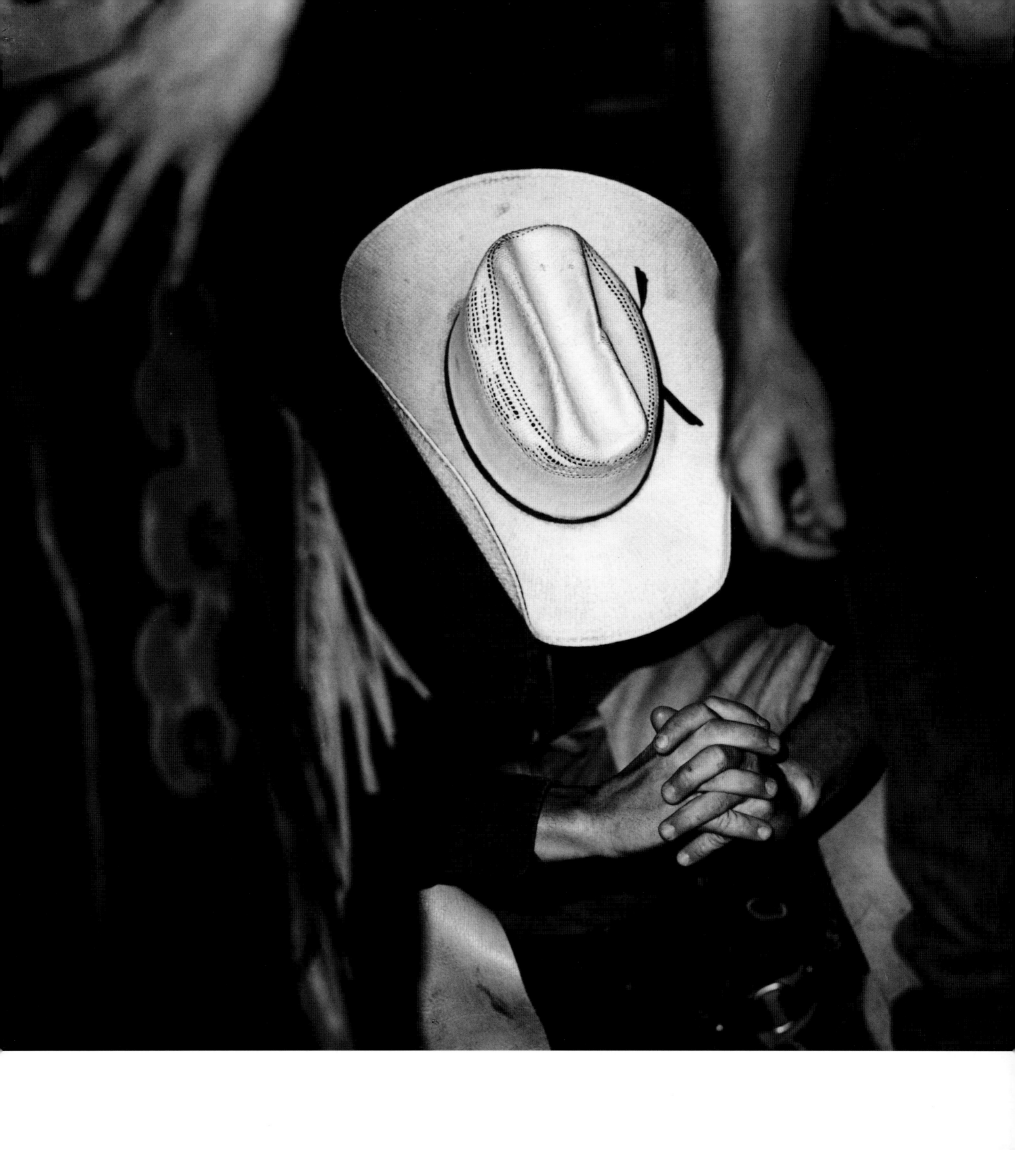

PHOTOGRAPHS BY **REAGAN LOUIE** • INTERVIEWS BY **BARRY DORNFELD**

REIMAGINING THE CITY

THE VILLAGE OF ARTS AND HUMANITIES

PHILADELPHIA, PENNSYLVANIA

The road to transformation of inner-city neighborhoods ravaged by neglect, despair, and economic failure is a hard one. Urban poverty and its poison partners, drugs and crime, may seem intractable obstacles, but the residents of such neighborhoods, who face terrific odds, also form a community of possibility. If they are nurtured and valued; if they gain the positive attention of the larger world and their elected representatives; if beauty has a place in their lives—individuals have important tools to turn the tide. The vision of the Village of Arts and Humanities in North Philadelphia is to engender these conditions, rebuilding community through creativity. The seeds of the Village lie in the belief that local hopes and dreams can be nourished through artistic practice—giving word and form, movement and voice, color and texture to the experience of living there.

Creative action at the Village opens and strengthens the inner life and potential of area children, teens, and adults while transforming their actual physical surroundings. Together with staff and volunteers, participants tap into their own resources to recast the face and future of a few blocks of North Philadelphia and a widening circle of people touched by this unique experiment.

What began as a park building project on a single vacant lot in 1986 by artist Lily Yeh, some neighborhood children, and a local handyman has burgeoned into many more community parks and gardens, as well as a comprehensive constellation of education, arts, neighborhood development, and outreach programs. Under Yeh's direction, the Village has reclaimed a small slice of Philadelphia's "badlands" with its funky, turreted stucco architecture, recycled-tire flower pots, vegetable gardens, and colorful public art—mosaics, murals, and sculpture that reflect the art and craft of Yeh, James "Big Man" Maxton, guest artists, and the community—especially the children.

Adjacent to public-housing projects and condemned buildings, the Village labors in a neighborhood where community cohesion and pride of place are alien ideals or distant memories. Periodically, the city demolishes the decaying brick townhouses, leaving unsightly and unsafe lots in their wake. The Village has reclaimed over fifty of these spaces as green spaces and sanctuaries distinguished by glistening handmade tile compositions and vibrant "Village angels." The Village also renovates the historic houses it can save, increasing quality housing for low-income residents. Villagers celebrate their work with festivals, performances, and other events that reflect their ongoing array of services and programs. Their commitment to youth and health, arts-based reclamation, and community capacities has attracted enough media attention to make the Village an unlikely tourist destination and modest national model. Through Youth Theater, publications, craft productions, and outreach efforts, Village residents extend their approach to building community through the arts beyond their own streets to other "villages" seeking to initiate their own renaissance.

Whether the Village is seen as the conception of an exceptional individual or as a groundswell of community inspiration, or both, its solutions reveal the potential of creativity to address both practical problems and the needs of the human spirit. *T.W.S.*

I've been here so long it's hard to put myself in the shoes of the person who's seeing the Village for the first time. I think, almost across the board, people are just totally astonished. I certainly was. When I first came up to North Philly, it was around five-thirty in the evening. Things were shutting down, and everything felt really desolate. I came down Germantown Avenue, and then I saw that mural. That's such a striking image, the bright color, in this otherwise desolate wasteland of space and broken-down buildings. The whole Village is this sort of jewel that's shining in the middle of an otherwise broken area.

When it's warmer weather and there's a lot of life in the street, it just feels good to be around here. There's a real sense of people saying "Hi" and friendliness and neighborliness. This is my neighborhood more than anything else. I think people sense that. I've had those comments made back to me, "Wow. This neighborhood is really an amazing place to be in, the energy here, the good will that you get around here." It's kind of like a little bubble. Go two blocks in any direction and you're away from it. You don't even see it, and it's strange how it's just nestled into this little North Philadelphia neighborhood.

There's been thousands and thousands and thousands of people come through, and everyone has expressed an appreciation for having it done. It's not about where it's at. Know what I'm saying? It's not about it being a part of north Philadelphia or a part of the Badlands or the horrid urban landscape. It's none of that. It's about an artistic presence, wherever it's found.

This is where art and society and politics and social work are all merging into one, and this is where the arts is the skeleton and the backbone of everything we deliver, whether it's transforming the community physically, in education, helping a teen to go to college, in everything that we do.

I always say that art is not just the product that we produce, like a mural, a park, and a performance. It's much more essential to our daily activities. Art is creativity in thinking, in methodology, in implementation. That's what we call art.

Guardian Angel Park, with its mural by Lily Yeh, marks the entrance to the Village.

Mosaic sculpture in Ile Ife Park by
Joseph "Jo Jo" Williams and James "Big Man" Maxton

Opposite: Big Man Maxton at home

Lily Yeh talks about Jo Jo Williams, her first community collaborator and supporter.

Joseph Williams. His nickname is Jo Jo, and his African name is Jabid. What was funny was that they said, "Oh, Jo Jo knows how to do some of the construction work. He will help you. He's lived in the neighborhood for a long time." But every time I'd go knock on his house—he lived right next to the abandoned lot, in a disheveled building—every time I'd go to find him, he wasn't there. Later on, I realized he was dodging me. He was saying, "God, who is this Chinese woman? I don't want to have anything to do with this crazy Chinese woman." So one day he was tying his shoes. He was one step too late. I said, "Jo Jo! You are Jo Jo. You have to talk to me!" Once I explained to him what I wanted to do, he was my fast friend, and he became the first person that came to help me. Some years later, his friend told me that in a way making this park saved Jo Jo's life because he was wandering. There was no aim, and then there were the drugs. This kept him focused; this gave him a place.

There was a touching story. He had stomach cancer, and he was in Temple Hospital. He just couldn't endure the hospital anymore, so when he was better he escaped from the hospital in his hospital gown. He took a bus and came back, and it was in the springtime. The sun was bright, and he sat on the bench in the sun basking in his hospital gown. That was just wild, just wild. That is how much he loved this park.

James "Big Man" Maxton describes how Jo Jo Williams, a neighborhood handyman, drew him into Lily Yeh's work in the community.

He'd talk about watching his back, and then he began to string together a very melodic kind of tale about Lily, this Asian lady who came and what she wanted to do for the community. I have to say the story was fascinating. Can you imagine Ile Ife Park when there was no trees, no benches, no nothing? It was just open space. We sat around a fire can, and he would tell these stories. Even in the state of mind I was in, I was impressed with the vision he painted of her. When she came around, I could see what he was talking about. Here's this lady with an overabundance of energy who was trying to do something positive. She was expressing an artistic vision, and it began to develop and grow as I watched and looked on. I became a part of that. I began to walk around inside her dreams, and it made me feel good.

Lily Yeh was formally trained in Chinese painting before she came to the United States. Her own art has evolved to become more personal and experimental.

The Village is about a different way of doing things, a different value system, and, like our stucco architecture that's all touched by hand, it's small-scale. Especially with globalization, and big huge-scale building, and mechanical materials and so forth—it's very, very important that many organizations or groups, like the Village, stay outside of the mainstream, so that people have a voice, and so that you open up the horizon, the depth and means of expression.

If you look at our architecture, the inspiration comes from Africa, comes from Islam, comes from American Indian, comes from Chinese, and Japanese gardens. I mean, it's true democracy where we're small people with diverse voices; it's truly democracy in spirit.

This project is rooted in the community, in the land nobody wants, full of chaos and decay. Being community-based becomes the nurturing element in this project, and then it goes in its chaotic, organic way, but defines this new light and air, and the nurturing elements it needs to thrive.

What's so interesting about the Village is that it's computer age. It's not linear thinking. It's not Newtonian logic. It's modern science, the modern way of doing things. It's taking everything about the organic community base seriously. And what is organic? It's chaotic, but it's an orderly chaotic growth, and it's powerful because it is nature and to survive you have to find where you can make a place, where you can find sunlight, rain, and all the conditions—like plants—that you need to survive.

It's about building a living community. People talk about community fabrics. We are weaving it. Everything you do, you put a little thread in here. You put your foot down. You put in another little thread. You put great labor in different elements. Eventually you have a multifaceted and rich fabric, and that's the community fabric.

Children working and playing on a soil heap at the Village's Tree Farm

Bahia Beasley and a woman tie ribbons on newly planted trees

Inlaid tile and stone floor of Meditation Park

Kitchen and entertainment center in a house being rehabilitated by the Village

Boys: I say, where is your fire?

Girls: I say, where is your fire?

All: You got to find it and pass it on.

You got to find it and pass it on.

Actor 1: From you to me.

Actor 2: From me to her.

Actor 3: From her to him.

Actor 4: From the son to the father.

Actor 5: From the brother to the sister.

Actor 6: From the daughter to the mother.

All: From the mother to the child.

Where is your fire? We say, where is your fire?

Can't you smell it coming out of our past?

The fire of living . . . Not dying.

The fire of loving . . . Not killing.

The fire of Blackness . . . Not gangster shadows.

Shadows, shadows, shadows.

Where is our beautiful fire that gave light to the world?

It's the richness of the color and the style of what we do, the images that we are presenting. Also we work not in a rich, giving environment like a suburban setting. This is urban America. It is raw. We're locked in. In and around the surrounding areas, they still deal with the drug problem, and you see the dilapidation of the buildings, people who couldn't keep them up, and people who didn't care about them, like the slumlords. While it still affects you, we effect change in the midst of all that. As soon as they see some change, people see hope, if not for themselves, then for their community.

Magical Garden tile mural designed
by Lily Yeh, Warnock Street

Neighborhood resident Devore Henderson playing guitar

Basilio and daughter, Ivelys Reyes,
live in the Village neighborhood.

Lily Yeh tries to balance the Village's need to survive and compete as a nonprofit with community-based process and growth.

You know where the real challenge is? The real challenge is how to deal with the bigger-power society that sees us as the Third World, the nonprofit. Everybody is anxious to send us technical assistance. I do want to learn everything, and I attend workshops and I go to talks. Everybody says, "This person can help you." So I've chased after numerous leads. Finally I said, "Mainstream society has not yet understood different kinds of capital, different kinds of resources that's not just a dollar, and is deeper and more abundant." There is no way yet to translate those resources into the system we have, but I am beginning to see the light, how to do that.

As the Village gets bigger and more visible, how do you get the right exposure so that more people know about us? We need the resources to sustain our staff and the Village crew, and stabilize the situation. We need to make it possible for young, inspired professionals to have a career here rather than losing them to the profit world or other places.

A thirty-year resident, Nora Gardner lives in a publicly subsidized house near a block she helped beautify.

Dorothea Bixby got me involved. I been knowing her for years, and she mentioned to me that they had the program at the Village. I'm walking past, in the neighborhood, not aware, you know, just from Huntington Street to Germantown, and not being aware of what was going on in the opposite direction. She said, "Nora, why don't you come around to the community meeting?" I said, "What community meeting?" When she explained it to me, I went around, and the rest is history. I met Lily Yeh and Inja, and I fell in love with these people because they were for real. I've been going ever since, and I love being involved with the community.

Heidi Warren is the managing director of the Village.

The community meetings formally got started because there were a lot of houses knocked down on Warnock Street. We had some volunteers working with us during that summer, and word was coming back to us through them—this very indirect "Heard it on the street"—of people grumbling about "What's the Village doing? We don't need more parks. They keep building parks, and we need houses around here."

We actually had nothing to do with knocking those houses down. We had wanted to try to save them, but the city just came, and no warning—boom—they were down. So we said, "Great. People are getting emotional about this. Let's seize that energy." And we started, "Come. Let's have a meeting. Let's talk about this. Tell us what you want." Out of that basically came our housing construction project. In that section of the neighborhood, we are going to build houses, and we've been having monthly community meetings since then, which is three years ago, so a long time.

Lily's very good at embracing whatever it is that comes to her, and just the act of embracing tends to create opportunities for dialogue. Sure enough, you find out that the grumbling is actually connected to something else, or that it is something that we can address or talk about. The sense of tension dissolves, because now we're communicating with each other, and you can find out that there's common ground. There's common interest.

Impromptu staff meeting with Jennifer Rulf, Lily Yeh, Lilly Toler, and Amy Fiske

Opposite: Pearline Hatten sitting on a stoop, Alder Street

Heidi Warren was studying the connection between art and social change at college when she first came to the Village.

I was able to see art as a bridge, something that is noncommercial and noncompetitive, and it's not a social service. It provides a common ground that people of very different backgrounds can meet on and feel much more like equals, and that has a tremendous power to then build relationships and build a sense of community, which is really what I was after.

Village staff members Sally Hammerman and Andres Chamorro performing with puppets on Earth Day

Opposite: *Tree of Life* mosaic in Meditation Park designed by Lily Yeh and executed by James "Big Man" Maxton

Melissa Talley-Palmer, education administrative assistant, came to work at the Village as an alternative to a corporate career.

I'm in my glory. I can smile a lot of days, let me tell you, because going from corporate America to this is so free. You have a sense of freedom, you know, the free spirit, the flexibility. There's not that confinement of what someone else expects you to do, the way they expect you to do it, all the time. Your opinion matters here, unlike in corporate America, where your opinion didn't count.

I love it here. I've brought my six-year-old here and watched him go from a fragile, apprehensive kind of kid to this butterfly that's into everything all the time, anywhere, with whomever, however. It's fun. There's so much variety. The vitality of the ceramics, the murals, the paintings that the children develop that have been made into life-size murals. The angels and the attitudes of the people here who work at something that they love. They're always willing to talk about what they do and to show you how to do what they do and to explain how it works and how it evolves and the whys and the what-ifs.

Christopher Nicoteria came to the Village through City Year Philadelphia, an AmeriCorps program. He works with volunteers, staff, and residents as they clean up and transform abandoned lots.

When someone comes from a different area it's the equivalent of Alice looking through the looking-glass. They say, "Wow, you mean I'm still in Philadelphia? Like, this place is beautiful—it's living art." There are homes with this undulating wall effect that go throughout; there's this sense of belonging at the Village; and there's a buzz and the hum of energy; and there's all this change going on. It's hard to believe that you're in the heart of a land that's economically a dried-out, barren wasteland because of different legislators and tax breaks that in the early 1970s brought all the big business out of North Philadelphia and basically, left it in the condition that you see outside of the Village today.

It's really hard to realize that you still are in that same area code, when you're in the Village and you see the work that the Village is

All of a sudden I began to dream about art. I became this kind of crazed monster. Sometimes I would work overnight, work through the night just because it gave me so much pleasure and so much joy. All of a sudden, where I always believed and thought that I would die addicted to drugs, to be free of that and to recognize the freedom and to totally enjoy it and, at the same time, find the positive energy to keep that freedom alive and constantly work at it, was like a reclaiming of myself and my history when I came to Philadelphia with starry-eyed visions. I have scars from not being able to pursue a professional football career that are deep and painful, and I kept them hidden and kept them masked. It was part of a cancerous kind of thing that began to eat away at me and that made me get lost in the whole drug culture. I stayed lost until Lily was able to bring out a creative side of me that I didn't know about, a side that she would nurture and applaud at every chance she'd get.

For me, Angel Alley was really my next evolution in the creative process. I had never worked inside of lines: I created my own borders, my own rhythms, my own flow to all the pieces I had done prior to that. Here was a chance to work within some of the lines Lily had set forth, because she did the illustration. I was excited by that kind of growth.

But it was a very painful cycle. In 1991, I had two years clean, and I had diabetes and my feet swelled, like maybe three times their normal size, and it was exceptionally painful. Since I was drug-free, I wouldn't take any kind of pain medication, and the only relief I could get was by soaking. So, I could only be out working for maybe an hour and a half, and then go soak for a couple of hours and then come back, maybe work another hour. That was the process. The community would continue to stop by and say, "My God! I don't believe how . . ." and that was like medication for me.

After Angel Alley was done, we had some sort of celebration. It was a winter harvest festival–type thing. It was just about dusk, and they had red, blue, and yellow lights hanging on the opposite wall in the alley. I came around the building and caught a glimpse of all the tiles, and everything seemed to be mirror and glass. The tiles had all these brilliant colors, and I was just blown away. I have to say, being a real man, being too emotional is not a good thing, but I was extremely choked up—just the overall beauty.

James "Big Man" Maxton has become a recognized
mosaic artist and public and community art specialist
since he began working at the Village.

People were getting filled up by what was happening, what they were seeing. For them, it was the first time they had been walked through a creative process. Then, to have a drug addict like myself to do that, they were both pleased and extremely impressed, making them take a little more notice. This very destructive individual they've known for years and years in this community was now taking a real positive approach to enrich and improve and begin the process of turning this into a celebratory place.

I got a lot of verbal appreciation from people, and to me that was totally without precedent. Know what I'm saying? These are people that come out and cling to their purses and pocketbooks. We're talking about both young and old. They come out, do what they're doing, and go straight back home. They ain't got nothing really to say to anybody. "Hi, how ya doing?" and they want to keep on going. But, people would stop and talk, and express what it made them feel. What it made them feel, know what I'm saying? How wonderful and how beautiful it was for the overall community.

Mary Mackie, a board member for City Year
Philadelphia and Philadelphia's Office of Community
Service, speaks at the Village's annual Earth Day
celebration, where a new community park and tree
farm were dedicated in 1999.

When I looked at the lot and saw what it could be, it reminded me of a line from Shakespeare, and the line was, "How brightly that little candle throws its beams. So shines a good deed in a naughty world." And so, for lighting a candle, for doing a good deed, for lighting up this neighborhood, we thank you.

Angel Alley murals designed by Lily Yeh.
Angel Alley (left), mosaicked by
James "Big Man" Maxton; *Angel Eyes*
(right) mosaicked by Carolyn Overholt
and Brother Mohammed.

German Wilson, education and theater director, founded and directs the Village's Youth Theater program.

I think education is the nucleus of this whole organization of the Village of Arts and Humanities. We're making sure that there will be a future, because we're helping to provide a base whereupon these people can say, "I'm worth something. I have something to live for and I can do that and I can be this and I can go accomplish this and come back and give back to this community," and therefore the community becomes stronger and more enriched. I think that's what's going on.

Girls playing on Germantown Avenue

We're doing something wrong, insane, ain't it?
Nobody has a heart, baby, quick to jump when they
    hear a gunshot.
The Village, don't you like my style?
The Village, here we go,
yo, the Village is my place to live,
coming in every day so I learn how to give,
like the lookout man from a steeple,
always keeping eyes on all my people,
yeah, I don't smoke cigarettes and I don't smoke crack,
you ask my friends and they go stand back,
don't you want to be a survivor all your life,
maybe in the future have a husband or a wife,
if you having problems I'll help you through,
if I ain't there they'll be there right for you,
we have all types of branches in these trees,
rappers, singers, and even emcees, yeah,
we just rapping in the hood,
know how we do it, it's always understood,
if you could, you could learn with me,
because I'm about to rip it off to my homey Willy.

Antonio Black, who is fifteen, participates in the Village's Youth Theater and other youth programs.

Sometimes I think that I need more rehearsal, I need more practice. We have something called a hype dance. What we do is we hold hands in a circle, or hold shoulders, and we kick and say, "Hype, hype, hype," and we get ourselves energized. We all take turns going in the middle, doing our own little dance and coming back. At the end, we pray, and we ask for support and help, just in case of anything. We have someone to look up to and look forward to. That's what I like.

In the school year they're very strict at the Village. They make sure that we buckle down and do our work. We have to be here by 3:30 to start on our homework, and then they tutor us by 4:00. They look over our home-work, help us with any problems. What they do is they focus on our hard subjects. They ask us which subjects we are having a hard time on, and we tell them. Like mine is geometry, and it used to be science, but it isn't anymore. I maintain a good average in geometry. I haven't failed any of my classes, and I'm looking forward to next semester so they can help me to go to college.

Casey Ayers (with blindfold) and Raheem Wilson
play pin-the-tail-on-the-donkey during a baby
shower given for a teen mom at the Village.

Jim Frazier is a retired newspaperman and shop steward who grew up in the Village neighborhood and frequents the local bar.

I'm glad they've got something working in the community. It's creating jobs; it's creating things to help the kids. The affairs they give are nice, and they give the kids some initiative, something to look for in life. All of them are dying young. If they ain't got no role model or something to look up to, people to help them, they're lost in space. They fixed up the garden, and now they have the kids cleaning up the lot over there. It makes them work. As long as you got somebody to give you an opportunity, you can do it.

Youth group cleaning up a vacant lot on Sartain Street

Barry Dornfeld talks with fifteen-year-old Raheem Wilson, who lives across the street from the main Village building. He started participating in Village programs when he was six or seven and is now a member of the Youth Theater.

BD: How would your life be different if you hadn't gotten involved with the Village?

RW: Well, I wouldn't know the things I know right now. I probably wouldn't be around here. I'd probably be in jail somewhere.

BD: Really?

RW: Yeah. If you ain't got nothing to do and you hanging on streets, you're either going to be selling drugs or doing something you're not supposed to be doing. You're going to end up in the wrong place. Then you going to be with the wrong person at the wrong time, and then you going to get caught—y'all going to get locked up. Or worse. You could get killed or hurt over something dumb, or get into something that you're not even in. That's why I try not to really mess with nobody, and then I try to be cool with everybody.

German Wilson, a director and playwright who founded Philadelphia's Venture Theater, came to the Village after recovering from cancer.

It took me a long time to get rooted with them because when you look at these young people, when they come to you, they come with fear, number one. They come with hurt, number two. They come in defense of themselves, but they don't know what this self is yet. So when you're talking about "I want you to do this," or "You've got to do this," they're looking at you with a very close eye and saying, "Now, wait a minute. You're sounding like you might be similar to what's going on out there already. You told me that I was going to be able to do all these wonderful things, and now you tell me I got to do this and I got to do that."

What has to happen is that they begin to understand that with freedom comes a sense of responsibility and discipline. You can't have freedom without discipline. You can't have freedom without a structure. I try to make them understand that. When you get the structure, there's room, and there will always be room for you to understand and appreciate that there can be somebody there that can love you. They begin to see that I love them, that I will do anything in the world for them, but I will not permit them to throw away their lives in connection with what I'm trying to do. If they want to throw their life away, they do it without being at the Village, not at the Village. They cannot do that.

When you look at this community, it's very open. It's very organic. There are always things going on. You never know what's going to happen the next minute. You have to be prepared, to be willing and ready to change with it and make adjustments because, if you don't, you'll become totally frustrated, totally out of focus, you will not be able to hang, and you will not be able to continue.

Casey Ayers and Ora Eldridge
at a teen group meeting

An after-school art class

Opposite: State senator Shirley Kitchen (with scarf) and Lily Yeh (center) join residents in prayer at the inaugural for the Village's Tree Farm.

Lily Yeh tells her story of starting and building the Village to college students volunteering during their spring break.

I didn't want to do this project. I very often felt frightened. I was scared, I didn't know how. Time and again, especially on the verge of a major break, my body hardens, my lungs harden, I just am plain scared to go forward. For two years I fought, not wanting to do it. Like when I first came here, this opportunity came and I didn't want to do it. I felt totally frightened. But the other thing drives you, tests you and drives you. You need to trust your intuition. The reason why you are here is because there is

Village youth actors perform "Catch the Fire"

ACKNOWLEDGMENTS

As a major national documentary project, Indivisible has been a complex and fruitful collaboration, and we have many people to thank. We are particularly indebted to the twelve communities portrayed here. Without their trust and cooperation little of this book—or of the Indivisible project as a whole—would have been feasible. The stories in *Local Heroes*, bearing witness to the shared understanding found in participatory democracy at the local level and within a national context, are the stories of distinct places and the individuals who live there—individuals who are the ultimate source of this work. Their full participation with the photographers and interviewers who brought their lives, surroundings, struggles, and successes to us in recorded voice and image is the centerpiece of the project.

We are also much indebted to the team of photographers and interviewers who took us at our word and created the remarkable body of work from which this book is drawn. Many thanks also to Ray Suarez for lending his voice to this book, both as writer of the eloquent foreword and as narrator of the audio collection.

In order to work carefully and effectively in each of the communities we relied on the generous help of a number of key contacts across the country whose guidance was regularly needed and always appreciated. They are Becky Anderson, David Arizmendi, Jane Arnold, Scott Asseng, Adriana Bartow, Rick Bass, Sharon Begay, Lee Bolton, Skip Brown, Pat Cabe, Dorothy Childers, Wiley B. Cooper, Juanita Valdez Cox, Scott Daily, David Glickman, Daniella Henry, Leni Hochman, Suzanne Jamison, Eric Jordan, Joanna Kramer, Glynis Laing, Careen Mauro, James Maxton, Kim McGill, Leslie Newman, Camille Odeh, Jaime Ortiz, Richard Overman, Debra Pascali-Bonaro, Terrell Piechowski, Charles Ridley, Ruth Rubalcava, Jason Singer, Heidi Warren, German Wilson, and Lily Yeh.

Since the beginning of the project in 1998, Indivisible has evolved through the labors of numerous staff members at the project's home, the Center for Documentary Studies (CDS) at Duke University, and with its museum and archive partner, the Center for Creative Photography (CCP) at The University of Arizona. The project staff at both institutions have worked to see this book through to completion, and their work is deserving of much more than the acknowledgment we give them here. Elana Hadler, the project coordinator, has been the captain of this immense endeavor, energetically and resourcefully holding together its many people and pieces. She and Rosey Truong, the project assistant, worked tirelessly with the photographers and interviewers and also managed over four hundred hours of taped interviews, which Elana artfully edited into the audio components for this book. Pat D. Evans and Janae Huber, assistants at CCP, have been meticulous in their research for the book and in the organization of the Indivisible exhibitions. Catherine Mills, our book designer, patiently finessed the diversity of text and images into a coherent whole. Iris Tillman Hill, director of programs and publications at CDS, and Alexa Dilworth, managing editor, worked together to turn an ambitious idea into a book. Lynn McKnight, communications director at CDS and for Indivisible, skillfully articulated the complexity of this project to a wide audience. Cyndy Severns, also at CDS, assisted in the making of this book in ways too numerous to mention.

Many others have worked on this project. At the Center for Documentary Studies, we thank webmaster Wells Tower; and for business administration, Greg Britz, Bill Butler, and Alice Huang. At the Center for Creative Photography, we thank the administration and budget staff, Nancy Lutz, Socorro Linnaus, and Terence Pitts; for communications, Jeanne Courtemanche; for exhibitions, Claudine Scolville, Betsi Meissner, Tim Mosman, Janice Collins, and Maria Harper; for education projects, Cass Fey, Roula Seikaly, Karen Jenkins, and Julie Steiner; for rights and reproductions, Dianne Nilsen, Denise Kramer, and Rosanna Salonia; for their archival work, Leslie Calmes and Amy Rule; for the postcard exhibitions, Ileen Sheppard Gallagher of ISG Productions; Ivan Arenas, James Biber, Michael Bierut, Suzanne Holt, and Jacqueline Thaw of Pentagram Design, Inc.; and Michael Sand of Rare Media Well Done, Inc.

The project's transcribers are Martha Adamo, Tracy Brown, Mara Casar, Shelley Castle, Frances Copeland, Julia Crocker, Jacquelyn Finley, Karine Gentil, Claudia Kaplan, Kathleen Kearns, Patrik Jonsson, Cathy Mann, Helene Montgomery, Laura Price, Sandy Tingle, and Alison Rebecca Waldenberg.

Many others contributed to Indivisible and this book, including Donnel Baird, Tammi Brooks, Amanda Capano, Laura Cheshire and the staff at Cheshire Films, Gary Covino, Ruthie Ervin, Maggie Golston, Tabitha Griffin, Maura High, Bill Kobasz, Joan Liftin, Jim Mairs, Resnicow Schroeder Associates, Danny Rosenbloom, Mike Stack, Mary Virginia Swanson, Eleanor Wilner, Elizabeth Wood, and Penny Waterstone.

The funding for this book and for the entire Indivisible project comes from The Pew Charitable Trusts. The earliest ideas for a documentary project looking at grassroots democracy came from the staff and leadership at the Trusts, and we are very grateful for their institutional and individual support. Three community-based organizations represented in this book have received support from The Pew Charitable Trusts either directly or indirectly: the Alaska Marine Conservation Council, HandMade in America, and the Village of Arts and Humanities. We thank particularly Rebecca W. Rimel, president and CEO; David Morse, director of public affairs; Ann Marie Cinque, public affairs associate; Jacqueline Flaherty, program associate, Culture Program; and Marian Godfrey, director, Culture Program.

Joe Wood, a brilliant writer and editor and our documentary colleague on this project, conducted fieldwork in Ithaca, New York, collecting voices for the Alternatives Federal Credit Union chapter. He disappeared while hiking on Mount Rainier in July 1999. This book is dedicated to him.

T.R. and T.W.S

CONTRIBUTORS

PHOTOGRAPHERS

Dawoud Bey

Dawoud Bey, a professor of photography at Columbia College–Chicago, began his first extensive project on the streets of New York City's Harlem in 1975. By the nineties, Bey had become known for his portraits of urban youth made with a 20×24 Polaroid camera. These images, and his earlier black-and-white work, have been published, exhibited, and collected extensively and were the subject of a retrospective exhibition and book organized by the Walker Art Center in 1995.

Bill Burke

Bill Burke is an instructor at the School of the Museum of Fine Arts in Boston. His first documentary commission was with the Kentucky Bicentennial Photo Project, the first of many grants and awards he has received. His books, *I Want to Take Picture* and *Mine Fields*, are a combination of artist's book and travelogue. Since the eighties, Burke has photographed extensively in Southeast Asia. His most recent project is a study of French colonial architecture in Cambodia, Laos, and Vietnam.

Debbie Fleming Caffery

Debbie Fleming Caffery began photographing sugarcane workers in her native Louisiana in the early 1970s while studying photography at the Rice University Media Center. Her monograph, *Carry Me Home*, features a selection of these images and other work from her home region. Caffery has extended her subjects to the cultures of Mexico and Portugal and to other American places. A teacher who is renowned for her expressive black-and-white printing, Caffery has work in many major museum collections and has been exhibited internationally.

Lucy Capehart

Lucy Capehart has worked as a curator since 1981, and is currently a contract curator at the Art Museum of Missoula in Montana. Her large color studies of domestic interiors and the American cultural landscape have been widely exhibited, including solo exhibitions at the Blue Sky Gallery in Portland, Oregon. Her work is featured on book and CD covers and has been published in *The New York Times Magazine*, *Architecture*, and elsewhere.

Lynn Davis

New York–based Lynn Davis began her career as a studio photographer of figures and objects. Since completing a series of photographs of icebergs off Greenland in 1986, she has concentrated on ancient monuments, sacred architecture, and natural water subjects around the world. Davis's work is represented in numerous public and private collections and is surveyed in her 1999 book *Monument*. Her photographs of Africa illustrate Henry Louis Gates Jr.'s *Wonders of the African World*.

Terry Evans

In her most recent books, *The Inhabited Prairie* and *Disarming the Prairie*, noted landscape photographer Terry Evans uses both aerial and ground photography, in black and white and color, to tell the stories of human change engraved on the prairie and the communities that live there. Evans was raised in Kansas and her long involvement with this unique ecology and culture has been the subject of recent solo exhibitions at the Art Institute of Chicago and at the National Museum of Natural History in Washington, D.C.

Lauren Greenfield

The photographs and interviews in Lauren Greenfield's 1997 book, *Fast Forward: Growing Up in the Shadow of Hollywood*, established her as a premier interpreter of American youth culture. A native and current resident of Los Angeles, Greenfield is a working photojournalist who has been recognized by many prestigious grants and awards. Her images have appeared in countless magazines and newspapers in the United States and abroad. At present, she is developing a major project on girls in America.

Joan Liftin

Joan Liftin is director of documentary and photojournalism education at the International Center of Photography in New York City. A freelance photographer, she has developed numerous projects and assignments. Her picture essays have been seen in *The New York Times Magazine*, *Creative Photography*, *Zoom*, and other publications. Currently, she is finishing a color book project on the drive-in movie experience in America.

Reagan Louie

Reagan Louie has been a professor of photography at the San Francisco Art Institute since 1976. His ten-year project photographing contemporary China, which began when he and his father returned to the village where Louie's father was born, is presented in the book *Toward a Truer Life: Photographs of China, 1980–1990*. A Guggenheim and Fulbright fellow, Louie has also received the Dorothea Lange–Paul Taylor Prize and the James Phelan Art Award. His next extensive project explores sex, sexuality, and love in Asia.

Danny Lyon

Also a writer and filmmaker, New York photographer Danny Lyon is well known for his frank and lyric vision. Many of his images have become iconic signs of their time and place, from the civil rights movement to Texas prison life. His landmark book, *The Bikeriders*, was recently reissued, and a photomontage memoir entitled *Knave of Hearts* was published in 2000. A retrospective Danny Lyon exhibition and book was organized by the Center for Creative Photography and the Museum Folkwang in 1991.

Sylvia Plachy

Born in Budapest, Sylvia Plachy emigrated in 1958 and lives in New York, where she is a longtime staff photographer at *The Village Voice*. Her three books are *Unguided Tour*, *Red Light*, and her 1999 monograph, *Signs and Relics*. A well-established photojournalist with a distinctly personal vision, Plachy has published extensively; her photo credits range from *Newsweek* to *Grand Street* to *Wired*. A Guggenheim fellow, she is represented in many museum collections and exhibitions.

Eli Reed

Eli Reed, a member of Magnum Photos, has been documenting the black experience since he first began taking photographs. His 1997 book, *Black in America*, shows the breadth and complexity of this sixteen-year exploration. His other books include *Beirut: City of Regrets*, *War Torn*, and *Homeless in America*. A much sought-after photojournalist, Reed covers national and world events for numerous magazines and organizations, and he has also contributed work to film projects. Reed has received a W. Eugene Smith Grant for Documentary Photography.

INTERVIEWERS

Merle Augustin

For the past eight years, journalist Merle Augustin has been writing extensively about Haitian issues in the United States and in Haiti. She is currently writing for the *Sun-Sentinel*, covering the city of Boynton Beach in Palm Beach County. Augustin is part of a team of reporters working on a year-long series about South Florida and the meaning of community in such a diverse region.

Dan Collison

Dan Collison, a regular contributor to National Public Radio, is executive director/producer of DC Productions, a not-for-profit organization specializing in radio and video documentaries about people and places overlooked by the mainstream media. His 1998 radio documentary *Scenes from a Transplant* received a prestigious du Pont-Columbia Award. The film version aired on the HBO/Cinemax Reel Life series.

Barry Dornfeld

Barry Dornfeld is director and associate professor of the Communications Program at the University of the Arts in Philadelphia. Dornfeld has been working in film and video for twenty years, producing and directing documentaries on a range of topics, including the Philadelphia Hmong refugee community, Ghanaian traditional performance in the United States, and an Appalachian Baptist Church. Dornfeld recently completed the book *Producing Public Television, Producing Public Culture*, an ethnographic study of the public television documentary.

George King

Trained as a documentary filmmaker in the United Kingdom, George King relocated to the United States in 1979. He works as a writer/producer of nonfiction projects in theater, film, television, and radio. King's recent work includes *Will the Circle Be Unbroken?*, the acclaimed radio history of the civil rights movement in five Southern communities, and *Goin' to Chicago*, a history of the African American "great migrations" to air on PBS in summer 2000.

Jack Loeffler

Since 1967 Jack Loeffler has recorded traditional cultures throughout the American Southwest, Mexico, Japan, and the Cook Islands. He is the producer/director of *Southwest Sound Collage*, a radio series nationally distributed by Pacifica Radio; *The Spirit of Place*, a radio series that addresses the relationship between indigenous and traditional cultures; and scores of other documentary radio programs. Loeffler's latest book is *La Musica de los Viejitos: The Hispano Folk Music of the Río Grande del Norte*.

Jens Lund

Folklorist Jens Lund documents occupational poets in the western United States and Canada, and has been involved in research on the traditions of Northwest timber communities, the folklore of Midwestern rivers, and Denmark's resistance to the Holocaust. His 1985 documentary film, *The Pearl Fishers*, about freshwater pearl fishing in Indiana, was chosen the "Best Ethnographic Film—The Americas" by the American Anthropological Association. He is the author of *Flatheads and Spooneys: Fishing for a Living in the Ohio River Valley*.

Karen Michel

For more than a dozen years, Karen Michel has been an award-winning contributor to National Public Radio. Recognition for Michel's radio work has come from the Corporation for Public Broadcasting, the National Federation of Community Broadcasters, and American Women in Radio and Television. She currently teaches at Columbia University's Graduate School of Journalism.

Daniel Rothenberg

Daniel Rothenberg is an assistant professor at the University of Michigan and a fellow in the Michigan Society of Fellows. He has also taught in the Human Rights Program at the University of Chicago and in the Department of Criminology, Law, and Society at the University of California–Irvine. His book, *With These Hands: The Hidden World of Migrant Farmworkers Today*, documents the world of migrant farmworkers through the presentation of a diverse array of personal narratives.

Jeff Whetstone

Jeff Whetstone has been documenting southern communities since he graduated from Duke University in 1990. His latest project is *Bringing Something from Home*, a documentary book on family dynamics of highly motivated high school students in Chattanooga, Tennessee. He is currently attending Yale University working toward an MFA in photography.

Joe Wood

For the past ten years, Joe Wood has been a prominent voice on contemporary American culture. In 1996 he joined the New Press as an editor of nonfiction books. His essays have appeared in numerous publications, including *The Village Voice*, *The Nation*, *The New York Times Magazine*, *Esquire*, and *Rolling Stone*. Joe Wood disappeared on July 8, 1999, while hiking on Mount Rainier.

Tom Rankin

Tom Rankin is director of the Center for Documentary Studies and associate professor of the practice of art at Duke University. He is codirector of Indivisible.

Trudy Wilner Stack

Trudy Wilner Stack is curator of exhibitions and collections at the Center for Creative Photography, The University of Arizona. She is codirector of Indivisible.

Ray Suarez

Ray Suarez is the author of *The Old Neighborhood: What We Lost in the Great Suburban Migration* and a Washington-based senior correspondent for *The News Hour with Jim Lehrer* on PBS.

LOCAL HEROES CHANGING AMERICA

THE AUDIO COLLECTION

1. **Introduction by Ray Suarez**

2. **Birth Stories: Stony Brook, New York**
   Interviews by Karen Michel
   Jane Arnold; Lise Golub and Sarah Matematico; Dr. Bruce Meyer; Lise Golub; Darlinda Donlan and Ana Fox Savillo; Darlinda Donlan and Ana Fox Savillo; Philip Mitchell

3. **A Traditional Future: Navajo Nation**
   Interviews by Jack Loeffler
   Sharon Begay; Leo Natani; Alta Begay; Terrell Piechowski; Sharon Begay; Antonio Manzanares; Terrell Piechowski; Alta Begay

4. **Faith, Race, and Renewal:**
   Eau Claire–North Columbia,
   South Carolina
   Interviews by George King
   Reverend Charles Austin Sr. and church congregants; Reverend Wiley Cooper; Henry Hopkins; James Soloman Jr.; Scott Trent Jr.; Henry Hopkins; Regina LaBrew; Henry Bracey

5. **Building on the Border: San Juan, Texas**
   Interviews by Daniel Rothenberg
   Olga Valle-Herr; Veronica Cruz; Yolanda Hernandez; David Arizmendi; Leslie Newman; Noe Hinojosa Jr.; Arturo Ramírez

6. **Growing Up, Coming Together:**
   Chicago, Illinois
   Interviews by Dan Collison
   Adriana Bartow; Sherry Brown; Camille Odeh; Andrea Shields; Héctor Rico; Alma Iris Montes; Dan Collison and Sylvester Carrizales; Cheryl Graves; Adriana Bartow

7. **A Forest Home: Yaak Valley, Montana**
   Interviews by Jens Lund
   Crash Karuzas; Rick Bass; Reuben Kneller; Jeanne Higgins; Mark Ewing; Rick Bass; Robyn King; Crash Karuzas and Shirley Karuzas

8. **Citizens on Watch: Delray Beach, Florida**
   Interviews by Merle Augustin
   Skip Brown; Chuck Ridley; Wilner Athouriste; Skip Brown; Lamousse Valcena; Richard Overman; Skip Brown

9. **Sea Culture: North Pacific Coast, Alaska**
   Interviews by Jens Lund
   Phyllis Clough; Stosh Anderson; Joe Macinko; Carolyn Servid; Julia Schmidt; Eric Jordan; Mary Jo McNally

10. **Youthline: San Francisco, California**
    Interviews by George King
    Chris Ramos; Ruth Barajas; Karma Bret Sweet; Janice Crotty; Aya Cash; Ruth Barajas; Karma Bret Sweet

11. **Local Money: Ithaca, New York**
    Interviews by Joe Wood
    Alan J. Cohen; Bill Myers; Leni Hochman; Paul Carubia; Gloria Molina; Audrey Cooper; Barbara Brazill; Leni Hochman

12. **Small Town Revival:**
    Western North Carolina
    Interviews by Jeff Whetstone
    Davitus Gosnell; Becky Anderson; Ray Rapp; Joe Penland Jr.; Becky Anderson; Ray Rapp; Joe Penland Jr.; Davitus Gosnell

13. **Reimagining the City:**
    Philadelphia, Pennsylvania
    Interviews by Barry Dornfeld
    Crowd at Earth Day celebration; Lily Yeh; Heidi Warren; Lily Yeh; James "Big Man" Maxton; German Wilson; Derrick; Lily Yeh

The audio collection was produced by Elana Hadler, with final assembly and mastering by Gary Covino at Popular Front Radio Studios, Haverhill, Massachusetts.